The Road Home
the journey beyond the spiritual quick fix

William Frank Diedrich

Book Design by Joshua Diedrich
Cover Design and Painting by Joshua Diedrich

Excerpts on pages 9 and 320 taken from The Illuminated
Rumi, by Coleman Barks, used by permission.

Isbn number 0-9710568-0-3

First Edition
Printed in the USA

Transformative Press
East Lansing, Michigan
www.transformativepress.com

For my children

Invitation

Open this book to any page and instantly step alongside William Frank Diedrich as he walks the path of divine transformation. After reading this book you will never again feel you are traveling this journey alone.

Grethel Ruth Brown

Contents

Introduction

I think about God every day. For many years concepts like God and spirituality rested on the periphery of my life. They were scenery that I could admire now and then. I was a spiritual tourist, an interested sightseer, spending a little time here and there, but always returning to my "real" life. Eventually real life became uncomfortable, and I looked to spiritual teachings as a tool - something I could use to get the things I wanted and needed. Life became more uncomfortable. Then I began to awaken.

The story you are about to read is true. It is a tale of a person becoming lost and then being found. It is the story of a person learning how life works. Spiritual growth is rarely easy. There is no quick fix. You do not get to snap your fingers and have your world change before your eyes. When I began my spiritual search it was the search for a cure. Wiser now, I realize there is no cure to life. The meditation that promises to manifest all of your dreams; the book or tape set that claims to be the answer; the belief system that promises salvation - all of these are but fragments of the truth. Yet, truths can be found and the quality of your life can change for the better. My life has changed dramatically in the past seven years. What was once an empty terrain struggling for sustenance is now a lush landscape, rich in spirit, filled with new life. As I look back I see that I am still me, yet I am more. I perceive and live life differently.

I began this book seven years ago. I did not wait until I experienced a great success, then looking back, wrote about how I did it. I wrote this book as I was learning. Often, I had to grow a little more before I could write a little more.

I cannot tell you what you should do. I can only share my experiences knowing that, if you are willing, they will lead you deeper into your own inner landscape. This is where the road home begins. You may choose to walk this road as a tourist, being just an observer, but something more profound is calling you. It asks that you walk this road as both student and pilgrim, that you seek experiences which teach and transform. We are all called by this inner Voice, but how many of us answer? How many of us are willing to break the mental bindings which limit us and separate us from ourselves, from each other, and from God? How many of us are willing to move beyond normalcy and become the glorious expression we are meant to be? This is the challenge now laid before us. Will we answer the call? Will we listen to the Voice of God within calling us home to our Self? I offer these pages to you as from one student to another. I wish you well on your journey home.

Many Blessings,

William Frank Diedrich

I HAVE LIVED
ON THE LIP OF
INSANITY, WANTING TO
KNOW REASONS, KNOCKING
ON A DOOR.

IT OPENS.

I'VE BEEN KNOCKING FROM THE INSIDE!

RUMI

From THE ILLUMINATED RUMI, by Coleman Barks and Michael Green, Broadway Books, New York 1997

The Road Home

The Journey Beyond the Spiritual Quick Fix

The Road Home

The Road Home

Chapter 1
Growing Up

Long Ago

Death frightened him. He didn't know what it was. All he knew was that one day a person was here, and the next, he was gone. One day a person could think and move and speak, and then there was nothing. He hoped that he would never die. Life frightened him, too. He tried hard to be a good boy, but he never seemed to be good enough. He was afraid that he was bad.

There were moments when he wasn't scared, like when he was at Grandma and Grandpa's house. Grandpa made him smile and Grandma always took care of him. Sometimes he would play under their back porch, digging in the dirt for hours. He loved the sweet smell of the dirt. He loved playing at their house. Then Grandpa died. At least that's what everyone told him. He prayed to God to bring Grandpa back, but God didn't answer. He never saw Grandpa again.

It was a sunny summer day in Woodmere Cemetery. Birds were singing, and a light breeze rustled the leaves in the trees. Grandma gave him the grand tour showing him where everyone was buried. How did Grandma know where everyone's grave was? She pointed out where his baby sister's grave rested.

She had been born dead. He wished she could have lived, even though he already had a new sister. Why do people have to die? Why did God make people die? He was afraid of God. They stopped at a small gravestone, and Grandma began digging in the dirt, planting geraniums. Geraniums smelled funny.

Billy: Grandma, is Grandpa under the ground?

Grandma: Just his body is buried here. Grandpa is in Heaven, Billy.

Billy: Where is Heaven?

Grandma: Heaven is up in the sky. Grandpa is up there right now, watching over us.

Billy: I wish Grandpa could just stay here instead of going to Heaven. Why did he have to die?

Grandma: Everyone has to die sometime, Billy. If you're good you get to go to Heaven, like Grandpa, and be with God. If you're bad you must go to hell. In hell people burn in flames forever. God doesn't like people who are bad, so he punishes them.

Billy: Will I go to Heaven, Grandma?

Grandma: If you're good, Billy. If you're good.

He grabbed a handful of the dirt from the grave and held it to his nose. It didn't smell sweet like the dirt under the porch. He wondered if this was what death smelled like.

Billy's Thoughts

If I'm good I get to go to heaven. If I'm bad I have to go to hell and burn. I don't want to die. When I die I'm going to take a knife with me. Then I can cut a hole in the sky and fall back to earth. I don't want to go to heaven or hell. I want to live.

Years Later

Bill: I just have a hard time believing in the Christian religion, or any other religion for that matter. I don't think you can use religion to justify war. We don't belong in that war.

Dad: You should believe. You should believe in your God and in your country!

Bill: I don't believe in either one.

Dad: You should!

Bill: Well, I don't! I can't believe in some god who sits on his throne and watches over creation. I don't believe people go to hell because they aren't baptized. It's so ridiculous! You're supposed to be a rational person, and yet you believe in this fairy tale about a god who sits up in heaven and judges us all. What do people do in heaven, fly around playing the harp and singing all day?

Dad: I believe in God and I believe in Jesus Christ. You will too if you know what's good for you.

Bill: Well, I can't. I'm sorry but I can't. I'd be pretending if I said I did. I'm not saying I know all the answers. I'm saying you don't know the answers either. I doubt if many people do.

      (Dad leaves the room red faced and angry. Bill steps outside, sits down on the porch steps, and begins to write in his journal.)

Bill's Journal

The Universe is incredibly vast. To have a single being with human-like characteristics, as its creator, judge, and father makes no sense to me. This god sounds more like an oversized human than something divine. I'm twenty years old and I don't know what I believe. I just know what I don't believe. Everyone acts like they have all the answers. It's all myth, dogma and rules. I don't buy it. I just don't buy it.

Twenty Something

Bill: You asked to see me?

Professor: Yes. I have the results of your MMPPI and your Strong-Campbell Inventory.

Bill: Yes?

Professor: You'll notice that your Strong Campbell reports that the profession your interests match up with is that of a minister. At the same time, your MMPPI shows a good deal of inconsistency and ambivalence regarding your attitude toward the subject of God.

Bill: And you're worried that I might have some unusual religious ideas that I may want to promote?

Professor: Well, we do need to check these things out. That's why we do a battery of tests. We screen all counseling candidates.

Bill: Well, you don't have to worry. I do have a strong interest in religions, and I read a lot on the subject. But, I would hardly make a good candidate for a minister. I guess I'm just a seeker looking for some answers. I have no interest in spreading the gospel.

Professor: I'm glad to hear that.

Bill: I know I contradicted myself on those questions. There must have been three or four questions regarding whether or not I believe in God. I answered some "yes" and some "no". That's how I feel. Sometimes I believe and sometimes I don't. Does that make sense to you?

Professor: Yes. It sounds like you're an agnostic. That's fine because we tend to stay away from religious matters here in the School of Counseling. You will be accepted into the Masters Program for Counseling.

Bill's Journal

Me, a minister? What a joke! I remember when I was eleven years old in my confirmation class at church, and the minister's wife said to me: " Billy, I think you have the makings of a good minister. Think about it, will you?" I was shocked to think of myself as a minister, but pleased to be recognized. I'm not sure what religion and God have to do with my life. Maybe I'll figure it out some day.

So, what do I believe in? I know I believe in the miracle of life. A couple of months ago I held my baby daughter when she was five minutes old. I was overcome by her beauty and the miracle of her birth. That was a spiritual experience for me. No church service and no guru ever made an impression like that on me.

I've read about Buddhism and Hinduism. Both talked about oneness, that all things are connected. I've felt that before. Once I was holding my son on my lap. He must have been about a year old. We were looking into each others eyes. I was overcome with this feeling that I was my Dad and my son was me. For a few moments boundaries were erased and we were one. We were all of the fathers and sons who had ever lived on this earth. That moment was a great gift to me. It was worth more than all the books I've read!

There are so many religions and spiritual paths. How can one particular path have all the answers? I had a discussion with a fellow school teacher. We stated our religious beliefs. She's a conservative Christian. I told her I believed there may be a higher power, but I couldn't believe in the Christian doctrine. She told me I would go to hell because I didn't believe Jesus died for my sins. She really said that!

When I was in college these two students visited me at my dorm room. They called themselves "Navigators". They wanted me to accept Jesus into my life. I did it. I prayed and followed the program. I really tried to get myself to believe. It didn't take. What about that? My path must be different. How can somebody tell me what I should believe? Isn't that between God(or whatever the Higher Power is called) and me? That's as far as I've come. I believe that a person's spiritual belief system is a personal matter. I believe there is something more to life than what we see. I just don't know what it is.

Turning Thirty

Bill's Journal

I turned thirty today. I don't feel happy. I have a family. I have a job. I have a home. I have enough money and I'm healthy. I love my family. I love my work. I'm not sure I love me too much. There seems to be something missing. I need something else. It's not that I'm bored. I just don't have enough intensity in my life. I want to feel things. I've intellectualized everything. I've read dozens of books on world cultures and religions, but I want to experience life. I don't want to spend my life just moving complacently from one day to the next. I want to feel alive. I want to live more intensely. I don't want to wake up when I'm forty and feel like I've wasted my life.

There is nothing wrong with my life. What's wrong with me? Where am I going?

Thirty Something

Bill: My wife and I seperated two months ago. I'm not eating and I'm not sleeping. I want to try and make the marriage work, but she says it's over. I hate being separated and I don't like being a weekend father. I feel like most of my life has been taken away from me - my marriage, my kids, my house, my friends. I don't know what to do. I want to love her, but she won't let me.

Therapist: How does she stop you from loving her, or from feeling the love of a father?

Bill: I can't be married by myself.

Therapist: Do you think you need to be with her to love her? Do you need to be living with your children to be their father?

Bill: It's hard not being with them.

Therapist: Yes, it is hard. That doesn't change the love you feel. Let go.

Bill: What do you mean?

Therapist: You don't own the people you love, and you can't make them feel the way you want them to feel. The only way to end your misery is to let go. Let go of your expectation of her to love you back.

Bill: I've never thought about that before. Maybe I do have to let go. I'll go crazy if I don't. I think I already have gone crazy. I can see now I've had the wrong goal. My goal has been to get her back. It's been so frustrating because I have no control over it. It hurts. I can change my goal.

Therapist: Your new goal is to let go?

Bill: Yes. I'm going to learn how to let go and love without expectation. I've been hanging on tight, thinking I could push us back together. When you said let go, a light bulb went on in my mind. I knew you were right. Thank you. I already feel better.

Therapist: You're beautiful!

Bill: Thank you, I guess. It embarrasses me that you say that.

Therapist: I'm telling you what I see in you. You have lost the love of a wife. Perhaps this is an opportunity to learn how to love yourself. You are worth loving.

Bill: I haven't thought about that. My energy is spent just trying to get through each day. I felt like I was truly crazy this week. I know I look like hell. I've never allowed myself to be crazy before. I mean, I've done a lot of crazy things, but I was in control. I've never felt so out of control as I do now.

Therapist: It's okay to be a little crazy. Let yourself go through it. You don't have to control how you feel. Just feel it, and control what you do. You can't see it now, but there will come a time when you'll feel stronger, better. Your wife's leaving is not just about you. It's about her. She has some things to work out, and she probably can't do it with you in her face. Let her alone to do her work. Focus on what you need to do for yourself, for your kids. Let go. Take care of yourself. Be yourself. That's all you can do.

Bill: Yeah, I should probably start eating again, too. It's been great for weight loss. I feel lighter. Thanks to you I feel lighter in my heart, too.

Therapist: Sometimes a little spiritual support can help. Have you tried praying?

Bill: I don't want to hear about God right now. My mother told me that if my wife and I had believed in God we'd still be together. I told her to mind her own business. And I'm asking you not to give me any God-talk right now. I don't have the time or the energy to deal with it. The way I figure it, this session is on my dime, so we'll talk about what I want to talk about.

One Year Later

Bill's Journal

It's been a tough year. I burned most of my journal. I drenched the pages in blood and tears, but I got it all out of me. I've been learning to let go, and I'm pretty proud of myself for getting through this year. I'm ready to move on now. To what? I'm starting to feel a spiritual pull. I haven't paid much attention to God and matters of the spirit these past several years. I've been too busy supporting a family, teaching school, and trying to keep my marriage together. Maybe it's time. It was several years ago, but I remember hearing about a spiritual teacher, an older woman named Marian. Maybe she can help me sort things out.

Bill: I've been separated for a year, now. It was a painful experience. So much hurt, but I made it. I did it myself, without God.

Marian: No one does anything without God, my friend. God is everywhere, including within you. You may not acknowledge God, but God is always guiding you.

Bill: That may be true. I haven't acknowledged God for a long time. It's kind of hard to acknowledge God when I'm not really clear about who or what God is. Lately, I've been feeling this urge to become more spiritually aware. That's why

I came to you. I thought you might help.

Marian: I'm glad you are here.

Bill: I had a dream.

Marian: Tell me about the dream.

Bill: I was walking down a dark street. Shadowy figures were passing me along the way. I was feeling fearful, but strong. I clenched my fists in case I had to protect myself from the shadows. I looked behind me to see if I was being followed. As I turned to look forward I walked right into this huge figure of a man. My face was pressed against his chest. He was wearing a soft flannel shirt, a very powerful figure. I was scared at first, but my fear left quickly. I began to awaken, and as I did, I heard a powerful, caring voice say, "Where are you going, Bill?"

Marian: Who was the powerful figure?

Bill: I don't know. Maybe it was God.

Marian: Maybe?

Bill: I'm not sure. The important thing is that I don't have an answer to the question. I don't know where I'm going.

Marian: Have you asked God for help?

Bill: No, I haven't. Like I said, I don't know who to pray to. I haven't prayed in years. When I did, I never felt like it did much good.

Marian: What are your thoughts about God?

Bill: Believing in God has not been easy for me. The God of my childhood was the God of vengeance. The one I was taught about in Sunday School. He was the Voice in the movie, *The Ten Commandments*. He was powerful and demanding. That's weird. I think I got some of my theology from Cecil B. DeMille. Those movie images were powerful. Anyway, the Old Testament God was a little too human for me to believe in. He seemed so arbitrary to me. I mean, there's a lot of violence in the Bible. I have a hard time with the idea that God would order one group of people to go kill another group. To me, he was sort of like the Greek gods, you know, toying with humans. So if you didn't want to be toyed with you better please God.

When I was older I read about the religions of the east. I learned that God was spirit. This God seemed so unreachable and impersonal to me. I tried meditating, fasting, studying, and listening to various teachers. I took Kundalini yoga classes. I spent ten days in the mountains doing yoga and listening to the teachings of a yogi from India. He was good, but his followers seemed so superficial. They acted like they had all the answers. I liked the teachings, but it was all too intellectual for me. I need spirituality with Heart, and I just haven't been able to find it.

I think what I need is a more practical God, one that can help me with my life. I need a God I can feel and know, one that I can experience.

Marian: God is both practical and knowable, and you can experience God personally.

Bill: Well, maybe you can shed some light on this God thing for me.

Marian: God is all there is, Bill. The Universe and all it contains is God. There is nothing outside of God. All is God and God is All. God is the only power at work in the Universe. God is all power, all wisdom, and all knowledge.

God is Love. Love is the creative power of the Universe. Love is the ever present energy of God flowing to us and through us. God's Love heals. It prospers. It creates. God loves you more than you can imagine. You are an individual expression of God, a part of the Whole. You are made in the image of God. Your God Self, your essence, is the real you. This Higher Self has never forgotten that it is an expression of God. As a human, you are an expression of God who has forgotten what he is. In Truth, you are God being you. You are a beautiful spiritual being having a human experience. You are on the road home to your Higher Self.

Bill: Wow! That's a lot to take in. I think my awareness of God has been pretty narrow. Tell me this: how is God practical? What does believing in God have to do with how well my life is going?

Marian: Your God Self knows only love, joy, prosperity, and peace. These qualities manifest in your life as you come into alignment with your true nature, your Higher Self. As you grow spiritually, the quality of your life improves.

Bill: Are you saying that by getting in touch with God I experience prosperity?

Marian: Yes. Not just money. Prosperity in all forms.

Bill: How do I do this?

Marian: First, understand that God is the Source of your supply. Your job or business is not the source of your supply. Prayers, affirmations, meditation; these will all help you to get closer to this understanding. An awareness of Universal Law is also important.

Bill: Wait up a minute! What kind of affirmations are you talking about?

Marian: Statements of Truth. For example: "I am abundantly supplied in all things." My statement is an affirmation of Truth. By affirming the Truth you teach your mind to believe in it.

Bill: Okay, and what is Universal Law?

Marian: A higher law that has universal application. For example: What you sow is what you reap. Your thoughts and actions are the seeds you sow; your life experiences are what you reap. Positive thoughts and beliefs create positive conditions. Unloving thoughts create unloving conditions. You know, Bill, if God had been at the center of your household, things would have been different.

Bill: I doubt that. I don't think that just because you believe in the same things that you stay together.

Marian: You may be right. What I'm trying to say is that if both of your minds were on God you would have created different conditions. At the very least, the parting would have been more peaceful.

Bill: I won't argue with that because God wasn't at the center of our relationship, and we did split up, and it wasn't peaceful. It just seems like there's more to it than agreeing to have God in your relationship. Was God at the center of your relationship?

Marian: God has always been at the center of my life and in all of my relationships. But sadly, my husband didn't see it that way. He wasn't interested in spiritual things, but he never interfered with my interests. He supported me and allowed me to do my spiritual work. He passed away last summer.

Bill: I'm sorry.

Marian: It's alright. I've been able to contact him through my spirit guides. He told me that I was right all along about an afterlife. It has been very reassuring to talk with him. I've always known that life continues after death, but it has been nice to confirm it.

My guides say that your relationship has been intensely emotional due to past life experiences together. You and your wife have been together before. You came together again to work out those issues.

Bill: You mean we have Karma?

Marian: Yes. Your respective souls made an agreement to come together to try to work out your Karma, your past issues. You two made an agreement to be together. You each did things that caused pain, and now you are trying to make it right.

Bill: So much for that. We've already filed for divorce. We still have to deal with each other because we have children. We don't seem to be doing such a great job. I try, and I know she tries, but it's still the same old stuff—pain, conflict, hurt feelings, guilt, resentment. These feelings keep coming up. I've worked so hard to be at peace about all of this, but I feel like I'm sliding back. I find myself feeling angry and hurt. I don't want to be in conflict.

Marian: Then be the bigger of the two, Bill. Let it go. Don't wallow in negative feelings. Forgive and remember the good times you both had. Get on with your life. The way to move beyond these lifetimes of relationship problems is to be at peace.

Bill: You're right. There has been enough suffering. Maybe I haven't done such a good job without God. I haven't been too successful on my own I guess, but I'm not sure where to go from here.

Marian: You must first begin to clean up your inner thoughts, feelings, and beliefs.

Bill: Yeah, well my thoughts have been a mess over the past two years.

Marian: There are thoughts, feelings and beliefs within you that need healing. Bill, you have some ugly "got-to's" to confront.

Bill: I don't get it. A got-to?

Marian: It's a compulsion. A have-to. Tell me, Bill, what drives you?

Bill: I'm not sure. Sometimes I think it's the need to get approval. I worry about what others think of me.

Marian: That's a good place to start. I have a book that might be of help. It's called, *What You Think of Me Is None of My Business.*

Bill:(Laughing)That's a good one for me. I'll read it.

Marian: Good! I have some others you may want to read, also. Here's one on prosperity.

Bill: Thank you. You've really helped me, Marian. You've given me a lot to think about. I'm curious though, what is it that drives you?

Marian: For me there has only been one goal in my life. I want to have a closer walk with God. I have spent my whole life in spiritual studies and doing spiritual work. More than anything I love God.

Bill: I would like to be closer to God, too.

Marian: You will. If you seek the Truth you will find it.

Bill: I'm not sure what truth is?

Marian: Would you like to hear a story about Truth?

Bill: Sure.

The Truth Story

Once, long ago, the Creator called for a gathering of all the angels at the center of the Universe. When all were gathered, a beautiful crystal globe was presented to the group. The Voice of the Creator spoke: "This globe is the Globe of Truth. A messenger is needed to carry the Globe of Truth to a small planet located in the Milky Way Galaxy. This planet is called Earth."

A young, rather brash angel raised his arm, volunteering for the task. Many were doubtful that he had the experience necessary for such an important task. He insisted that he was the one to take the Truth to Earth. He was chosen for the task.

Careful instructions were given. In his excitement he only half listened. At the appointed time, he flew off with the globe in his arms. After a time, he came upon the planet called Earth. It was beautiful. He felt both excited and honored to be the deliverer of Truth to this beautiful planet. He began his descent.

As he descended upon the Earth plane he forgot that the Earth was spinning on its axis. The spin caused him to lose his balance as he landed. He stumbled, losing his grip on the globe. The beautiful globe hit a rock and shattered into thousands of pieces. A wind swept up the many tiny crystal shards and scattered them across the surface of the Earth.

Since that day, on every continent and island, upon every ocean and sea, men and women have been finding those shards, picking them up and saying, "I have found the Truth." And others would say, "No, I have the Truth." In reality, each has only found a part of the Truth, and no one has it all.

Bill: I like the story. Does that mean I'll only get part of the Truth from you?

Marian: You may learn some Truth through me. But, you will need to look within, to your God-Self, for the whole Truth. Perhaps I can help you learn more about looking within.

Bill: You have been very helpful. I have one more question for you. Do I have a destiny? What do your guides say about that?

Marian: There are many possibilities in a person's future. Your choices will decide your fate. My guides tell me I am to work with teachers. You are a teacher. You have the potential to be a spiritual teacher in the coming new age.

Bill: What does that mean?

Marian: Many souls have come to earth having the potential to be teachers for the new age. You are one. But first you must deal with many issues. As we discussed earlier, you have thoughts and feelings that need healing. It is difficult, as a teacher, to give what you don't have. How can you lead others down a spiritual path if you are not spiritually and psychologically healthy? Learn how to trust God. Of yourself, you cannot successfully lead anyone. Now it is time for you to go. Thank you for coming.

Bill: Thank you for your help.

Bill's Journal

I'm not real sure about reincarnation and karma. Is it real, or do I just want to believe in it? It makes a lot of sense. Oh well, the important thing is that I have finally found an idea about God that I can accept. God is Spirit, not some great being in the sky. The Spirit of God lives in each one of us. Our thoughts make our life. Therefore we can create whatever we want in life. We can also un-create the things we don't want. I am going to grow spiritually and create prosperity in my life. There is a God! It just fell into place for me today. Eastern thought meets western thought — like two pieces of the same puzzle.

I am voraciously consuming these books Marian has given me. The daily affirmations are helping me. More money is coming in. I never thought I'd own a new car, and now I'm driving one. The idea that there is a connection between my spiritual life and my financial life never occurred to me. This is exciting. I think I'm ready to experience more prosperity.

Three Years Later

Bill's Journal (Summer)

Each morning I wake up filled with fear. My life is a mess. Money, relationships, health, and career are all in state of chaos. I have no money and no home of my own. This relationship I'm in is crazy. One day I'm in ecstasy and the next day I'm in hell. I have no job, and a shattered, broken hip. How did I get into this mess? More importantly, how do I get out of this mess? Why is all of this happening to me?

Once upon a time I was married, working, healthy, and my financial needs were met. I can't believe this is happening. Instead of finding my dream I'm living my nightmare! Wasn't I better off before I started seeking spiritually? I'm not giving up, but I wonder. I wonder why, if God is supposed to be my Source of all Good, did my life get worse when I turned to God?

I have practiced affirmations and prayer. I have read books. I have taken action whenever I could. Miracles have happened. To my surprise, unexpected money arrived. A friend offered me a place to live. My body is now functioning fully within two months after the fall that broke my hip. My hospital bills are paid off in full, and I received some money to live on. A mountain of debt and personal problems are still here. Is there no escape from this? For years I have imagined a life in which I am in a happy relationship, financially taken care of, and doing work that I love. Why am I not living this life?

Bill's Journal (Winter)

It is winter. The cold gray skies enclose me like a prison cell, and I'm a prisoner of my own life. I can't seem to get out. I feel like I'm in a deep hole without a ladder, and I keep sinking deeper. The roller coaster relationship I was in is over. Emotionally and physically I wanted the relationship to continue. Mentally, and perhaps spiritually, I knew it was time to end it. So I let go. All these years I have told myself that I am a seeker of Truth, that I'm a spiritual person. Have I been? Let's be honest, Bill. The truth is, I have centered my life on a person I've felt attracted to. Why was I so attracted to her? Why did I set aside everything that was important to me just so I could be with her? Maybe I thought I could find love in her, that she would meet my needs. I thought it was a deep love, but was it just an addiction? I mean, I had to have her, to be with her. The sex and affection were so important. She was my drug. It was exciting and fun. My life was falling apart around me, but when I was with her, I could forget about it all. I thought I was putting my faith in God, but my actions show I was putting my faith in a person. Did I really believe she could save me? Funny thing is, I think she thought I would save her. It's good that she is gone. I used her to avoid dealing with myself.

I look back over the past few years and I can't believe how I have lived my life. What the hell was I doing? I ignored the needs of my children. I gave up my career. I spent all of my money. Creditors have been calling me weekly. I still don't have a steady income. I'm embarrassed, and I feel like such a fool. How could I do this when I intended to make my life better?

Bill: I asked God for help. I stepped out in faith and I fell on my face.

Voice (within): *You did not step out in faith, Bill.*

Bill: I didn't? I thought I did. I prayed. I affirmed. I read spiritual books.

Voice: *You have not listened. You have read your books and done your affirmations, but you have not listened within.*

Bill: Who are you?

Voice: *We are the Voice within you. We are your Guide. We are the feeling that urges you to make the best decision. We are intuition. We are the urge to read a particular passage on a page in a particular book. We are Spirit within and around you.*

Bill: Who is we? Which one of the "we" is addressing me?

Voice: *Your Soul, along with your Teachers and Guides. We speak with one voice. We represent the One God that is within you and all around you. We are the "One" who is addressing you.*

Bill: Where have you been all of these years? Where were you when I fell on my face? Where were you when I needed you?

Voice: *Right here, Bill. With you, around you, continually guiding you and protecting you.*

Bill: Maybe you're not so good at guiding. I mean, look at where I've been.

Voice: *We do not choose the territory, Bill, you do. We just guide you along the paths that you choose.*

Bill: What about protecting me?

Voice: *It is difficult to protect you from yourself, but believe it or not, we have done that, too. You could have been killed that time you fell. You were fortunate it was only your hip. The insurance money that came through to pay for your operation - We were there. You have free will. You learn by experiencing the consequences of your decisions. We give guidance, but we do not make you take it. You are aware of spiritual principles. You know that a person reaps what he sows.*

Bill: I practiced spiritual principles, but still my life came crashing down around me.

Voice: *Listen within, Bill, and learn. Many times you have felt that an action was not in your best interest, yet you did it anyway. Other times you felt inspired to take an action, but you held back out of fear. Most of the time you were afraid to look within for guidance. You did not want to know. Trust, Bill. Remove the barriers you have put up between you and God and trust that your answers are within you. You have much to learn. Your life will improve, although you may continue to struggle for awhile. It does not matter.*

Whatever is going on in your life is your spiritual course work. You cannot avoid doing the work. Do not worry; you will learn. You will grow. Be at peace, for you are loved and you will be shown the way.

Bill: That's not what I wanted to hear. I mean, yes, I want to be shown the way. I don't want to continue to struggle.

I want things to be better right now. I want my debts paid now. This is too hard.

Voice: *It is what you wanted, Bill. Yes, you have struggled and experienced much pain, and you will grow from it. No matter how bad things look, keep your vision. Your vision of a joyful, loving, prosperous life is not that far off. Find the calm place within you now. Clear your thoughts. The struggle you are experiencing is just thought. Let your troublesome thoughts pass and find a quiet place in your mind. Listen within and do what you feel is right.*

Bill: What I feel is right is to earn more money so I can start paying off these debts. I also need to be alone. The last thing I need right now is another relationship.

Voice: *So be it.*

One Year Later

Bill's Journal

My life has improved. I worked hard for several months and received help from my family. I have found a job that pays well, but my past is still here in the form of unpaid debts. I have no significant relationship in my life, but I think I'd like one. I am glad things are getting better, but I want it all. I want to be free of my past mistakes. I want my dreams of success and happiness to come true.

Bill's Journal

A couple of years of steady paychecks and here I am again. These past seven years have been like a white-water-rafting experience, with me falling out of the raft many times. I've been tossed about on the rapids of life, crashing into barriers, practically drowning in my problems, veering out of control, direction unknown.

I want to do something about this, but what can I do? I've tried everything. I've read dozens of books on spiritual ways to achieve a better life. One book told me to affirm my success and it would manifest. I tried that. At first, I did find success. Then the roof caved in and my life fell apart. Another book told me that if I had problems it was because I wanted them. I doubt that I really wanted pain and struggle. Did I? Others told me to love my problems away. Well, I surely don't love having problems. I read and I practiced, but nothing seemed to work.

I have tried more action-oriented books, too. I have written down goals, made action plans, and taken action. I have visited spiritual readers and psychics. They have told me of the wonderful things that will happen in my life. They never say when these great things will happen. They say, "someday". When will "someday" get here?

Bill: Success seems to elude me. I've been in therapy. I have learned a great deal about myself. Many of the problems I carried over from childhood were identified and worked out. I have felt an increase in confidence, but my life conditions seem to change very little.

Voice: *The Universe knows what you want Bill. Relax and be yourself. Do not work so hard. You struggle so much! It is not necessary. People learn through joy or through pain. It is a choice you make.*

Bill: I want to learn through joy.

Voice: *Then give up the struggle.*

Bill's Journal

There are so many thoughts bouncing around inside that I often don't hear my inner voice. When I am able to listen answers do come to me. When I pay attention and do what I feel guided to do, things seem to work out.

Listening has not been easy for me. So often I have done what I thought I should do, or what someone else thought I should do.

I keep telling myself that each day is another step closer to understanding Life and to understanding myself. I have traveled so many roads that have led nowhere. Looking back at a few years ago, I feel I have come so far. At the same time it seems I've made little progress. I'm not there yet, but I'm learning. Did I need to take all those nowhere roads just to find out where they led?

What road am I on now? What is my destination? That's part of my problem. I don't really have a road. I just want to be happy.

Voice: *What would happiness look and feel like, Bill?*

Bill: I would feel at peace. I would feel loved. I would feel a sense of control in my life. I would be financially secure. I would have a loving marriage in a loving home of our own. My relationships with my children, family, and friends would be loving. I would be doing work that I love, making a positive contribution to the world. My work would contribute to building a more peaceful world. It would help others to grow and learn. This is what I want.

Voice: *Now you know what road you are on. Your life has been chaotic because your thinking is chaotic. Chaotic thinking creates and maintains fear. Decisions and behavior have arisen from these thoughts and feelings. Know that to teach peace, one must become peace. To offer and accept love, one must let go of fear. To live in a loving world one must love one's self unconditionally. Completely fall in love with yourself now and your vision is manifest. For to love a situation unconditionally, within the space of moment, will transform it.*

Bill: I don't think I can love myself unconditionally just because I decide to. I wish I could.

Voice: *We do not expect you to do it immediately, yet, we say it is possible. Fear stands in your way. You will learn to overcome your fear of life, your fear of facing the reality you have created. We are here to help. We will guide you along this road if you desire it.*

Bill: I can use any help I can get. What do I need to do first?

Voice: *Listen. Turn within and listen.*

Chapter 2
I Want Success Now!

The Dialogue Continues

Am I crazy? I was just laid off for the second time in two years. I have no money, a lease on an overpriced apartment, two children to support, and I'm starting a business. On top of that I just ended a relationship. Am I destined to struggle forever? Will I find the financial success I have sought? Will I ever find the right relationship? Every day I affirm that I will succeed, that more clients will come. People say it takes time to grow a business. Time I have. It's money that I need.

I feel like everything is tied to my financial success, or lack of it. In order to have a healthy relationship with a woman I need to be at least somewhat successful, don't I? What woman wants to get involved with a guy who's drowning financially? What kind of father am I if I can't help support my children? I want success now. I'm not good at waiting.

I have this vision. In it I see myself self employed, teaching classes, consulting with managers, and giving workshops. I've had only a couple of short term clients, and I need to make a living. I have responsibilities to meet. Maybe I should find a full time job and do this business on the side.

I am successful. I am totally open to receive my

abundance. I deserve success and I rejoice in it. I've said these affirmations thousands of times. I've really been giving it my all. Why isn't it working?

What is it that you think is not working?

The idea that if I affirm enough and create the right attitude I can make it happen.

You are making it happen. That is, whatever is going on in your life or in your business is being created by you. When you say the word "make," it sounds as if you want to force something into being. In that sense, you can not make it happen. Manifestation of desires is not caused by mental coercion. Spirit takes the form and direction of your thoughts and, of itself, finds the way to manifest.

It seems that I've spent a lot of time in the past few years wondering what has happened? How do I make things happen?

You can not make customers call you. You can not make them pay you on time. You can not make people want to use your services, and you can not make them like you. You can create a situation where more customers are attracted to you. You can believe in yourself and in your services. You can demonstrate that belief in all that you say and do. You can put your trust in God to help you.

So, am I wasting my time doing all of these affirmations?

Just because you do not see success does not mean it is not on the way. Yet, sometimes your affirmations accomplish very little.

Then why do all the books I read say that affirmations will bring me prosperity?

Many people do achieve results from affirmations. Often it is only temporary.

I don't understand this.

You do not make it happen. It is already happening. You have only to claim it. The Universe is continually supplying you with an abundance of all good things. What you are "making" is your consciousness.

I read about that too. Everyone talks about consciousness. What is consciousness?

It is your view of yourself and your world. Your consciousness includes the meanings you attach to thoughts, feelings, situations, people, and objects. Your consciousness is your personal world. It is a combination of your perceptions, awareness, understanding, and knowledge. It is the way you respond to the world physically, mentally, emotionally, and spiritually. Your consciousness sets the tone for all of your relationships. It is the determinant of 100% of your experience. All experience is interpretation. Your consciousness is the unique way which you identify, evaluate, and give meaning to your world.

Your experiences in the world are a reflection of what you think you are. For example, if you think you must struggle to make a living, then you attract experiences that reinforce that point of view. If you believe making money is as easy as tying your shoes, then you will find money coming to you easily. (Of course, that is assuming you can bend over and tie your shoes easily). Your life is a reflection of your consciousness.

Okay. I understand that my consciousness creates my experience, and I've been trying hard to change my consciousness. I thought that affirmations would do the trick.

Let us address two things: trying and affirmations. First, you do not try to change your consciousness. You do not try to start a business. You do not try to get customers. Do not try, do. Trying is so tentative. It implies a holding back. When you say you are trying you are preparing yourself for an excuse: "Well, I tried!"

Well, I have tried!

Stop trying and do it! Say: "I am changing my consciousness."

I am changing my consciousness.

What are you changing it to?

I am changing my consciousness to one in which I expect wealth to come to me easily, but I'm not there yet. That's why I say I am "trying."

If you were there you would not be working to change it. It might be better if you said "I am building a wealth consciousness." If you walked past a construction site and the foreman told you he was <u>trying</u> to build an office complex what would you think?

That he doesn't know what he is doing.

So, if you are trying to start a business you do not know what you are doing and you hope everything comes out well. What kind of confidence does that inspire? Build a consciousness centered on God, and you can know things are turning out well. God is the divine power that lives within and around you. Whatever you would build upon this power is like the house built upon the rock. It can withstand all storms. Know this power is in you and let your confidence proceed from it.

Okay, I get it. I won't try anymore; I'll do it.

Good. Now about those affirmations. You spend a lot of time saying them by rote.

I know. I feel like a kid practicing his multiplication tables.

Constantly affirming may bring temporary results, but it is difficult to create lasting results by mental work alone. Change your approach. First, see that you have a genuine intent to shift your consciousness. For example, if you are ill, your intention would be to be whole and well. Healing is all that you want. Your intention focuses your energy. Often you have conflicting intentions. For example, one moment an ill person wishes to be well, and the next, he is using his illness to get sympathy. Be clear on what you want. In your business, one moment you think you can do it, and the next you doubt yourself. Let thoughts of doubt float by as drifting clouds. Let your intention be as the sun, always there, always shining.

Second, if you are going to practice affirmations, put some emotion behind them. Say your affirmations with feeling. Your emotion will convince you of your intent.

Third, recognize that God, or Spirit, is doing this work through you.

Fourth, make your every thought and word an affirmation. Whenever you talk about your business, speak with confidence, no matter how bad things seem to be going.

I do try to say affirmations with feeling.

You try?

Okay, you got me. I don't always say them with feeling. Often I have felt uncomfortable when I do affirmations. There is this little voice that immediately reacts. I say "I am a rich child of God, open to my abundant supply", and the little voice says, "No, you're not, and just saying it doesn't make it so." Then I affirm harder or try to push away the negative thoughts. This only makes the little voice stronger.

If you get a headache every day you may take an aspirin. In taking the pill you have addressed the symptom only. The cause remains. Perhaps your headaches are caused by stress or something harmful you are doing to yourself. The way to end the headaches is to remove the cause.

With financial issues, or any life issues, it is the same. The cause in your consciousness that creates the experience of insufficiency may have very little to do with money. It may be a feeling of worthlessness. It may be unforgiveness for another person or yourself. It may be anger or resentment you are holding. You must seek out the barriers you have created and eliminate them through forgiveness, prayer, and self understanding. Once you have let go of these feelings and beliefs, you can build your sense of worth through affirmations.

Always ask God for understanding. Second, pay attention to how you feel when you say affirmations. When you feel uncomfortable or resistant, you have run into a belief, thought, or emotion which contradicts that affirmation. Deal with this underlying problem.

Your consciousness is a system of thoughts, emotions, and beliefs. The harder you push on it, the harder it will push back. If you are straining and pushing on this system, it will fight you. This is why people who work very hard to change themselves often find their situation worsening. Stifling thoughts and emotions you do not want makes the unwanted thoughts and emotions stronger. Become aware of your thoughts. If they are unproductive or unhealthy, acknowledge that they are unhealthy. Simply acknowledge that they are thoughts. Relax yourself. Love and accept yourself the way you are right now. Know that you are imperfectly perfect. When you push you are trying to make it happen. Accept yourself and you allow change to happen. Your goal is not to change who you are; it is to love who you are. Love is based on self acceptance, not rejection.

One of the most loving things you can do for yourself is to find joy each day. Find things that make you smile and laugh. Live your life right now. This "someday" philosophy is destructive to you, Bill. You have this idea that you do not deserve happiness until you attain a certain level of success. Be happy now. More money does not bring you more happiness, but more happiness may bring you more money. You do not have to wait for money to be a good father. Just be one now. You can be a loving partner to a woman regardless of money and success. Everything is tied to your business and financial success because you have tied those knots. There are no physical contingencies for happiness. Happiness is now. It is a result of the thoughts you choose to dwell on in this moment. There are no physical contingencies for prosperity. Prosperity is now. It, too, is a result of the thoughts you choose to dwell on in this moment.

I think I contradict myself a lot. I spend fifteen minutes saying affirmations, which makes me feel pretty good. Then, later on, I find myself worrying for an hour.

Bring your everyday thinking and feeling into alignment with your affirmations. What do you think about all day? Do you worry about finances, relationships, or health? Are you filled with resentment because you do not have what you want? Take an accepting, non-judgmental look at your daily thinking and feeling. As you discover thoughts and feelings that are contradictory to the positive experiences you desire, acknowledge them. In fact, welcome them. They are signals that something is amiss in your perception.

That sounds strange. I'd rather get rid of these worries and fears.

Stop fighting your experience. Your business and financial situation is not the problem. The problem lies in how you are viewing the situation. Say in prayer: "Help me to view this situation differently." When you say an affirmation and feel discomfort, welcome the discomfort. When you feel worry, thank yourself for the signal. Face the emotions you have and accept them without judging yourself. Resist or judge your emotions and your "unpleasant" experience will tend to persist. Face and accept your worries and fears. They are gifts. Behind each gift is a lesson for you to learn, an experience for you to enjoy.

What kind of lesson?

Lessons about the false foundations upon which you have built your view of the world.

Please explain what you mean.

Let us take your issue with money. How do you feel when you can not pay your bills?

Embarrassed. I don't feel good about myself. I feel angry at myself. I feel guilty.

You judge yourself. Look at your life. You are not starving. You have shelter. The people you owe money to are not starving. You are doing your best to meet your responsibilities.

Your goal of paying people back is honorable. Your idea that something is wrong with you because you have debts does no honor to you. You are not your situation. When you identify with your situation you help to maintain it. To lay guilt on yourself and mentally beat yourself up for your past mistakes helps you convince yourself that you are not a good person. Your guilt becomes a seed that grows and is reaped as new experiences of owing money. You continually recreate situations that reinforce your view of self.

So what do I do about this?

Forgive yourself. The past is over so why focus on it? Focus on now. Today you are being responsible. Today you are doing your best to pay off debts and manage your money. Think well of yourself and move forward. Focus on what you have control over: your present thoughts and actions. With your present thoughts you can reinterpret the past. See the good that was there. You can see yourself as an honorable person, a child of God. Take action based on these thoughts.

How will I know what action to take?

Ask within:"Is there anything I could be doing right now that would bring me closer to my desire?" Pay attention. Sometimes it may be difficult to distinguish between an urge to action based on a "should" you feel inside and an urge coming from your intuition. If you find that you are pressuring yourself to take a particular action, it is probably not your intuition speaking. Intuition tends to be more gentle. Listen to your intuition and do what "feels" right to do. It may not appear logical at the time, but do it anyway. Many people who are frustrated with lack of progress from affirmations and prayers are those who are sitting around waiting for something to happen. Often you are called upon to do something to make your desire manifest. Do what is before you to do.

Taking action helps to indicate your level of commitment. If you have a tendency to feel fearful, taking action will help you to focus your fearful energy on something positive. You want more business. You can not make business come to you, but you can talk to people. As we have already said, make your every word to others an affirmation.

Check your words, your voice tone, and your body language. Are all parts of you speaking the language of success? Act as if you are already successful. Talk to people in business. Explore their needs and see how you might be of service to them. Find ways to serve.

What if I get a feeling, act on it, and make a mistake. How can I be sure? What if I don't hear anything?

Always be open, ready, and willing to take action. Practice will help you to discern between effective and ineffective action. Practice trusting your gut feelings.

I can talk to more people. I can do all of the things you have told me, but there is no guarantee that the right people will hear my message.

You do not trust the Universe to supply you. For you, praying or affirming for some desire is like casting the dice, hoping your number will appear. The Universe does not work that way. Hoping something will happen is not enough. You must learn to get beyond the hoping stage to feeling faith and trust. Shift your belief system to a higher level of thinking where you absolutely trust the Universe to supply you with what you desire. Absolutely trust that you are intimately connected to this infinitely providing Universe.

There are two things you can do to help yourself. First, recall unexpected good things that have happened to you in the past. These are proof that the Universe does respond to you. Second, as we have already said, act as if you already are the successful person you want to be. This does not mean that you spend money you do not have. Give of what you have. Bless what you have. Pay those to whom you owe money without feeling anger. Be glad to give them what is theirs because you have what is yours. This is how you demonstrate your faith and trust.

I can't make problems go away by saying affirmations. But, there are things I can do to move forward:

- Create an intention to make a change.
- Put some feeling behind my words of affirmation.
- Realize that God works through me.
- Make sure my every word is an affirmation when speaking to others.
- Seek out the barriers to success I have created; acknowledge and release them.
- Acknowledge my successes.
- Accept myself and love myself as I am.
- Forgive myself and release guilt.
- Take action as indicated by my intuition.
- Trust God

One of the most important things is that I begin to live what I am affirming. If I affirm that I am wealthy, I need to act as if I already am.

What about prayer? Should I pray for more money?

No, Bill, ask God to make you ready for more money. Ask for help in eliminating the barriers to greater wealth that you have created.

Okay, I hear what you are saying. I will approach affirmations and prayer differently, but I still have doubts about their effectiveness. All of the books I've read present affirmations and other techniques as a way to achieve success. I read a book by a well known author, for instance, who enthusiastically presented affirmations for achieving success. I practiced those affirmations. I thought, lived, and breathed those affirmations for a month. Nothing happened.

Sometimes people do experience quick success when they use a new technique. Most people find that there is a lot more to it than saying a few affirmations.

The author told about one person after another who experienced something wonderful after doing affirmations. She said that some found success in a day or two.

Many people, yourself included, have layer upon layer of beliefs and old feelings that block you from receiving much of your good. It is unrealistic to think that you can make it all go away with the saying of a few affirmations. You must be patient with yourself.

I know I'm not patient with myself, and I have lost patience and respect for "success" authors. They make it sound so easy. It's not easy!

You were feeling desperate, which made you vulnerable. In your vulnerability you were willing believe whatever you were told. You put your faith in the advice givers instead of in the Voice of God within you. Whenever you put your faith in something or someone outside of yourself you are setting yourself up for a fall. No person or book is perfect. No technique is a cure-all. God is in you. Put your faith in God who is in you.

I wanted the words I read to be true. I wanted to find success quickly.

It is okay to want that. The principles you learn in books are true. It is the application of principles that is difficult, as you know.

That should be explained better. The author should tell about the failures, too. How many people try these techniques and don't succeed? It's dishonest.

There are no failures, only people in process. Everyone will understand all there is to understand eventually. You have all of eternity. Mistakes and failures, as you call them, are important learning experiences. They allow you an opportunity to make changes and grow. As for dishonesty, it depends on your perspective.

My perspective? Dishonesty is dishonesty, isn't it?

That is a judgment on your part. Have you ever talked to a good baseball player?

What does that have to do with it?

If he is hitting .300, he is considered a successful hitter. He does not go around saying he makes seven outs for every ten times at bat. He simply tells the truth: "I am an excellent hitter."

So what's the point?

Perhaps the author in question just has a good batting average. Enough of the people she has worked with have experienced success to give validity to her ideas. She talks about the hits, not the outs. There are hundreds of success writers out there. They all talk about the hits. There is a tendency to express their words with great enthusiasm. The reader, then, begins to think: "Here is a quick answer to my problems. Here is how I can get out of this mess."

Thinking, both conscious and unconscious, created the mess. Therefore, thinking must be changed. Not a single one of these authors can tell you exactly how to achieve success in your life or how long that success will take to manifest. They can only provide you with principles, tools, and encouragement. The rest is up to you. You adapt the tools to fit your life. You supply the desire and the intention to create change. Change and growth are very individual things. What works for one person will not necessarily work for everyone else. There is no one right affirmation, prayer, lifestyle, diet, religion, or belief system. That is why you ask God for help—that you may be led to finding what is right for you.

So, there is no right answer in those books?

There are many answers. Find which ones work for you. Each person's life is like a book. For example, whoever may read these words may find some helpful ideas. They will certainly find Truth Principles. They will not necessarily find their truth. Each person must read their own book, metaphorically speaking. You will find truth within you. The holiest book is the book of your Higher Self, engraved deeply upon your Soul. It is your memory of what you are.

I think I'm reading that book.

Pray. Meditate. Write in your journal. Contemplate who you are. Understand yourself. Love yourself exactly as you are right now. Know that the conscious you is but a small part of who you really are.

How do I find out who I really am?

We have answered that. Love yourself unconditionally. Find the barriers you have created to loving yourself and release them. The road home is the road to Love. Love is your salvation, for it is the stuff of which the Universe is created. God is Love.

The Bible says that God is Love. What about the Bible?

It is an interesting and inspired book. Many people get a lot out of it. Others do not. It was written to be of help, and it can be. Your truth is still within you. That is the place where you make contact with God.

All of my life the Bible has been presented to me as <u>the</u> authority.

There is nothing wrong with the Bible. There is much authoritative information in it. It is written on many levels. The dedicated student may discover great insight by diving deeply beneath the words on the surface. At the same time, the human race is evolving. You are moving into a stage of evolution where you no longer look to outside authorities like the Bible or preachers to tell you what to do. Everyone has access to the Voice of God within them. That is where you find your authority.

So, my opinion is better than the Bible?

Your opinion is based on judgment. Seek the Voice of God within you. It is loving and nonjudgmental. Where did Jesus say that the Kingdom of Heaven is found?

He said it lies within.

Then look there. Where do you think many of the authors of the Bible found their information? From oral history and inspiration. Inspiration! The act of drawing in. Metaphysically— Divine Guidance or influence exerted directly on the mind and soul of humankind. Do you think only Jesus and the various prophets had the ability to draw in God's wisdom? Are you not made of the same stuff as they? Read all you want. Go listen to great teachers. Know that the answers you seek are within. A Zen Master once said: "Do not mistake the finger for the moon."

I'm not sure I understand.

The finger pointing at the moon is not the moon itself. Books and teachings are like fingers pointing at the moon. They give you directions on how to get there. They are not the goal itself. The goal, the Truth, is within you. Like a road sign they may point the way, but you must take your own journey. The Bible may express the word of God, but it is not God. God is God, and your point of contact with God is within you. Respect the Bible. Love it if you wish. Honor it, but do not worship it. Those who would have you worship it would have you worship their interpretation of the Bible.

Although ministers, priests, spiritual teachers, authors, and religious organizations all have God within them, their words are not God. They are not to be worshipped; they are to be questioned. You must discern for yourself what is Truth. You do that by seeking confirmation within.

If the Truth is within us, why do we need books or teachers at all?

Good question. The answer is that they can be helpful. You may find some great tools and learn some important Truth principles in books or from teachers. You may be guided by your intuition to a particular book or phrase in a book. In this way you will often find the Truth. The origin of your individual Truth, the Truth of your being, is within you. Your success does not come from something outside of you. It comes through you. Do you refrain from stealing and killing because the Bible says so? You do not do these things because you have learned that they cause pain for you and for others. The Bible has great words in it. Your local minister, priest, or rabbi may have great words to offer. None of these things lets you off the hook. You must take responsibility for your thoughts and actions. Part of life is about learning personal responsibility. Many leave the care of their souls to the Bible and the clerics. They leave the care of their bodies to the doctors. They leave the running of their organizations to managers. They leave the running of the world to politicians. If you must leave your decision making somewhere, leave it with God.

You, Bill, have refused to make ministers, Bibles, doctors, and politicians your gods. But you have engaged in magical thinking. You have mistaken the finger for the moon. You treat affirmations as if they are some kind of incantation. Affirmations are not "abracadabra." They do not bring you anything. Affirmations are a tool for changing your consciousness. Your consciousness is then reflected in your experience. The Good you receive comes through you, not from some outside force. There is no magic involved. There is no Celestial Being sitting up in the clouds judging your affirmations and prayers to be worthy or not. You affirm to make an impression on you, not on God. God already loves you. God is already supplying you. If you are not receiving the supply you desire it is because you have been unwilling to receive. You are not separate from God. See yourself as unified with God, therefore you are unified with your supply.

In other words this is another aspect of reaping what I sow.

Yes. Your thoughts and feelings are the seeds. Your life experiences are your crop. The problem is not that you lack money. The problem is that you are not living consciously within the Law.

What is the Law?

You just stated it. What you sow you will reap. You do not need magic or any special tools. The value in using your affirmations is that they are a way of taking responsibility for what you think, feel, speak, and do. Everyone lives within the Law. Most people are not aware of it. You are aware of it yet you still allow yourself to think and feel in painful ways.

Maybe I don't believe in it fully.

You do not jump off of tall buildings. Why?

I would crash and die.

You know and believe in the law of gravitation. The Law of the Universe is even more certain than the law of gravitation. People have fallen out of airplanes and survived in spite of gravity. No one has ever beaten the Law of the Universe. No one is above it. Like attracts like. You reap what you sow. The Law of Cause and Effect. Call it what you want. It is.

Bill's Journal

To get keys for unlocking Truth, read books or listen to teachings. The doorway opens inward. Why have I always looked to some authority or technique for my answers? How do I learn to trust what is inside of me? I really don't think that I've been unwilling to receive, because I do want a better life. But, I reap what I sow. My thoughts are the seeds that grow and become my experience. I am not exempt from Universal Law.

I think it's starting to sink in. I have been reading all of these books and attending classes expecting the teachings to work for me. Then I get angry at the books because I don't succeed. I get angry at myself for foolishly thinking these techniques would work. My lack of success is my own fault.

You are so hard on yourself. A great many people approach New Thought and New Age teachings expecting them to work for them. They will say, "This stuff really works", or "This stuff does not work." God always works. The purpose of affirmations and other techniques is to align your consciousness with God. When you do that, your life works.

It sounds so simple.

It is simple. You are only a thought away from it. You are but a thought away from solving every problem you think you have. Shift your thought and your feeling, and your life is transformed. The difficulty you find is of your own making.

Why is it so difficult?

You have created the difficulty with your attachment to what you think is reality. That attachment is reinforced by your society. The more you believe in struggle, lack, disease, and conflict, the more life experiences you attract that tend to elicit your negative response

Does that mean that experiences of lack or disease are not what they appear to be? For instance, if I have no money in my bank account, I only think I am experiencing lack?

Yes. It looks real; it feels real; but it is not. Poverty and lack are not in your situation; they are in your perception of the situation. In other words, the real experience of poverty is in your mind.

Okay, let's say I go into a poor part of a big city. The buildings are falling down, abandoned. Some people are living on the sidewalks. They have no money, tattered clothing, and no where to go. Am I in the midst of poverty?

You are in the midst of an experience you have labeled as poverty. Perhaps the people you mention have labeled it as poverty, too. We cannot take that experience away from you, because, you think it is real. Know that prosperity is there, but neither you nor they can see it.

This does not make sense to me.

Think about electricity. It has always been here. Some people in the past were aware of it, but no one knew how to use it. Edison and others discovered ways to make use of it. Today the world is full of electrical technology. Yet, there is no more availability of electrical potential today then there was 2000 years ago. Your people on the sidewalks are living in the midst of God energy, Divine Substance. They are not aware of it, but that does not make it not there. It is there and it is available to them.

There are ideas for your prosperity, people who need your services, and possibly, people who want to give you money. If your mind is not tuned into these possibilities, does it make the prospering possibilities not there? You are unable to see what you do not yet believe in.

When you are in the state of mind where you recognize that God is your abundant supply and that you are deserving of this supply and grateful for it, then these possibilities will become realities to you. You will experience prosperity.

So, my experience of financial lack is an illusion?

Yes. You imagine yourself to be poor, and so your circumstances seem to match your imagining. Were you of a prosperity mindset you would see the prosperity in your present circumstances and give thanks for it. You would be open to ideas which are ever present, and you would think and act upon a brilliant idea.

So, all I need to do is to imagine prosperity?

That will help. At any given moment you are bombarded by thousands of stimuli. Your conscious mind perceives less than one tenth of one percent of all stimuli in a given moment. The stimuli you perceive are those which fit your belief system. The others, you miss. There may be thousands of ideas for obtaining money right in front of you. You will perceive and act upon the ones your belief system is willing to accept. As you become more loving of yourself, more grateful for the good you already have, more trusting of the Universe, and able to express more faith in both God and yourself, your belief system expands and can accept more options. Then you may be inspired to take actions you have never thought of previously. When you are in this consciousness, your imagining, combined with actions you are guided into taking, will manifest prosperity.

Bill's Journal

I am in the midst of God Energy. It conforms to create situations that I interpret according to my consciousness. If my consciousness is of lack, I will attract situations that my belief system interprets as lack. If I am conscious of prosperity, my situation will conform to my idea of prosperity. It makes sense to me. Or, is it that I just hope it's all true? I know it's true somewhere inside, but I'm having a hard time proving it to myself. Maybe if I say it enough I'll believe it. If I keep reading and studying, maybe that will help me believe. I can't help wondering: what am I not seeing? One thing is clear. I have read so much I could teach a lesson to anyone about prosperity, but I still don't have any money! All that I know to do is to keep on praying and visualizing my good. I won't give up.

I want to change my consciousness. Everything you say makes sense, but I don't seem to be getting it.

Look at the areas of your life. Think of financial well being, relationships, work, and physical health to name a few. Which one offers you the least amount of problems?

Physical health.

Does this mean you do not have problems in this area?

No, I have problems, but they don't seem to be a big deal. When I broke my hip it hurt and I was scared. Once I got clear on the healing process I was fine. I did what I needed to do and I healed.

Tell the story.

I was in the emergency room the night I broke it. A doctor told me my days of playing sports were over. My hip was in pieces and needed to be pinned together. I thought about what he said and found it to be unacceptable. I looked him in the eye and told him I would be playing sports again soon.

I had my operation with another doctor. He told me to spend six weeks on crutches. After that I had exercises to do. After six weeks I threw away the crutches and painfully did my exercises. Three months from the day of my fall I was playing full court basketball.

You saw your physical condition as a challenge. You believed 100% in your ability to heal. You listened to professional advice and did what was before you to do. You did your personal work (managed your emotions, eliminated thoughts contrary to healing). You left the healing to God.

Yes, I did.

There are no levels of difficulty in God's healing. You can heal your finances as well. Believe; do what is before you to do; do the mental/emotional work; and let go. Have you noticed that some people you know never worry about money, and they always seem to have it? Some of these same people experience poor physical health. Everyone has their own challenges. Use your success in physical health as a model for the other areas of your life. Use the success of others as your model. You will learn.

You must be frustrated with me that I am such a slow learner.

Actually, we find you quite interesting and rather humorous.

I make you laugh?

When you get it, yes, you make us laugh. We laugh with joy when you realize something new. We laugh when you love. We smile when you earnestly seek answers. This is a funny arrangement. It is as if you are lost in a forest, but here we are above the trees. We see you walking around lost, so we do our best to tell you where the path is. We do not mean to be insensitive, but it reminds us of an old parable:

The Fish Story

Imagine you are watching over a pool of water. You see a fish and you tell him that he is surrounded by water. He does not quite realize what this means. The fish tells you he is looking for water. He swims in every direction in search of it. He goes to the fish library and researches data on fish lore, studies fish psychology and philosophy, and works very hard to understand just where the Waters of Life are and how to approach them.

A wise old fish tells him that in ancient times fish knew about a so-called Ocean of Life. It was prophesied that fish would eventually live in the Waters of Life happily. Our little friend gets together with his friends at a fish seminar. Together they roll their eyes, wiggle their tails, and begin to chant: "O Water, Water, Water, we beseech you to reveal yourself to us. Please flow around and through us. Thank you. Amen". You smile at the fish and tell him that water is already flowing around and through him. He gives you a puzzled look and swims off.

Bill, you are immersed in the waters of infinite life just as fish are in the ocean. Life flows through you and around you. God, the Spirit of Life, permeates everything. You do not have to go looking for God, or for prosperity, or success, or health, or love. It is all here.

Then why don't I see it?

You think the answer is somewhere outside of you. You search far and wide for what cannot be found outside of you. You seek answers that you already have. You chase prosperity that is standing before you.

You make gods of people and things that cannot possibly meet all of your needs. You search for love when all you need to do is give it. We do not laugh at you, but sometimes we laugh at life on earth. We love it when you laugh at life.

I would like to laugh a little more.

There is much to laugh about, even when things seem terrible.

Bill's Journal

Maybe if I laughed a little more I'd be happier. Life is kind of silly. We wander around looking for things we already have. How ridiculous! I get upset. I feel hurt and anger. Maybe it's really funny, but I don't know it.

As you know, I read a lot of books. Am I wasting my time?

Books can be of great value if used well.

How do I use a book well?

First of all, question the ideas you read in books. Contemplate them. Take them within and experience how they feel to you. Do they feel right? Do they feel off the mark? Do you feel fearful when you think about a particular idea? Are you experiencing fear because you do not wish to accept the truth? Or, are you experiencing fear because its implementation would take you farther away from your desired closeness to God?

I used to challenge spiritual ideas when I was an agnostic. Since then I have wanted to believe so strongly, that sometimes I try to force myself to believe in things.

You owe it to the integrity of your mind to question ideas. If you force yourself to accept ideas your mind will reject them. You have been given a thinking mind. Think. Just accepting ideas is not thinking; it is parroting. Simply rejecting ideas you do not like is not thinking; it is rebelling. Consider, weigh, and contemplate ideas. Allow your intuition to speak to you, then decide. Know that the path of the believer and the paths of the agnostic and the atheist are equally valid. Each must be true to himself. Believers often gloss over their doubts. Doubts must be faced.

Bill's Journal

It is clear to me that I have been looking outside of myself for satisfaction. Life is an inside job. I thought that if I became successful in business, earned plenty of money, and had wonderful relationships, I'd be happy. Things don't work that way. The outside doesn't create the inside; the inside creates the outside. My thoughts and feelings create my life experience. The answers to my problems are inside of me, not in books. When I first started the spiritual path, my motivation was a spiritual longing. Later, I became caught up in the idea that I could improve my financial circumstances through affirmations and prayer. I saw wealth in my future. I saw happiness. Maybe I am just a thought away from solving all problems and finding happiness, but the gap between my thoughts and "the Thought" looks like light years to me. There must be a way for me to let go of my old thinking and feeling — a way to let go of worry and fear.

Your original motivation was a spiritual longing. What is it now?

More of a material motivation than I would like it to be. It is difficult to shift to purely spiritual motives when I am struggling to survive. I have to pay the bills.

Realize that you are experiencing "life." There is no pill you can take that will make all of your troubles go away. Each situation that confronts you helps you grow. Imagine that whatever is going on for you is a situation perfectly crafted for your learning and enjoyment. So go ahead, experience and enjoy. Life is not about finding the right affirmation, the right book, the right religion, or the right answer. It is about choices. From moment to moment, you choose what to think, how to act, and what to say. Your choices determine the course of your life. Choose to listen to intuition and divine guidance or choose to do it on your own. Choose to be happy, and happiness is yours. Choose to be successful and you will be. Choose to focus on God as your source, or choose to focus on people and situations. Choose to see yourself as loved, or choose to see yourself as unloved. Your circumstances will reflect these choices. Things do not just happen to you. Your experiences are results of your choices and perceptions. Embrace your experiences and learn from them. Know that even struggle is a choice.

Didn't I already choose to act successful and then fall on my face anyway?

You said the words, but in your thoughts and feelings, you did not believe it. Also, you did not ask for guidance. You can choose to let go of your fears, Bill. You are surviving much better than you think you are.

Chapter 3
Learning to Let Go

I have listened to what you have said. What can I do when there appears to be no sign of improvement in my life? I feel frustrated, almost hopeless, and scared. I feel like I am at the end of my rope! I dream so much of a better life, yet it seems to elude me. Every day seems to be the same old stuff, but I know I've made changes in my thinking. I look back over the past few years and I see growth. Yet, my conditions have changed very little.

Know that there is a Loving Presence within you that has not forsaken you. You are loved, guided, and protected. As long as you continue to focus your energy within on God as your Source, you can expect to receive what you need. Do not be concerned about how it comes. It may come in the form of ideas, but ideas do not enter the mind that is tense. You must relax your mind and trust that the right ideas or opportunities are present. You have tossed your thoughts and feelings into the pot, and now you are watching for them to boil. You are not the cook. Let God do the cooking. God does not need you standing over His shoulder.

We suggest you do the following:

1. Let go. Give up everything to the Infinite Intelligence within you. Contemplate what that means. Ask: Were I to let go and leave everything to God what would that look like? Would I continue to feed worrisome thoughts? Would I be angry when money does not get here as fast I think it should?"

2. Love yourself. This means to stop all self-criticism and criticism of others. Focus on what is right about you. Embrace yourself and your life. Love the fact that you are in the process of proving God in you.

3. Be you. Quit trying so hard and begin to express who you are. You are a child of God with God-given talents. Express those talents now. If you want to be a writer, write. If you want to be in business, do business. If you are a singer, sing. Express you. Follow your inner desires for expression.

4. Acknowledge what you already have by expressing gratitude daily.

5. With quietness and firmness, ask for direction. Listen to your intuition. When you are able to set fear aside and trust your inner wisdom, it will come. When you truly want the answer, it will come.

Grateful! Why should I be grateful when I don't have enough?

That is part of your problem. You think you do not have enough.

I don't, so why does God need me to be grateful?

God does not need you to be grateful. You need to be grateful. What you hold in your mind is demonstrated in your life. If you spend your time thinking about what you do not have, and feeling the hurt or angry feelings that go with that, you will create more conditions that seem lacking. What you focus on in thought will expand in your life. Focus on the blessings you already have, then your blessings will be increased. You see what you want to see. If you want to enjoy prosperity then start seeing and acknowledging it. What are you waiting for? Worrying about what you do not have is fear. Can you name even one person who has increased his wealth, who has enriched his life through fear or worry? Fear creates more fear in your life. Expressing true gratitude for your blessings is love. Love creates more love in your life.

You, who want more, must first acknowledge what you already have. Acknowledge the portion of your body which appears healthy. Acknowledge your friends, your money (even if there is little), and your surroundings with deeply felt gratitude. Go back into your past in your mind. You will notice that even in painful situations, there were ways in which you were guided and supported. If this were not true you would not be here now. Express your gratitude for all of the times you made it through a tough situation. Gratitude is love. Build an attitude of gratitude and you will never lack for anything.

Think back, Bill, to the time you were homeless, penniless, and physically broken. You were at the bottom, but you were given help. A man opened his home to you. Money came, maybe not as much as you thought you needed, but it came. Your body healed. Eventually you found a well paying job and a home of your own. You could have been left at the bottom. Are you not grateful for all that you received? Are you not grateful that you arose victorious from the bottom of life? Or do you spend your time hurting over what you still do not have? If your attitude is that what you have been given is not enough, then you will continue to perceive and demonstrate "not enough" in your life.

Can you love the miracles that have happened for you? Can you love the fact that you made it out of the pits? Look at the world around you. Notice how fortunate you are. Look around this apartment in which you live. Notice your furnishings. Are you not kept warm in the winter? Do you not have enough food to eat? Are there not friends and loved ones in your life? Be grateful that you are you and that you have what you have. Bless your life, and bless others. Love in this way and your harvest of joy and prosperity will be great.

You're right. That time when I had the broken hip was miraculous, but I didn't realize it. I had come back to my home state penniless. I prayed for a place to live, because I didn't want to sleep in my car anymore. An old friend came to mind.

This man had told me I could stay with him if I ever needed a place. He was glad to see me and to give me a room. A week later I was working to earn some money, and I fell off a one story roof onto the pavement. I broke my hip. I received good care and I healed quickly. Unknown to me, the guy that owned the commercial building I was working on had me covered under his insurance policy. All of my doctor and hospital bills were paid in full. I received a small income to live on for a few months. I didn't focus on all of the good things that happened. I mostly focused on what was wrong with my life. I focused on my debts and my relationship problems. I was embarrassed that I had made such a mess of things. I desperately searched for answers to these seemingly overwhelming problems, but ignored the blessings I was receiving. Why didn't you tell me about gratitude back then?

We were there, Bill. You prayed for answers, but you did not listen for them. You acted as if God was some kind of slot machine in the sky. Put in a prayer, pull the lever, see if you are a winner. We are grateful you are beginning to listen now.

Bill's Journal

It is true; I haven't been very grateful. Many people don't have a home or money, and many don't have food. I have so much more than that, and yet, I have not felt gratitude for it. When I look at where I have been, and where I could have ended up, I do feel grateful.

After our talk I was feeling good yesterday. That all changed this morning. I woke up feeling depressed. My body ached, my nose was running, and I was filled with frustration. My world looks dark.

I look at myself and my life, and I ask why am I here again? Why do I continue to experience the same conditions? I have worked hard. I have studied. I have stretched. I am tired.

Tired of struggle. Tired of pain. Tired of seemingly falling on my face. I am tired of my life always looking like its falling apart. Tired of telling this to you.

For eight years I have been working spiritually to create a life that is God-centered, prosperous, joyful, and love-filled. I see that I have little financial security and sporadic income. My back aches. Why can't I make progress? What can I do?

The spiritual journey often includes dark nights. Your pain feels very real to you, and it is a sign of good.

A sign of good!? I don't think so. This "be positive" stuff is really annoying. I've prayed for progress, change and spiritual growth. I want these repeating life cycles of pain to end. Yesterday I prayed that I would just as soon end it all rather than go on like this. I keep asking myself: "Is it really worth it?"

We heard you and cannot answer for you. We see worth in your life. We ask you: "Is it worth it?"

I keep thinking it's going to get better. I'm not going to kill myself because I might miss out on something. I'm just depressed.

Things often appear to grow worse before they get better. Positive change often involves a period of seeming chaos. The old thoughts and beliefs are hanging on. The new you is desiring to emerge. Old thought forms want to pull you back into your old ways. Do not fight them. Stay firm in your resolve to become God-centered; to welcome your new life; to love and be loved. The change is happening. The chaos you are experiencing is proof of it.

I thought that I had let go, and that things would improve immediately. Maybe I haven't let go all the way. I mean, if I still feel anxious, then I obviously am not letting go at that moment.

Yesterday you were feeling a new sense of gratitude. Today, a part of you that needs healing rises up to challenge those thoughts. It is appearing in order for you to deal with it. When you ask for change, or make a change in your thinking, the barriers to change you have created are shown to you. Give thanks for this. Tell yourself it is safe to feel the feelings, then release them. Remember that it is only your thoughts that are creating these feelings. Take time each day to face your thoughts, then allow them to pass.

I don't know how I can truly change a painful physical condition or a desperate financial situation. I feel like I have so little control over these situations.

You are not changing the conditions. You are changing your thinking. When you let go and trust Spirit, you change your point of focus. You have complete control over this. You are only a thought away from this change. Change your mind and your life will follow. Do not worry about the physical changes. Focus on what you can control-your thinking, your emotional state, and the actions you take as a result.

It often feels like my thoughts and feelings control me rather than me controlling them.

It is a combination of desire and discipline. The more you want the change, the more willing you will be to discipline your thinking. Some people need an absolutely desperate situation before they can want to change. Do you need to hit bottom again before you desire change enough to change your thoughts?

No, I don't want that again.

Deep within you want to create change. The conditions you are experiencing help to create a sense of urgency in yourself to want to shift your thinking. Pay attention to your thinking. Be very conscious of the thoughts you entertain and the emotions that result. Come to recognize repetitive thoughts that create fear. Catch yourself thinking these thoughts and remind yourself that <u>you</u> are doing the thinking here. <u>You</u> are creating the emotion. Fearful people often pray and affirm *with great effort, only to tire of it and give up in anger or frustration. They feel this frustration because they believe that what they need comes from something outside themselves. There is no outside; there is only the inside. All that you experience comes through you. Face your thoughts which cause fear.*

One of my thoughts is that I am not doing enough. Then I begin to criticize myself for not doing everything I can. This creates an uncomfortable tension in my solar plexus. As I continue to think these thoughts the uncomfortable feeling moves into the rest of my body. Soon I am filled with this fearful feeling.

Next time you begin to feel fearful stop your thinking. Recall that you are the author of these thoughts and feelings. Identify the thought: "I am not doing all that I can." We would ask a question here. You are not doing all that you can therefore what?

Something is wrong with me. I'm useless and incapable. I'm unsuccessful.

These thoughts bring no value to you. Look at your life. If you are doing all that you can, then your thought is incorrect. If you are not doing all that you can, then what else can you do? Acknowledge what can be done and do it. You are using your current situation to support an old belief (useless and incapable). The opportunity has come to let this thought go. Condemning yourself is not an effective motivator. Do what is before you to do. Leave the results to God.

Take time each day to visualize and imagine the joy and peace you will feel knowing that God is always there for you. Imagine what it feels like not to have to worry or be fearful. Imagine what it feels like to have every need fulfilled, to have a whole and healthy body, and to have relationships that work.

You want me to fantasize that I am filled with joy and peace?

This is no fantasy. Joy and peace are real and available to you.

Only think joyous and peaceful thoughts and the experience is yours. We say for you to <u>imagine</u> because in your present state you believe in your physical situation and the experience of it which you have created. So, imagine these feelings every day. Teach yourself to be joyful, peaceful, and loving. Focus on God's Grace.

What is God's Grace?

It is God's unconditional love for you. It is continuously radiating to you and through you. As you continue to turn your attention inward to God as your source; as you recognize your connection with your Higher Self; and as you focus on the incredible and powerful love God has for you; you begin to create an opening for God's love to pour in. As it begins to pour into your consciousness, that love is manifested as the answers to the needs and desires in your life. Before that manifestation ever happens, you will begin to feel a sense of peace and understanding. At first you may wonder why you are not worried when everything appears to be falling apart. If you are not careful, this wondering may cause you to worry and act out of fear. Just enjoy the new sense of well-being. The manifestation will follow. The important thing is to take your mind off what you think you want to have happen, and focus on God's love for you instead. Stay focused on God.

So, if I want more money I shouldn't think about wanting more money?

You are not trying to get more money, better health, or any specific situations. Do not try so hard to get them. Your goal is to know and love God within you, and to know and love yourself. Do this and you will reconnect with your Source. When you place God first in your life, all else is added. You may think about having more money, but do not worry about it. Practice the feeling of already being prosperous.

It sounds like a paradox. If I want more money I need to stop wanting it so much?

You need to stop focusing on what it is you want and focus on your connection with God. Focus on the Spirit of God living and loving in you and through you. At the same time you need to take care of yourself. If you are fearful about money, you can find work and earn it, or find another legal means to obtain it so you can reduce your fear. If you are experiencing illness, do everything you can to enhance healing, including seeing a doctor or taking medicine. In your present state of consciousness, God may supply your needs through a job or through the hands of a doctor. Do not do these things out of panic, but do them because they are logical means to improve your situation. Before you make a decision, ask for guidance; then do what feels right. Do not stop taking care of yourself because you feel lost. Do your best, all the while knowing that God is guiding you now.

Also, take care of yourself emotionally. Let yourself be loved. If someone wants to help you, let them. Do not allow pride to prevent you from receiving love and care. Care for yourself in your thoughts by refusing to be critical of yourself. Stop dwelling on mistakes.

I do feel better when I consider what you have said. What do I do when I feel myself slipping back into worry and depression?

Acknowledge your feelings and your doubts. Face them. They are symptoms reoccurring. Do not make yourself wrong for having them. Shift away from your unhealthy thoughts to more healthy thoughts.

Bill's Journal

I know why I keep getting frustrated. I push too hard. I think I have to have it yesterday, and when it doesn't come as fast as I want I get upset. I get angry at myself and at the Universe. Letting go is tough. I seem to think that I must worry about a situation for it to improve. Why do I always need to struggle so much?

Chapter 4
Learning to Release
Fear, Pain, and Struggle

I feel like I should be farther along than I am. I feel like a failure.

Your process is unfolding. That is why you are here. You are experiencing what you want to experience.

What do you mean?

You have created this life and all of your experiences to date. You brought your state of consciousness into this life. As you look around you, you see the physical forms and experiences that represent your thoughts and feelings about you. Your life is but a mirror of who you think you are. All that you think, feel, and believe is reflected back to you. You came here because you wanted to grow and learn. You wanted to see, in physical manifestation, your perceptions of yourself. Look around you. This is what you think you are. The joys, the sorrows, the pain, the good times, the bad. It is all part of your perception of you.

I thought this life was supposed to be all illusion.

It is not all illusion. Love is not an illusion. True joy is not an illusion. Peace of mind is not illusion. These are real. Loving, joyous, and peaceful thoughts are reflections of the real you. Your other experiences are reflections of illusions you hold about yourself.

What illusions do I hold about myself?

You doubt your value. You think you have to prove it by hard work and struggle. You seek after recognition to affirm your value. You measure your value in terms of your financial success and by the approval of others.

You are valuable. To doubt your value is to have an illusion about yourself. Your experiences that seem to <u>prove</u> your lack of value are reflections of how much or how little value you place on you.

So, you say that I don't value myself?

We see only value in you. We love you. We love your illusions, too. You want them and we want what you want.

But, my illusions hurt me. Do you want me to be hurt?

You cannot be hurt. You are Spirit. Any number of things may happen to you in life. You will still be Spirit. Your body may die, but you can never be hurt. The hurting you are experiencing is by choice. It is your right to feel hurt if that is what you want.

When will the hurting stop?

When you truly want something else more, like love or joy.

What can I do?

Stop condemning yourself. Your fears and self-imposed pressures are a result of self rejection and condemnation. Spirit never condemns you or rejects you. You are not judged by Spirit. Your self-imposed judgments of yourself help to create your conditions.

I am pretty hard on myself. I know I would feel a whole lot better if something good would happen. Instead each day seems like the day before. Each day my fear seems to grow. It is like my fear rules me. I feel powerless at times. Paralyzed.

Fear is about the future. You fear the future will be like the past. In the past you experienced lack. You are afraid of going there again. Do not allow your memory of the past to cloud your vision of the future. You are learning and growing. You are experiencing life, and fear is part of life. You see your situation as unfavorable yet it does not compare with the suffering you once experienced. This is progress, is it not?

You can learn to handle the fear. When you become filled with fear, immediately focus on the physical sensations of fear. Just experience the sensations. Feel the fear sensations in your body. Stop thinking. Or at least stop thinking the thoughts that have brought you pain and discomfort. Your body will work through the uncomfortable feelings. They will go away. Fearful feelings are fed and expanded by fearful thoughts. To release your fear and pain feel the fear and pain. At the same time, cease feeding these emotions with fearful thoughts.

So, if I just allow myself to feel the discomfort of fear it will go away?

Yes. First you think a fearful thought such as "What if I can not make enough money to pay the rent?" Next your body tenses up, your breathing becomes shallow, and you feel great discomfort around your solar plexus. Then you frantically search your mind for answers, hoping to find a way to pay the rent, to alleviate the feelings you are experiencing. Then you think about how time is passing you by and still you have not found the prosperity you seek. These thoughts create more fear. This is how fear paralyzes. What do you think has created this fear?

Not being able to pay the rent.

No, Bill, your thoughts have created this experience. Yet, you have made progress. In the past you would have anesthetized your feelings with food, or if available, the company of a woman. Now you allow yourself to feel the feelings. That is good. Now take the next step. Recognize the thoughts and beliefs that create the uncomfortable feelings, and make a decision to let them go. Then take time to feel the feelings in your body. Just feel them. Experience them. Think about where the tension is and know that you can feel it and still be okay. When people feel this discomfort they do not have to reach for food, or alcohol, or a drug, or sex, or a cigarette. Everyone has a choice. You choose what to do to your body. You choose which thoughts to think. In this way you choose your emotions. You are not the victim of your emotions. You are the creator of them. Therefore, pain is a choice. When you feel pain, recognize that your thoughts are creating it. Pain is not bad, and it is often a good teacher. Let it teach you, then be done with it.

So, I think worrisome thoughts which cause me physical discomfort and emotional and physical pain. If I keep on thinking those thoughts I am choosing to feel pain.

Yes. Recognize those thoughts. Discern whether or not they have value for you. Do these thoughts help you to grow, to be healthy, to learn? Do they help you to accomplish your goal or solve the problem? If they do, then by all means keep them awhile and ponder them. If they are but self torturing thoughts, then choose to let them go. Just feel the physical experience of discomfort, without the painful thought, and the pain will go away.

Okay, great. So I feel better. Great! What about the rent? I still have to pay it.

When you have emptied your mind of worrisome thoughts ask the question: "How can I pay the rent?" Once your mind is clear of worrisome thoughts there is space for new ideas. Thank God for meeting your needs and refuse to worry about the rent. Keep an open mind to new ideas and do what is before you to do. Be patient and be willing to take action.

I can manage fear by refusing to think worrisome thoughts when I feel fearful. My body will process the fear feelings. When I empty my mind of worrisome thoughts new ideas can come in. I was able to let go of my thoughts for awhile and a thought came to me regarding how I could earn the money to pay the rent. I offered my services to a friend of mine who is a builder to help him increase his business. I told him I would help him increase his business through getting the word out to the community. I asked for $1000 in return. He liked the idea and paid me the money up front. I've paid the rent and a few other things.

If I trusted God I wouldn't worry. Part of the problem is that I've always taken care of myself. I've prided myself on being independent. After all of the times I have fallen on my face it seems like I would have the humility to let God take charge.

Do I lack humility?

What is humility to you?

It means I know that I'm not always right, even if I feel like I'm completely right. I guess it means being willing to listen instead of blocking out the views of others.

It is being deeply grateful for the blessings you have. It is always being willing to forgive. It means refusing to be critical of others or yourself. Humility is recognizing that all power, all wisdom, and all Good come from God, not from your personality.

Humility is refusing to see yourself as better than or less than someone else. We are all connected. We are one. Humility is recognizing the oneness of all people with each other and our Creator. Humility is openness. There is always something for you to learn from every situation and from every person. Good can come to you from any direction. Humility is a willingness to let go of your preconceived notions about what should happen or what should be.

Humility is loving God more than you love your own opinion. This means that you become more focused on the value in another person than on what you think they should do or be. Do you think you are humble?

I am learning. I am continually releasing my need to have things my way. The other side of this is that I recognize that hanging my head in shame, or feeling guilt for mistakes, are not ways of expressing humility.

Being humble, you have no need for great riches or fame. You have moved closer to God. When you give up the thought that you must have this thing or that situation, and place God first in your life, everything you require is added.

I say I want to put God first, but something is getting in my way. This is difficult to admit, but I realize that I feel angry. I am angry at myself, angry at God, and angry at life. I am angry that I have invested so much time and energy into spiritual growth with little to show for it.

You wanted an immediate return?

Yes I did. I still do. I must sound like a spoiled child who rants and raves when he doesn't get what he wants.

You are not that child. It is only one part of you. What does that child in you need in order to feel better?

Success. Manifestation. A visible return for efforts expended.

Let us be more specific. What can you do to help that scared child within you?

I don't know.

You cannot ignore your anger. It must be faced. The way you
*face it is to acknowledge it. Say to yourself, "I feel angry. I realize that
I have chosen to be angry. I am willing to let this anger go and to
choose something else (like love). Do this each time anger arises. Once
you have done this you may find that the energy from the anger is still
there. Use the energy for something productive.*

Bill's Journal

By loving myself more, I will grow and learn. I cannot
ignore my anger. I must acknowledge it and release it. There
seems to be so much of it in me. I can't place positive thoughts
on top of anger and expect I'll feel better.

Many teachers have told us we must not allow negative
thoughts to come into our minds. This is a good practice.
However, negative thoughts would have little meaning if there
were not fertile ground for them to take root. It is this negative
fertility I must attend to. What I think about is based on what
I think I am.

Every decision I make, every opinion I hold, and every
word I speak is based on my self image. As I change my self
image, the way in which I view myself, I change my life. As I
identify with love, with my Higher Self, with abundance in all
things, my life becomes a reflection of these ideas. It becomes
easier for positive thoughts to take root.

I can use affirmations or any tool, but the real power is
within me. It is my conviction that gives the tool power. If the
tool happens to work, only my belief and conviction can make
the healing stay.

It is time to stop fighting my thoughts and emotions.
This causes me pain. Uncomfortable emotions are coming up
so I can take care of them. Instead of pushing them down with
positive thoughts, I need to acknowledge them and release them.
Force does not work. I am not my anger. I am not my hurt.
These are only emotions I have expressed, not the truth about
me. They are symptoms of something amiss in my thinking.

I acknowledge and I release, but the negative stuff comes back. What do I do?

The spiritual path can be rocky at times. It is your resistance that makes it so. As you approach higher levels of learning the unhealthy thought forms of your personality will fight to hang on to control. These thought forms may lead to illness, financial lack, conflict in your relationships, or other problems. These are appearances and not the truth about you. Remain steady in your desire to grow closer to God. Acknowledge and release again. Do this as many times as it takes. Expect good things.

You can tell me to expect, but that doesn't work for me. How do I expect success when failure seems certain?

A basketball player was asked what he expected his shooting percentage to be in an upcoming game. He replied, "100%." His interviewer said that no one makes every shot he takes. The player answered "I know that, but I expect to. I would never take a shot at the basket unless I thought I could make it." Did you expect to fail when you asked your friend for the $1000?

No, I felt very confident. I just don't seem to have a very good track record. I have failed a great many times.

Your track record is not what you are counting on. God has a perfect track record. No miracle is too big or too small. Nothing is impossible. Trust in God's ability to come through, not on the ability of your personality.

Trust God. Let go and let God. Ask God. God, God, God, God, God! God is this impersonal essence. God is in everything. God is everywhere. How can I talk to this God who is everything and everywhere? How do I talk to this God who is so impersonal? You talk about God as if God was a person. God is not a person. If God is not a person then who do I talk to? Who do I count on? Why pray at all if God is not a person? Why ask anything if God is not a person? If God is everything then how do I have a relationship with Everything?

When we speak of God we speak of Mind. This Mind of God is everywhere present. When you are willing to place your trust in God you express your willingness to set aside the thoughts of your personality. The thoughts of your personality are very limited and are restricted to current knowledge that you have stored. When you are open to the Mind of God you become like a radio receiver. As a receiver you have access to new thoughts, inspiration, and intuition. Your prayer has no effect on God. It has a great effect on you. It serves to align you with the thoughts, the love, and the answers you need which are always available to you.

God is a presence. God is the Presence. To be continuously aware of the presence of God is to practice the Presence. Be always aware that this Presence, called God, is here now. Therefore, bring your thoughts to the here and now. Let go of past regret and your worries about the future. Be here now

Know that you are not separate from God, therefore do not think that God judges your worthiness. God does not withhold your good. God does not choose one person over another to receive good. God is. The word "God" is a but a name, and a name is limiting. We, in order to communicate with you, must use a limiting name in order to describe that which is unlimited.

Then to whom am I speaking when I say the Lord's Prayer?

You speak to God, All That Is. "Our Father, who art in Heaven" refers to the Source of all being who is constantly in a state of perfection. The Lord's Prayer is as much an affirmation of what is as it is a prayer. You pray to align your thoughts with the Mind of God. With the Mind of God thinking in you your prayer is answered. When you pray, you may also speak to your Higher Self, that part of you which has never forgotten that it is part of God. This will help to make it more personal for you.

When you pray, know that God, the Universe, does not intervene in your personal affairs. God gives you that which you ask for, whether you know you are asking for it or not. God seeks to express through you, but only with your permission. God always provides you with what you need. God continually loves you.

Then why talk to God at all? If my prayers don't make an impression on God, why pray?

As we have said, you pray to align yourself with God. In your present state of mind, you believe you are separate from God. You pray to build a relationship with God. As the relationship strengthens, you come to realize your oneness with God. Since you are connected to God, you are connected to God's all knowingness. Therefore you are connected to the answer to all problems, to creative ideas, and to that which will meet your needs at all times. Prayer teaches you this.

So, when I pray, God doesn't do anything He isn't already doing. God is already answering me; I'm already connected to the answer; and prayer just makes the connection complete.

Yes. God is within and all around you. It is only your thought which keeps you from the realization of God. Prayer helps you realize God.

What about you? Do you intervene?

We do intervene at times. We, as angels, spirit guides and teachers often help you. Sometimes because of your prayers and sometimes not.

You help me? How?

Think of the intensity of your negative thoughts over the years. Had you reaped exactly what you had sown your life would have been much more difficult. You may not have survived. We, including your Soul, have served as a filter to lessen the intensity of your thoughts.

Thank you. I remember spending whole days in intense negative thinking. Can you tell me of a specific time where you helped me?

Many years ago you were driving your car on your way to a party. You were about to make a left hand turn, but you hesitated. At that moment a car sped by your left side. Had you made the turn in your normal fashion you would have been hit and probably killed. Why did you hesitate?

I'm not sure. I had a thought that I should wait, so I did. The whole incident took only a second. I was very relieved that it happened that way. You had something to do with that?

We put the thought in your mind.

Why? If all that happens is a result of our thinking, then wasn't I supposed to be hit?

No. It was not your time to go. Before your birth we made an agreement with your Soul to protect you from these kinds of things. Do not test us. If you try to drive off of a bridge we will let you fall. We do not interfere with your free will.

So, you were my guardian angels.

We still are.

There have been times when I wanted you to intervene. I wanted you to save me, but you didn't.

We do not contradict your free will, and we will not take away that which you need. Often you have chosen to suffer. The suffering has been part of your learning. If we were to take it from you, you would not learn.

Bill's Journal

As I look over the words I have written I just have to shake my head. I know how Universal Law works. I can recite the importance of love and self love. I can think of dozens of affirmations for wealth, health, or harmony. I am real "smart" about what it takes to change consciousness. I know that God is perfect and that God is in me. I have learned many of the basics about what it takes to live a life that is spiritually rich, financially prosperous, and full of love. There seems to be a big difference between knowing about these things and living them. To a degree I guess I am living these ideas. I'm ready to move up to a higher level. I'm willing to do the personal work that will help me grow and find greater contentment in life.

It would be great if I could just fall in love with myself. Why can't I just look at my self and my life with total unconditional love? I've been told that this kind of love is all it takes. Look upon my self and my situation with complete unconditional love and healing will happen. What prevents me from doing this?

Chapter 5
Love and Forgiveness

Friend: Hey, Bill. Are you okay? You look like you're in pain.

Bill: I am. I woke up this morning with a tremendous pain in my lower back. I can barely move I'm so stiff. I don't know how this happened.

Friend: Why don't you ask it?

Bill: What?

Friend: Why don't you go into a meditation and ask your lower back why it hurts?

Bill: That sounds a little strange to me. Is that what you do when you're in pain?

Friend: Yes, and it works. I get an answer.

Bill: Okay, I asked my back why it hurts. I didn't get an answer.

Friend: Be patient. It'll come.

Next Morning

I know the answer. I can't explain how. The first thought that came to me this morning was something to the effect that I don't feel loved. I asked myself: "What does that have to do with my back pain?"

In the physical world physical phenomena are manifestations of thought. Often that thought is subconscious. Something you have buried is now rising to the surface. Recently you asked the question: "How can I love myself unconditionally?" In order to love yourself unconditionally you must remove the barriers you have created. Your pain is an opportunity. We recommend you receive help on this one.

I was hoping you would help me.

We suggest you receive human help. You need a healer. Sometimes you can not just think away problems, Bill. You can analyze and figure all the reasons why your back hurts. You can come up with all the answers, but it still hurts. You can affirm health and deny pain, but the problem, the cause is still there. You need help. Go see a counselor.

Yeah, I do need help. I need a counselor who understands both spirituality and psychology. I need to see someone I can feel very comfortable with. Who should I see?

You know who to see. You heard her speak last summer.

Yes, maybe she can help me. She spoke at my church, and I was very impressed with her. She said she does spiritual counseling. I'll see if I can get an appointment.

The Session

Bill: And it came to me that this pain in my back is caused by a feeling of a lack of love and support.

Counselor: Are you in a relationship now?

Bill: No. I had one that just ended after three years. We ended on good terms.

Counselor: Tell me how you felt unloved in that relationship.

Bill: When you asked that question I found thoughts and feelings moving to an earlier relationship that ended several years ago.

Counselor: Let's go with that. How did you feel unloved in that relationship?

Bill: Nothing I ever did was good enough for her. I never could seem to please her. No matter how hard I tried, it was never good enough.

Counselor: You tried very hard to please her, didn't you?

Bill: Yes, I did. I wasn't accepted for who I was. It seemed like everything I did was criticized. I made a lot of changes, but she kept raising the bar.

Counselor: Close your eyes and go back to that situation. Feel that feeling of being unloved and unappreciated again, of not being accepted for who you are.

Bill: (Closing eyes) I feel it.

Counselor: You've felt this before.

Bill: What?

Counselor: You have felt these feelings before. This isn't the first time you felt this pain. Go back to when you were a child. Go back to a time when you first felt unloved and unacceptable. Go back.

Bill: My father, I can, I can hardly talk. I never do this! Never!

Counselor: Never do what?

Bill: Cry! I'm sobbing and I can't stop it. It's embarrassing.

Counselor: I'm hardly noticing your tears. Tell me about your father.

Bill: When you asked me to go back my mind raced to a time when I was about two years old. I don't think my father liked me. I never felt that he liked me. When I was little I felt resentment from him. The story was that I looked a lot like my mother, and not like my dad. I guess people used to tease him and ask who the father was. Those comments hurt and embarrassed him. It seemed like he took it out on me. I wasn't able to meet his expectations as far as I knew. He never complimented me, or told me he loved me, or touched me in an affectionate way. I can look back, as an adult, and understand, but as a two year old, or even as a teenager, I just felt like something was wrong with me. I tried to look good in his eyes, but I wasn't successful.

Counselor: You tried very hard to please him, didn't you?

Bill: Yeah, I did. It never happened though. He died a few years ago and I really didn't feel anything. We never had much of a relationship. He was always closed off to me, so I closed off to him.

Counselor: Where did you feel safe and loved when you were a child?

Bill: Sometimes I felt it from my mother, though she never said the words either. My grandparents! I felt loved and safe at my grandparents' house. They were my mother's parents.

Unfortunately my grandfather died when I was four and my Grandmother died several years later. But I spent a lot of time with them when I was little. They thought I was special, and they made me feel special. I feel warm when I think of them and their house. My father didn't like my grandparents. My mother complained that they spoiled me. She said it took awhile to get me to behave after I spent time with my grandparents. My home was very restrictive. I think I resented the restrictions after experiencing the freedom to be myself at my grandparents.

Counselor: Bill, perhaps your grandparents didn't spoil you. Perhaps they just loved you generously.

Bill: I like that. So, what do I do now. I don't hate my father, and I'm not really into blaming my parents for what's going on in my life. I want to move on. I really thought I had already worked out this parent stuff.

Counselor: In your childhood a pattern was established which included being rejected and feeling hurt. You have brought that pattern into your adult life. You are continually recreating situations where you feel this pain. You set up situations where you are unable to meet the expectations of another person.

Bill: Why?

Counselor: As a child your interactions with your father convinced you that you were less than worthy (of being loved), that the only way you could prove your worthiness was by meeting his expectations. Since you could not meet his expectations you believed yourself unworthy. As an adult you continue to prove your unworthiness by finding people whose expectations you cannot meet. You will continue to recreate these situations until you can work out the feelings of being unloved.

Bill: How do I work it out?

Counselor: You learn to love and approve of yourself. I want you to do a visualization with me. Visualize a time in your childhood; let your mind choose it. See that child who is you, your small self. Go to him as the adult you are and talk with him. Let him talk to you and listen to his feelings. Give him whatever he needs: love, affection, compliments. Tell him how much you love him. Can you think of anything you did well when you were a child?

Bill: I had a very creative imagination. I often lived in it.

Counselor: Good. Compliment him on his imagination. Tell him how great you think it is. Give specific examples of his wonderful imagination at work.

Bill: Okay.

Counselor: Now I want you to visualize the Christ. How do you see the Christ?

Bill: I see a figure clothed in light.

Counselor: Now see the Christ approaching you. See and hear the Christ telling both of you how beautiful you are. Hear him say that he loves you dearly. Feel his love. See it in his eyes. Feel it in your heart. When you are ready, open your eyes. I want you to do this exercise every day for at least thirty minutes. This will help you to overcome that lack of love you feel as well as heal the past.

Bill: What happened here? I mean, you said a few words and suddenly my body was shaking with sobs.

Counselor: Your feelings of being unloved were imprinted in your body. You just released some of it. Do the visualizations. They will help to heal your mind and your body.

Bill: I will. I feel better. Thank you.

Counselor: You are welcome. Call me if you need me. And God bless you.

Bill's Journal

I thought I was all done with this emotionally abused child stuff. I thought all was forgiven. I'm happy about how this all turned out. I guess a back pain is more than a nuisance; it's an opportunity to learn something about myself. The pain in my back is gone. As I peel away these layers of consciousness it seems like all that I find is more layers. When do I get to the real me, the loving, strong and spiritual me? Just when I start thinking I'm becoming spiritually evolved another issue comes up.

Months Later

I think I understand forgiveness, now.

Tell us what you think it is.

Forgiveness is letting go of resentment and anger. It is not holding a grudge against someone.

That is certainly part of it.

But not all of it?

True forgiveness is the realization that there never was anything to forgive.

That's like saying that the mistake was all mine.

The mistake was in your perception of the event.

I don't get it! Someone does something hurtful to me and it's my error?

Who created the feelings of hurtfulness in you?

I didn't ask the person to hurt me. I didn't want to be hurt.

Who created the feelings of hurtfulness in you?

The other person did by their unkind act.

No, Bill. Their act may have been unkind, in that they did something that led to a situation of great inconvenience for you. Only you have the power to create or release your feelings about the situation. Only you can define the situation as good, bad, horrible, devastating, or joyous. You decided to be hurt. Maybe you wanted to understand what being hurt felt like. Whatever the other person did, you gave it the hurtful meaning. It may have been very painful at the time it happened. Perhaps the hurt came so quickly you had no time to decide differently. What about now? Does it still have to hurt now? Do you still want to play the role of being hurt and angry? Do you understand what we are saying?

Yes and no. I know that I am responsible for me, but I still feel the person in question did things that hurt me. I don't know why I would <u>want</u> to be hurt.

Then you have not forgiven yet.

How do I forgive someone who continues to treat me in an unkind way?

Have you tried hard to forgive them?

Yes, I have.

Perhaps you try too hard.

How can that be?

Forgiveness involves a process leading to an event. The process begins by acknowledging how you feel. If you feel anger, then admit it to yourself.

Does that mean I should express my anger to her?

If you are in a close relationship it is important to express your anger, but not in a way that attacks the other person. Just say that you are angry and why. If you are no longer close to this person, there are other ways to deal with your anger. You may want to yell at an empty chair you imagine her to be sitting in. You may want to write a letter that expresses your anger, but do not send it. You may want to express it to a trusted friend or a therapist. If you are angry, be angry. You must acknowledge that it is there. When you try to pretend it is not, the part of you that is angry becomes more angry. The problem with anger is not that you have it; it is in what you do with it. Acting it out on a person or stuffing it inside are not healthy ways to handle anger. At some level you wanted to experience hurt and anger. So go ahead and experience it. Your resistance to your emotions delays your release.

So, I acknowledge my anger, and I express it in a safe manner. Then what?

Then you forgive yourself for what you have done to yourself through anger and your uses of it. When you have expressed it sufficiently, you release it. You will release it when you truly want to release it. You will come to a point when you have had enough of it, when you understand that you have no use for it. Imagine yourself pouring love into the situation, the other person, and yourself. Remember this is a process. You can begin forgiving yourself while you are still angry. Finally, you must practice thought management. That is, if unforgiving thoughts arise, remind yourself that you have no use for them

This doesn't sound easy.

It must be done. Forgiveness is the only sane response to a situation.

Tell me, how do I forgive myself?

Acknowledge that you are imperfectly perfect. You are a child of God in the process of realizing your perfection. While in process, you cannot realistically expect yourself to think, feel, and act perfectly all the time. Drop the expectation. Accept yourself where you are now. Acknowledge your hurts, fears, angers and guilt. Also, acknowledge the good in your life. There is much. You are loved and have been loved by many. You have loved many people.

It sounds like a big job.

Begin with the first step.

I am angry with my ex-wife. When I see her she treats me with obvious disdain. I think I will write that letter.

After you write the letter you will. . . ?

Throw it away or burn it. Then I will forgive myself for all the misery I caused myself through my anger, and for feeling guilty about my anger. Then I will forgive her.

That will be the end of it?

No, it won't! I know it won't be the end. It will come up again.

Why will it not go away, Bill?

Because I don't want it to! I don't want to forgive. She makes me feel small. I've made mistakes and she won't let me forget them. What about all of the things she did to me?

Did your mistakes cause her pain?

Probably. But I've changed. I'm not making those mistakes now. It has been a long time.

No, I haven't. I feel terribly guilty. There was a period of time when I didn't help support the kids. I left town and I wasn't available as a father. I was wrapped up in my own stuff. But, I made up for it. I paid all the money I owed and I took responsibility.

You definitely made a comeback. Now you expect her to forgive you, yet you have not forgiven her. You still speak of her past acts. We would suggest that the problem is not her unforgiveness of you. The problem is your unforgiveness of yourself. She is but a reflection of your disdain for yourself. Guilt is a harsh master who exacts punishment. Your ex-wife's anger, your seeming inability to stabilize yourself financially, your back pains—these are the ways you punish yourself. You believe you must pay for the mistakes you made and so you do. Were you to forgive yourself healing would begin. You are fighting this situation, yet it is you who has set it up.

You tell yourself that you deserve to be treated with respect. Yet, how are you respecting yourself? She reflects your guilt back to you, and you resent her for it.

Well, she judges me, but I've never heard her take responsibility for her actions.

You have no control over her sense of responsibility. If you would like her to take responsibility, and to give you respect, then demonstrate how. Be what you want from others. Let go of your patterns of guilt and resentment. It is painful when someone we have loved is unable to acknowledge the greatness in us. You must acknowledge your own greatness and self worth. Then, you can acknowledge another's greatness.

Okay, I see your points. I feel guilty. I feel resentment. There is something in me that blocks my ability to forgive. No matter how many reasons I come up with to forgive, no matter how hard I try, I end up feeling emotionally locked into this pain.

That is one of the patterns you play out in your relationships.

What pattern is that?

Everyone has patterns they play out in relationships. A pattern may be bitterness, resentment, disappointment, envy, pessimism, doubt, guilt, loneliness, isolation, superiority, animosity, or unworthiness. It could also be love, joy, optimism, or easy-goingness. One or more of these is your pattern which you are playing out now. Guilt and resentment come up in this situation. Have you felt these emotions in other relationships?

Yes, in all of them to some degree.

You create thoughts of unworthiness with guilt, then you battle them with resentment. You resent others for not giving you the approval you desire. You resent them for not releasing you from your guilt. You set up situations where you feel guilty and resentful. What you call real life is like a dream. Dream interpreters say that when one dreams, all of the characters are the dreamer. We would say, that in this dream you call physical life, all of the characters play roles designed by you. You invite people into your life whose behaviors spark your barriers to love. Guilt and resentment are your barriers. This is why it is difficult for you to love yourself: You do not want to love yourself.

Yes I do because I've worked on these issues. I did those visualizations.

You did well, and you still have more work to do. You have continued to set up situations in your life where this need to feel guilty, and powerless to do anything about it is expressed. It continues to come up so that you can forgive; so that you can learn to let it go; and so that you can learn to love yourself whether you are given validation from another or not. You can learn to love another without the expectation that they must love you according to the way that you think they should love. Do guilt and resentment come up in a present relationship?

I find myself feeling resentment. If something goes wrong, I usually think its my fault. If there is nothing to resent, I find myself fantasizing situations where I am "wronged" and feel hurt and resentful. No matter how much I practice forgiveness, a pattern of guilt and resentment keeps returning. There must be a more effective way to let it go than forgiving every person I think hurt me, only to have it pop up over and over again.

Perhaps we can offer you some ideas for working through this pattern of unworthiness/guilt and resentment in relationships.

1. Acknowledge your tendency to feel guilty and to resent others. Stop making yourself wrong for feeling it. You are not wrong. This pattern is one of the reasons you came into physical form. You have created a pattern that has you thinking, feeling, and acting automatically. As this pattern begins to take off stop it in mid flight. Realize what you are doing. Say to yourself: "There I go feeling guilty (or) resentful again."

2. Stop making other people wrong for what they have done. You, in your desire to work out your negative feeling (in this case, guilt and resentment), have drawn these people and their behaviors into your life. They are mirrors of your emotional disturbance, not the causes of it. Catch yourself blaming the other person for how you feel. Note we said "catch", not "judge". We seek that you would be aware of that which you do to yourself.

3. In your mind, thank these people for helping you to learn and become stronger. Acknowledge that you were also attracted to each of them to help them learn and become stronger. Also, think of the good they have brought to you in this lifetime. This gives you a new, and more useful perspective on the person.

4. Love the feelings you have. Love your resentment (or any other emotional disturbance you are experiencing), your unforgiveness, and the experiences you created as a result of these feelings. The way that you do this is to simply say that you are sending love to the feelings, to the time in the past when the hurtful events took place, and to the physical area in your body where you experience the emotional disturbance. Allow yourself to accept and be grateful for the situation. Love this situation because it is your teacher. Love this person, because she is your teacher.

5. When you feel the negative emotion coming on, know that you have a choice. You may go ahead and express the emotion. Or, you may recognize it, and tell yourself the following: "In the past I have chosen to feel guilt or resentment in situations like this one. Today I am making a different choice." Then choose to respond with love instead. Practice this and you will experience more forgiveness. You will teach yourself to let go of hurtful feelings.

Bill's Journal

I want to release my need to experience guilt, anger, and resentment by acknowledging and expressing these feelings in a safe way. As I release my hurt and anger I will forgive myself and all others who I think have hurt me.

When I am able to forgive and to love others I feel better. It is painful to face the truth that, sometimes, I don't want to forgive. I want to be right. I know this gets in the way, but I keep on doing it. Books and teachers tell us to forgive, to love others, but they don't say how. To forgive, you have to want to forgive. How do I get myself to want to forgive?

How do I become a more forgiving person?

Look upon your world with love.

What do you mean?

The actual circumstances in your life are a result of the reality you have created in your mind. Your inner reality is not of love, or you would not be so dissatisfied with your life. Your present inner reality involves fear, distrust, and a devaluing of who you are. Thus your experiences match your reality.

So how do I change my reality?

What you really want to know is how to change your mind, and you begin with forgiveness. What most people call forgiveness is really granting a pardon.

How are pardoning and forgiving different?

To pardon someone is to say that they did something hurtful and now you are going to let them off the hook. To forgive is to say and believe that you created your own reality. Therefore, the other person never did anything to hurt you in the first place.

I can see how I created the situation we just discussed. I set it up. You're saying that if someone intentionally hurts me I should pretend it didn't happen.

Do not pretend. Realize that you helped to create the situation. Somehow, obvious or not, you drew it to you, and you created your own reaction. You are not to blame for what happened. You are responsible. This means that at any time, from this moment on, you have choices regarding how you respond. If something hurtful happened, and it is over, then you have choices as to how you respond now. You have choices regarding what you do with your feelings and how you behave. You choose what to think.

So, if someone hurts me I should just forget about it? I don't think so. What about their responsibility? Shouldn't they have to pay for what they did?

The Old Testament says "Vengeance is mine sayeth the Lord". What do you think that means?

It means that God will handle it, and I shouldn't worry about it. The other person will "pay" but not by my design. My only job is to let it go. I worry about the fact that they might do it again.

You have no control over what people do. By you letting it go you not only heal, but you assist the other person in healing. By hanging on to the sense of being wronged you extend your own pain as well as support their pain.

So, are you saying I should just let people do whatever they want to me?

We are saying do not take the Law into your own hands. There is a Law of Cause and Effect of which you are very aware. People are punished by their sins, not for them. When you step in to repay someone for what they have done you interfere with that Law and set it in motion for yourself. Your negative reaction will be returned to you. Forgive and love, and that, too, will be returned to you.

Of course, you do not let people do whatever they want to you. You set limits and make those limits known to others. You think about situations before you get into them in order that you may avoid repeating hurtful results.

You are responsible for creating your own reality. You must realize that in seeking your desired outcomes you disconnected yourself from your Source. You made the outcomes you thought you wanted more important than your relationship with God, your Source. You made your need to be right, to be admired, to be loved by a particular person or to be rich, more important than God. The outcome you thought you wanted with the "problem person" or "problem situation" has become your god, your center of focus. You release this false god through forgiveness.

Forgiveness is a process that looks something like this:
• Acknowledge that you created your reality. All of your experience is created by your thoughts. Thoughts can be changed.
• Acknowledge the feelings you have and express them safely, then let them go. Allow yourself whatever time you need.
• Let go of the expectation of what you thought should have happened.

- *Ask (Spirit, God, Christ, Holy Spirit) to change your perception.*
- *Reestablish God as your Source. In other words, you do not need for things to have happened differently. The person, situation, or outcome is not your god.*
- *Recognize how the situation has contributed to your growth. Celebrate what you have learned. Celebrate and give thanks for your healing.*
- *Extend Love to the one you are forgiving. That is, wish them only the best.*

Bill's Journal

Through forgiveness I can learn to love myself. I can see how forgiveness applies to my life, because I see that I have created at least most of my problems. But I can't imagine believing, much less saying, these words to someone who is truly a victim.

A friend of mine, a woman, was sleeping in her apartment. A man broke in, beat her and raped her. In her physical and emotional state how would she forgive the perpetrator? How could she conclude that the perpetrator never did anything to hurt her? I can't imagine saying that to her.

Forgiveness is the only way to heal completely. You can not expect her to accept this idea immediately. Her emotions, whether they be of fear, anger, grief, sadness, or despair are part of her experience. You can not take this away from her. The loving response on your part is compassion. See her as one who would benefit from your love and understanding. Love and understanding are expressed as deep listening and being present.

You help her to heal by the way you perceive her. See her as a child of God, a powerful spiritual being. Rape and beating do not change this. Do not see her as a victim, as helpless. You need not give her advice nor try to motivate her with positive talk. Love and honor her where she is right now. Love and respect her reaction to the event no matter what form it takes. It is not your job to fix her or make her okay. She is already okay in spirit. Be still and call upon God for thoughts on how you may be helpful. She is a spiritual being, of great strength and highly honored. Let your words, your voice tone, and your body language reflect this Truth. Whether you are speaking to her, about her, or thinking about her, let your words reflect the Truth about her. Empathize, but do not pity.

It is enough that one must suffer the pain of such an event. To continually replay it in her mind for years to come causes her more pain. This is why she forgives—to let go and be whole. Physical attack on someone does not change her spirit, her essence. It does create trauma for the soul. Determination to forgive and heal will produce freedom. She does not forgive in order to do her perpetrator a favor. One forgives to help one's self. Her soul can heal. The perpetrator benefits only if he desires forgiveness for himself.

So, if someone hurts me, I really don't need to do anything?

You really do not need to do anything to him, except, of course, set limits and make wise choices.

You're telling me that forgiveness is just another way of letting go and letting God. It's faith. Faith that God will take care of things. I don't need to seek vengeance, punish, or judge anyone?

Forgiveness requires that you understand that no one can truly hurt you unless you give them the power. Power that really belongs only to God. You always have God. Therefore, no one can take anything of value from you, nor can you be abandoned unless you choose it. Even when you choose it, it is not real.

It takes a lot of faith to live that way. A hell of a lot.

Faith is more than trusting God to meet your needs. It is knowing and feeling that God does love you, and because of that love, God will take care of you. It is knowing and feeling that you are one with God. There is no separation. If you are having difficulty forgiving, the problem is not an absence of faith. You have plenty of faith. Unfortunately your faith is in negative outcomes. Your problem is not enough love.

I don't have enough love?

You have enough love. You do not feel or express enough love. There is no lack of the presence of love in the Universe. There is only the lack of accepting it and expressing it.

How can I accept and express more love?

Make a clear decision that you want only love. (This means that you no longer wish to express or feel hate, resentment, hurt, fear, anger, poverty, or lack of any kind). Notice when your thoughts are critical of your self and others. Ask yourself: "Is this the way I want to think? Does this help me?" Then let those thoughts go.

When you are feeling unloved think about someone, past or present, who loves you. Feel that love. Feel the confidence you have in that love. Know that God loves you even more. Feel confident in God's Love. Express gratitude for all the ways God loves you. Choose an image such as an angel, Jesus the Christ, or other great being. Picture yourself talking to this being. Feel the love and understanding you receive from this totally loving being.

You do not have to entertain fearful, angry, or hurtful thoughts about any person or situation. Pray that you may see the situation with love. Begin to pour as much love as you can into the situation. Love is not something that happens to you. Love is positive energy that is always available. You need only accept it. The only thing standing between you and love is your need to feel or express something else.

Notice the love people are giving you now. Notice every kind word or smile, every tender voice tone, every expression of concern about you, even if it is expressed in anger. Everyone is loving you right now in the best way they can.

How can I believe that God loves me more than any person has? How can I feel confident in God's love? I know we've moved past that anthropomorphic God sitting on a throne, but I was taught God throws you into hell if you screw up. Imagine disobeying God for fifty years and then the price is an eternity of suffering. How loving is that? I wouldn't do that to my child no matter how badly they acted. How do I believe in God's love with all of these images in my mind? I don't believe in the God who sends people to hell, but to really know, deep within me that God loves me—I don't know how to feel that.

Humans have created a god who sends people to hell, because that is what they would do. Humans think everyone who does bad things should be punished. You know this is not God's nature. God's nature is love. God wants for you what is in your highest good. God is love and you are part of God. You are love. Today you do not know how to feel that love. One day you will. Just continue to practice love. It grows exponentially when you practice it. Love's purpose is to give of itself. Give it and you will feel it. It will grow and prosper within you.

It is difficult to feel love unless you would build a relationship with that which you want to love. Build a relationship with God. Talk to God. Think about God. Practice putting situations in God's hands. Over time you will begin to feel love for God.

Bill's Journal

I have plenty of faith. My faith will work in positive ways when I accept and express more love. Love will grow in me as I continue to practice it. I hope so! Thank you, God, for loving me. Throughout my life journey you have loved me. Often I have not recognized your Love or I have turned away from it. I have complained about my life. But you still loved me. Your Love got me through. No longer will I say "My life is not good enough for me." Instead I will say, "There is good in this, and I am grateful." Then I will consciously identify the good, ask for more good, and give thanks.

Thank you, God, for loving me. As you have loved me, asking nothing in return, so I will love you. As you have loved me, so I will love others. So be it.

I've done a lot of work on myself. I've forgiven much of the past. Do you think I'm ready for a loving relationship? I went to a workshop given by Alan Cohen. He presented the idea that I could write down what I am looking for in a partner. So I wrote it down. I read it every night before I go to sleep. I feel very strongly that I am going to meet this person. Is this real, or just some new age fantasy thing?

It is as real as you want it to be. You are not doing magic. You are clarifying your intention. You are asking for the perfect person for you to manifest in your life.

Bill's Journal

I met the woman of my vision within two months. It's funny, she went to an Alan Cohen workshop in a different city, the same month I did. She also wrote down what she desired in a partner. I don't know if we'll be life partners, but I think it's possible. She's beautiful. My intention for a loving partner is manifesting. In my business, clients are just starting to come. Maybe I need to clarify my intentions in those areas, too.

Chapter 6
From Victim to Victor

I read in a book that we always get what we want. It doesn't seem that way to me. Most people don't want to suffer pain. Most people don't want to be poor.

The problem for many is that they do not know what they want. What do you want in life this moment? What is your intention?

I want to get on top of my financial situation. I want my debts paid off, my bills paid on time, and money to meet my needs and desires. Also, I want to grow spiritually.

Let us look at the financial intention first. An intention is an aim. It is what you want to come of your efforts. You have stated your intention to be on top of your financial situation. If your intention were 100 %, your desires would be manifest. That is the law. You have other intentions that conflict with these. Your conflicting intentions are your hidden wants.

What else could I intend?

Listen to yourself. When you talk about your challenges, how do you sound? Is there hurt in your voice? Or anger? If someone asks how business is going, do you feel compelled to tell all of the things that are going wrong? Your words, your tone of voice, and your body language will be evidence of your intentions.

Does that mean that I shouldn't tell anyone when things aren't going well?

It means that if things appear not to be going well you might refrain from telling everyone. It only serves to strengthen your hurt or anger. Tell someone who is supportive of you, like a good friend or a therapist. This will help you to release the feelings and get a better perspective. If you go around telling everybody, then you will only feed your negative thoughts and feelings. Part of you delights in telling the drama of Bill. Poor guy, he tries so hard but to no avail. He keeps getting up and life keeps slapping him down.

You're being a little hard on me, aren't you?

You wanted to know if what you see around you is what you want. We are responding to your request. Shall we continue?

Please do. I understand what you're saying. I do hear myself sounding hurt when people ask me about my situation.

What is your expected payoff?

There is no payoff. I'm just answering their question. I don't want to be perky and positive when people ask me how things are going. Things aren't all that positive. I'm being honest.

Be honest now. What do you get from explaining your drama of life?

I don't know. You tell me.

There is a payoff or you would not be doing it. When you use your hurt voice to tell about a situation, what are you hoping to get in return? What is your payoff? What do you want?

I guess I want sympathy. I want people to feel sorry for me or to admire me for being so brave in the face of great challenges.

Your intention, then, is to get sympathy for your struggle. This is one reason why you struggle. Know that you can not have it both ways. You can not have the sympathy and the prosperity. Choose one. Which do you want, sympathy or healthy finances?

I want healthy finances.

Then you must stop seeking sympathy. Does a well-to-do person need sympathy for his financial conditions? Perhaps now you understand what is meant when it is said that you always get what you want, including your problems. Poor me thoughts and feelings serve to create poor me circumstances. On a practical level, potential customers do not want to help you out by giving you business. They want you to help them out. They will pay you to help them if you can inspire their confidence in you. Misery has a payoff. You are receiving something you think you want or you think you should have. When you make a clear decision that healthy financial conditions are more important than sympathy, you will be on your way.

I guess I've been sabotaging myself all along.

True change and true empowerment begin with honesty. It is difficult to see one's self with total honesty, but it must be done if you want change.

I do.

If you want prosperous conditions, let your thinking, feeling, words, and actions be in alignment with that desire. To have wealth see the wealth you already have. Enjoy it and be grateful. By sounding hurt when you talk about your money problems you may be hoping someone will feel sorry for you and give you money. Or at the very least, they will agree that you are suffering misfortune, therefore you cannot be expected to meet your financial responsibilities. You do not have to create financial insufficiency in order to receive caring attention. You do not earn love by creating the image of poverty and humility. You are entitled to have your needs met now. Groveling, hostility, aggressiveness, and laying guilt on those who have money are inappropriate ways of gaining money. These behaviors arise out of victimhood. You are not the victim of your circumstances. You are the creator of them. Acknowledge your self worth. Begin now to identify with Spirit. Begin now to look at your life and affairs with love. Let your behavior reflect a consciousness that knows it deserves total well being.

The principle is the same in all aspects of life. To have totally loving relationships become totally loving. Does a totally loving person need to feel hurt? Does a totally loving person need to create hardship in order to get love? A totally loving person thinks, feels, speaks, and acts with confidence and love. This is all possible because you trust the Creative Intelligence of the Universe to meet your every need. You see your self as totally connected to this Power, totally loved and supplied by this Power.

Some people become ill or injured to get love. Being ill, they are taken care of. If no one takes care of them, it supports their belief that no one cares. Getting well involves loving yourself and acknowledging your self worth. It involves the intention to be well and happy. It often involves forgiveness. It means knowing that no one has to prove their love for you through care taking or sacrifice. You do not have to injure yourself or cause illness in order to deserve love. You deserve love now.

If you want a change you must make a commitment to yourself to not be a victim in any situation. Success in the financial area requires a commitment to success. It requires that you focus your vision and energy toward success. Refuse to waste time and energy wishing things were different. Continue to discover and face conflicting intentions.

Spiritual growth also requires a commitment. You make a commitment to your path, whatever it may be. We have spoken often about this Power we call God. Know that it is the only power at work in your life. Victimhood comes from giving power to other people, to situations, and to things. Take back that power now. Do not make situations or other people your gods.

Let me see if I've got this right. If a person is in a bad situation he should just suck it up. If I feel bad about my circumstances I should stop feeling sorry for myself and move on. Is this what you are telling me?

The path from victimhood to victory is often difficult, but always rewarding. When you are a victim you have no power. When you have conquered your sense of being a victim you are free. Victimhood is habitual and serves to keep people right where they are. The past is gone. Right now, in this moment, you have the power to respond to what is. We are not telling you to move on. We are suggesting that if you are ready to move on, if you truly intend to experience greater well being, let go of your victim thoughts. Start being what you want to become. You want to become more prosperous. Act as if you already are. You want to feel more connected to God. Act as if you already are. Let your thoughts, your words, and your behavior be in agreement with your stated intentions. Be congruent in thought, word, and act.

Okay, one more question. Are you saying that if someone is sick, it's because they think like a victim?

Sometimes this is true. At the very least, thinking like a victim can be counterproductive. We say that all illness is for a purpose. There is something to be learned or a gift to be given. An illness or injury can be a teaching vehicle, both for the soul experiencing it and for those around him. Self blame or a "Why me?" attitude will create more suffering. Find purpose in your suffering and rise from victimhood.

Bill's Journal

My consciousness is reflected in my words, my voice, and my body language. When I no longer need to be a victim, I will be empowered to change. I'd like to make a commitment to myself to make the necessary changes in my thinking that I may move from victim to victor.

People often believe themselves to be victims of their respective situations. They are victims of their illnesses, of the economy, of other people, of their own bodies, or of their circumstances of birth. Sympathy, admiration, being taken care of, being right, being excused of responsibility, and attention of any kind are all payoffs. I can hear the sense of ownership people have over their aches and pains. I can see the enthusiasm people feel for their personal dramas. I've seen these things in myself. We maintain unhealthy situations because we are usually getting something out of them. What we get seldom brings us true joy.

I don't want to be a victim. How do I move forward when I feel so much fear? All of my life I have lived with fear. Most of the time when I accomplished something it was not because I felt great confidence. I acted in spite of my fear. I can't think of too many times in my life when I haven't felt fear in my body.

You have overcome fear many times. We acknowledge your bravery. Yet, we ask of you, is it healthy when fear is normal? Is it healthy when you become accustomed to the tension in your solar plexus? Do you enjoy being nervous about each encounter and each decision?

I don't enjoy it. Fear has always been a big part of me. I've used the technique you taught me for releasing fear feelings. Is there a more proactive way of decreasing the power of fear in my life?

Stop being a victim. It is your thought that your needs are met by other people, situations, or events that creates your fear. This causes you to spend your efforts attempting to please others, making a good impression, manipulating situations, and hoping for positive responses. When you give your power to external sources you will inevitably be disappointed. When you give your power to external sources you will inevitably become a victim. Focusing on external sources creates fear, because you have no control over the outcomes they produce. Fear creates victimhood and victimhood creates fear.

Examine your past. Whenever you were hurt by others in work or personal relationships you made certain outcomes your gods. For example, you gave your power to a woman when you made her love for you a necessity, a god. You could not live without it. When she did not love you, you were a victim. You feared rejection and it inevitably occurred. When a business deal fell through you were in terror. You thought you had to have it in order to make a living. In spite of the fact it fell through you are still here. In spite of the fact that certain women could not give you the love you thought you must have—you are still here. Bill, you constantly set yourself up to be a victim. This creates constant fear. This is why we ask you to place God, the Creative Intelligence of the Universe, the One and Only Power, first in your life.

This is your quest. Learn how to turn within to the Power that is you, that expresses as you. Trust in God within you. Listen to God's voice. Worry not about outcomes. Cease trying to manipulate the world, because even if you are materially successful, you will not experience true joy.

You will transform yourself from victim to victor. We say this can be instantaneous, yet we know it will take time. We see you as already the victor. To us, you are whole and complete.

Be not dismayed, you are opening to greater wisdom and understanding. Make a commitment to this quest and we will help you. Without a commitment your intentions will be divided.

I don't want fear to be normal. I don't want to be a victim.

My Commitment To Myself

I promise to get to know myself. I will face conflicts rather than avoid them. I will seek out every area of my life where I feel discomfort. Asking God for understanding, I will confront each situation.

I will remind myself that in any problem situation in which I find myself, I am responsible. This means that I am able to respond. I will not respond without first seeking guidance.

I refuse to blame another person for any conflict or problem. I refuse to blame myself. Each of us is acting out of our respective consciousness at the moment. I give up my need to be right. I give up my need for someone else to be wrong.

Whenever I see a problem, I will recognize that my perception *is* the problem. My job is to change how I see things. I do not have to do this job alone. I ask God, Infinite Intelligence to show me who and what I need to forgive. Then I will forgive. I will continue to forgive so long as I feel areas of discomfort, anger, resentment, bitterness, sadness, or hurt.

I will respect myself. I will respect and acknowledge my feelings. If I am angry or hurt, I will not pretend I am not feeling those emotions. I will acknowledge how I feel and seek to release all anger and hurt. I will not try to make someone else feel guilty for my feelings. I will pour love out to myself and into each situation.

I will hold my head up high each day. I will not do this out of pride, but rather out of love and respect for who and what I am:

- I am a holy child of the Creative Intelligence of the Universe.
- I am a spiritual being having a human experience.
- I am God expressing as me.
- I am prosperous, healthy, whole, joyous, and at peace. Each day I will do my best to think, feel, speak, and act in ways that match these statements:
- I love myself. I extend this love to all others.
- I forgive myself and all others of all blame.
- I will think, feel, act, and speak with love.

I am responsible for my reality. I am responsible for how I feel. I am responsible for what I think. I am responsible for what I do. I reconnect to my Source, God within. I commit myself to these ideas. I commit myself to remaining connected to my Source. I now go forward with a spirit of enthusiasm, excitement, and expectancy.

I like this commitment. It will help me to stay on track. I need to make a commitment regarding my spiritual path, also.

Your commitment is about your spiritual path. Psychological wholeness is part of your spiritual path. Everything we have discussed is your path. It is common, in your world, for people to see spirituality as a compartment of life. Spirituality is the whole of life. Everything you think, feel, say, and do is your spiritual path, because it affects your Soul's growth. The spiritual path is not a small part of a human life. A human life is a small part of the spiritual path. You are so much more than your little human awareness. We welcome your commitment to spiritual learning.

My Commitment To Spiritual Growth

I am a spiritual being, an expression of God. God is my Source. I place this source first in my life, before all else.

I experience unhappiness, usually because I am putting something or someone before God. The answers are not to be found outside of myself. I will turn within. Rather than focusing on problems, I will focus on God as my solution. This Creative Intelligence will provide the idea or the opportunity.

God is a word for perfection. I commit myself to seeing and knowing God in me. I commit myself to always seeing and knowing God in all others, no matter what their values or beliefs.

I will love God with all my heart, all of my mind, all of my soul, and all of my strength. Whatever is going on around me or within me, I will see God there. I will bless the situation and call it good. I recognize that God is omnipresent. God is everywhere present. There is no place where God is not. There is no separation between what I am and what God is. We are one.

God is omniscient. God knows all because God is all. The all knowingness of God is available to me within me.

God is omnipotent. God is the only power there is. There is no real power called evil. There is no real devil. All other "powers" are illusions, dreams, and the creations of people. God is the only power.

The ever presence, the all knowingness, the all lovingness, and the all powerfulness of God are always expressing in me and through me. I commit to aligning myself with all the presence, power, love, and knowingness in the Universe. I commit to aligning myself with the incredible power of love expressed by God to me, through me, and as me.

God in me is my Higher Self. I commit to becoming my Higher Self. I do this by always turning within to my Higher Self for the answers I need. I release my fear of hearing the solution. I release my fear of knowing the answer. I release my need to hang on to old and familiar ways of thinking feeling, speaking, and acting. I recognize, accept, and desire that with each loving thought; with each loving feeling; with each loving word; and with each loving act, I become my Higher Self.

We honor your commitments. We see positive changes coming more rapidly. This will please you. More importantly, we see greater awareness and wisdom. We see you overcoming fear and becoming love. You will experience a shift from fear filled thoughts to love filled thoughts, from a fear filled life to a love filled life.

Chapter 7
The Prodigal's Brother-
Learning to Receive

Now that I have made a commitment to God and myself I find that resentment and disappointment are coming up more often and with greater intensity.

Whenever you resolve to move forward in your growth those aspects of yourself which need healing will come forth. This we have already discussed. We believe you will find insight into your resentments and disappointments in the story of the Prodigal Son. Do you remember it?

Yes, I do remember it. Let me reread it.

The Prodigal Son

A man had two sons. The younger son said to him, "My father, give me the portion which is coming to me from your house." He divided to them his possessions. The younger son gathered everything that was his share and went to a far country, and there he wasted his wealth in extravagant living. When all was gone there was a famine in that country, and he began to be in need. He accepted a job feeding corn husks to swine. He craved to fill his stomach with the husks the swine were eating; and yet no man would give to him. He thought of his home. He thought to himself: "My Father's servants live better than I do. I will return home to my Father's house and beg that he will let me work as a servant".

And so he returned home. When he was still a distance away, his Father saw him. His Father came out and welcomed him home. The Father was so joyous at his son's return that he had the servants kill a fat ox for a banquet in his son's honor. He gave him a new, beautiful robe along with a ring and new shoes.

Now the older son was arriving late from his work. He heard the sounds of celebration and inquired of one of the servants what was going on. He was told that his brother had returned and that the fat ox had been killed. The older son became very angry at this. The Father came out and asked his son what was wrong. The older son asked, "How many years have I served you and never disobeyed your commandment? Yet, you never gave me even a kid, that I might make merry with my friends. After this son of yours took his money and spent it on harlots, you have killed the fat ox."

The Father replied, "You are always with me, and everything that is mine is yours. It was right to make merry and rejoice; for your brother was dead and has come to life; and was lost and is found."

I have always seen myself as that younger son. I left God and tried to make it on my own. I failed and returned to God. It's the story of all of us.

You identify with the lost son. What about the son who stayed home?

I don't think I'm very much like him.

The older son resented the fact that he had been loyal to the Father, yet he had never been rewarded. No feast had been prepared for him. He was angry and hurt. He did not understand the love of the

Father. Had he understood his Father's love, he would have felt the same joy the Father felt at his brother's return. He may have joined in the celebration. Instead, he chose to separate himself. In other words, he was pouting.

Well, maybe I'm like that sometimes.

The older son judged that his brother was unworthy, and that he was the worthy one. To him, the situation was unfair. As soon as he judged the circumstances as unfair he prevented himself from learning. He could not understand his brother or the Father because he was blinded by his feelings of injustice. As soon as you judge a situation as being unfair, you stop learning. There is no humility in resentment, only humiliation.

Humility is an openness to learning. It is being willing to look into the situation for the lesson. Can you think of a situation in your life that is similar to that of the older son?

I guess if I'm in a situation where someone else is being acknowledged and I feel that I should be the one who is acknowledged, I would feel disappointment and some resentment.

If you choose to resent another's good fortune are you not being like the older son? In the older son world view you may cry out "I have been good. Why am I not rewarded? Why does someone less worthy than myself get the reward?"

You fulfill the irrational beliefs that say: "I am good but no one appreciates me. I sacrifice my own needs and yet I get nothing in return. The world is unfair." Each time you are disappointed the anger and the hurt grow.

The Universe reads your irrational beliefs and provides you with more opportunities to experience and change those beliefs. The Universe does not supply you with a hurtful situation. You make the choice to be hurt. The Universe provides you with an opportunity to change your interpretation. You can continue to feel hurt, or you can choose a more loving response. Situations in which you feel resentful tend to recur in your life until you learn to respond with love rather than hurt, fear, or anger. Can you give us a more detailed example of this?

I desired greater responsibility in a job I once had. I really believed that I was qualified. I had been loyal. I had worked overtime. I had always given my best to the organization. Someone else was brought in from the outside and offered a position that was over me. I didn't feel this person had better skills. He was puffed up with self importance. Also, his salary was two and a half times mine. I was hurt. I was angry that management overlooked me. I was embarrassed that this person was now my boss. I thought to myself, "That's it. No more overtime. No one appreciates me around here. Its not what you know or what you do that counts. It is how cocky and confident you can act! This just isn't fair."

Like the prodigal's brother, you had an opportunity to grow and to love. The degree of suffering experienced by you was equal to the degree of resistance to the lesson. This is a lesson most humans resist. You have judged others to be unworthy. You have believed certain others do not deserve to receive. Who were you to decide that your colleague was unworthy of a high salary? Did you expect that he should be perfect to deserve his position?

You're right. I could have focused more on my performance rather than my perception of his lack. Three months later I lost that job. Honestly, I was ready to leave.

What did you learn from the situation?

I learned that things aren't always fair, and it was really time for me to move on. I no longer fit in that organization. I didn't like the way people treated each other. A few months after leaving that job I found one in a much healthier organization where my skills were acknowledged and appreciated.

What appeared to be a bad situation turned out to be a blessing. You were able to move on to something better. Be aware that there was an opportunity you did not consider.

What was that?

Your fears and resentments prevented you from asking a very important question. The question was: "How can I profit from this situation? What can I do to create a positive situation for myself, this new person, and the company?" Had you contemplated those questions some interesting answers may have come your way. If you look for unfairness in a situation you will certainly find it. If you look for an opportunity to learn and grow, you will make gains you never thought possible.

I felt I had been treated unfairly, but I was relieved to get out of there.

The prodigal's brother judged himself to be treated unfairly even though he lived right in the midst of the Father's goodness. He could have enjoyed the riches of the Father at any time, and you can, too. The abundance of God is always available to you. Know who you are (Spirit, the Christ). Express who you are (Love). Be who you are (God expressing as you). Do this and you will be heir to the abundance of the Universe.

How can I do this?

When you are feeling that things are not going your way, that is the time to turn within and ask for help. Things are not always as they appear. Rather than placing your faith in appearances, place your faith in God. Continually remind yourself of who you are. Ask God to help you see the situation differently.

Whenever you feel discomfort, or a lack in your life, stop and ask for greater understanding. You want to know what the lesson is, or better yet, what the opportunity for growth is. Listen within for the answers. Acknowledge that God is the answer to your need, the solution to your problem. Give thanks that it is done. Then move forward, loving the situation, loving yourself, forgiving all concerned, doing what your intuition indicates for you to do, and expressing joy.

Do not forget to express gratitude every day. We have talked about this, and you did express gratitude for a time. Then you stopped. Expressing gratitude is not a technique for gaining wealth or improved conditions. It is not something you do once or twice yearly on Thanksgiving Day. It is a higher level of consciousness, a way of life. Express gratitude every day for what you have. Gratitude is Love. If you want to grow spiritually and be prosperous, gratitude is a requirement for moving up to the next level. Whatever happens, whoever enters your life, give thanks. Giving thanks fills you with love and helps you to release fear. Often other people will not have your best interests at heart. God, the Creative Intelligence of the Universe, always loves you and wants what is best for you.

Often I see God as the strict parent and me as the child. I feel that God is holding back from me. I do everything I think I am supposed to do but God doesn't respond. I feel that I am supposed to be rewarded for being good, and I get mad when I don't get what I want. Maybe I am a lot like the older son. The older son just hangs around doing what he thinks he is supposed to do. When I was a child I was taught that I would go to Heaven if I was good. I was taught that good people were rewarded and bad people were punished. The world doesn't seem to work that way. Seemingly good people suffer and seemingly bad people reap rewards.

Bill, spirituality is not about being good so you can be rewarded. That concept is more in the realm of religion. Religion, at its best, is a tool for spiritual growth. It is an opportunity for like minded people to gather together to honor God and each other and to learn spiritual principles. At its worst, religion imposes controls through guilt, judgment, and exclusion. Traditionally religion has taught its followers that they are rewarded for following the rules. This totally ignores the importance of seeking within. It teaches you to ignore your Inner Voice. When you experience disappointment in life it is not because you were not good enough nor is it because God is withholding from you.

The prodigal's brother behaved well. He did all the right things, but he did not understand his Father's love. The prodigal son misbehaved and made a mess of his life, yet he chose to come home. He demanded nothing, and he was willing to give everything. True success in life is inner success. The great job, the big contract, the wonderful relationship, the beautiful family are all manifestations of something deeper. They are results of a deeper connection with Spirit. Behind every desire is a feeling. It is that feeling you really desire.

What do you mean?

You have desired financial abundance. You did your affirmations, you prayed, and you did every thing you thought was right to bring that abundance to you. When it did not come how did you feel?

Frustrated, disappointed, angry. Like God was withholding it from me for some reason.

You looked to particular situations to satisfy your desire. When those situations fell through you were disappointed. You made those situations and the resulting income your source. When your "source" did not perform, you became angry.

So, I reacted just like the older son.

Yes. Although you were standing in the midst of God's abundant good you assumed that because this or that situation did not work out that you were being denied what was due to you. Your reaction demonstrated your lack of trust in God. The prodigal son realized that there was nothing "out there" that would fulfill him. He could only be fulfilled by returning to the Father. Once he chose to serve the Father he received what he needed and more.

You are again telling me to put God first and all else will be added.

Yes. Turn within. Spiritual growth is not about being a good little boy. It is about becoming a powerful child of God. The Parable of the Prodigal Son is your story. You are the prodigal. You abandoned your inner wisdom, your inner connection to Spirit, and followed your urges and emotions. This created suffering. Suffering has driven you inward. You turned within to find answers. You decided to take the road home. You are also the older son in that you think you should be punished. This is your guilt. You are angry at yourself for being irresponsible, for making poor decisions. The Father (God) wants to give you everything, but the older son says you do not deserve it. The older son insists that you have to prove yourself worthy by creating external symbols of success. Of course, you can not create these external symbols with these conflicting intentions. You intend to succeed and you intend to punish. Desire for good and resentment for self battle each other. You blame God for withholding from you, yet it is the older son in you who withholds through guilt and resentment of self.

Find the feeling underlying what you want, be it love, joy, peace, or fulfillment. When you tell yourself that you must have a certain situation in order to be happy you are setting yourself up for failure. Externals will always fail you in the long run. Only God will never fail you. When you place conditions on whether or not you can be happy you deny yourself the happiness you seek. God does not deny it; you do. The older son could have had whatever he wanted from his Father. He chose disappointment, anger, and resentment over his Father's goodness. The older son did not realize that he had also abandoned his Father. His self righteous judgment was his "far off country". He spent his inheritance on bitterness and resentment. He lived on the corn husks of self satisfied indignation. He lived in the poverty of lovelessness.

If you spend your energy judging the worth of yourself or others, you are in poverty. You are choosing guilt and resentment of self over success. People have made rules about who should or should not receive rewards. These rules do not come from the Creator. For a moment, see creation as we do. We see each and every soul on earth receiving an infinite supply of love. Your souls are surrounded and permeated with the love of God. It is everywhere you turn. Yet, you deny yourself this great gift. Breathe in the air. You are breathing God. Look in every corner of this room. God is there. Where God is, there is love and abundance. Were you to know this for a moment, you would feel great joy. Your desire for joy and freedom would be met immediately. Spend your energy, your thought, contemplating the constant flow of God's gifts to you and through you. Life is a gift. Everything that happens is a gift. Be thankful. Cease denying yourself this gift and let it flow.

Wow! You say that I am denying myself what I want. You say that all that I could want is right here right now. I'm missing something. How do I get myself to enjoy the gifts instead of denying myself?

What is it that you want, Bill?

I want prosperity.

How would you feel if you were prosperous?

I would feel good.

Be more specific.

I would be proud of myself. I would feel confident. I would feel appreciation for myself. I would have freedom. There would be a sense of joy that comes from being able to do what I want. I would feel like I have no limitations. I would feel strong because I would be able to help my children more. I would feel focused, on track. People around me would have confidence in me.

More money would do all of that for you?

Yes, I think so.

Without money, you are unable to feel those things?

Well, sometimes I do feel those things.

You do not feel those things as much as you would like, and you believe that the reason is because you do not have enough money. If you only had money these feelings would come rushing in and everything would be wonderful. You would be happy. Do you believe money makes people happy?

No, I don't, but I think it would help. I rather be unhappy with money than unhappy without it.

Unhappy is unhappy. Joy, freedom, and confidence are the feelings you desire. God is not withholding these feelings from you. God's love for you is unconditional. How about your love for you? Is it unconditional? Or are you withholding love from yourself until you earn it via your financial standing? Are you not denying yourself these feelings?

I see what you mean, now. I've been looking outside of myself for validation.

You think you need to prove yourself in the physical world before you can grant yourself the gifts of love, joy, freedom, and confidence.

Yeah, I guess I do.

You have the same choice the older brother had. You can go off and be angry, waiting for your Father to throw you a party or, you can receive the invitation, gratefully accepting what is now available to you. You can focus on the good that is at hand, or you can focus on what you do not have. Cultivate the feelings you want right now. Act as if you are already prosperous, because, in Truth, you are. Give thanks for your prosperity. Celebrate the prosperity of others. Rehearse the feelings you desire every day. Practice by visualizing yourself as joyful and peaceful. Remind yourself that when you feel down you can choose peace or joy instead. Know that God puts no conditions on His love for you, no terms for deserving.

Bill's Journal

I thought that God was withholding from me, but it was really me all along. So where am I? I have learned the importance of gratitude. I have increased the love I feel for myself. I have let go of the payoffs I was getting (pity, etc.). I have learned that I must look within for my joy and freedom. I have begun to practice the feelings of joy and peace every day through visualization. I have begun to let go of guilt, disappointment and resentment. If my income is my barometer, then I am seeing slight improvements.

What else do I need to do?

Fear is scattering your energy. You say you are in business for yourself, yet you are applying for jobs that would take you away from your business dream. Why are you doing that?

I feel pressure from people close to me to create a secure financial situation. I fear not having enough.

Their idea of security is a job working for an organization. Is that what you want?

Not really. I want to be in business for myself, doing what I like to do, and making a good income.

You say you are intending to have a successful business. At the same time you hedge your bet by looking for a full time job. Stop scattering your energy looking for things other than what you want. You have a business. At the same time you hunt for a job that you do not really want. Focus your energy on what you want. The Universe does not know what to bring you if you do not know. Your mixed energy brings you mixed results. Move forward, focused and confident.

My strongest desire is to be a self employed consultant and speaker, but sometimes I feel that is an irresponsible choice.

The irresponsible choice is the one that feels wrong inside. If it feels right for you to grow your business, trust that feeling. Trust that you are in your right place living your purpose.

Bill's Journal

I am scattering my energy. Why not go for what I really want. I have the qualifications and I know I am capable. I need to make a choice—go for a job or grow my business. I can't worry about what others will think.

Later

I am amazed. I made a clear decision to focus on my consulting business. Within the week I got a phone call from a customer. I was asked to do a major project which pays very well. Several other projects have come my way. On top of that I have found ways to bring my monthly expenses down.

You supplied yourself with confidence. Work came your way. Your performance and the customer's response reinforced your confidence. There is nothing amazing here. It is only God supplying you abundantly. It is only you learning and growing.

Bill's Journal

I am grateful for all that I have. One thing that not having much money has taught me is that I truly appreciate what I have now.

Now you are aware that you have been receiving what you needed all along.

I am? It would have been a lot easier if I had achieved success earlier.

That was not what you needed. Had you received more you would not have felt the gratitude. You would not have had the opportunity to let go of your resentment. You would not have understood the importance of clear intentions. These things you have learned were part of your healing experience. Today you are finding more prosperity and joy. Money without wisdom or joy has little value.

You are always supplied with everything you need. Do not place your faith in appearances. Appearances change.

Bill's Journal

Yes, appearances do change. Now I have a good income stream. I am confident it will continue. I am doing work that I love, speaking to groups, working with organizations to help them improve. How did I get here? I learned to be grateful. I learned about letting go and turning within to God, my Source. Earthly situations are not my source. I learned that I am responsible for my conditions, not the victim of my conditions. I discovered that loving myself on the inside draws more love to me from the outside. Forgiveness clears away internal barriers to joy and prosperity. Releasing resentment opens me up to receiving goodness. Eliminating conflicting intentions helps me to focus my intentions and energy toward what I want. Grateful; let go; God as my only Source; personal responsibility; self love; forgiveness; releasing resentment; and focused intentions. Eight steps to greater prosperity! Sounds like a book.

Why didn't you tell me this formula when I started out?

There is not formula for prosperity that fits all people. You needed to discover your own steps. We see your thought forms and we are pleased to see less fear and more love. Everyone has work to do, and you have done yours well.

Thank you. I feel different. I feel more aware, stronger.

It's not about the money, is it? Money, financial conditions, they were just symptoms of my fear of life.

Your financial struggles were created by you. As we speak, new dramas are being created to help you learn more about loving you and others. Fear has played a big role in your relationships. Now it is time to heal this fear.

Chapter 8
Relationships

You have progressed well growing into your prosperity. You have learned to place more trust in God, to be grateful for your abundance, to be confident in yourself, and to ask God for help. This growth has created work that you enjoy doing and a more than adequate income. We believe it is time to take a deeper look at your relationships.

We have dealt with forgiveness.

Past patterns that create conflict for you in relationships are recurring. It is time you addressed these issues. In your consulting business you teach others how to communicate more effectively. Part of the reason you are called to this teaching is that through teaching you will learn.

So, when I do workshops and consulting I'm really teaching myself?

Yes. A true teacher is a student. What better way to learn than to teach what you need to learn. Let us examine what you have learned about relationships.

I have learned much through relationships. Why do I continue to create relationships that have the same kinds of problems?

You resonate to another person whose behaviors activate your issues. You do that for each other. Spouses, children, bosses, and friends are great activators. You will always attract into your life people who activate your ideas about who and what you think you are. If you feel unworthy, you will attract people who help you feel unworthy. If you feel well loved, you will attract people who help you feel more loved.

It is not the people who cause your feelings. It is your interpretation of your interactions with them. Your interpretation of the actions of others is either healthy or unhealthy, loving or unloving. Relationships become repetitive because thinking is repetitive. You must take responsibility for your thoughts.

So, if I am unwilling to take responsibility for what was created in a past relationship, I will probably recreate the same problems in my new relationship?

Anything unresolved from a past relationship will show up, in some form, in a new relationship.

Do I need to completely forgive myself and all others before I can have a new, healthy relationship?

You need to feel a sense of completion about the past. This includes understanding how you contributed to the dynamics experienced in the past relationship. This is why it is usually a good idea to spend some time alone before engaging in a new relationship.

I did that. After a time I met a wonderful woman. We have been trying to make this relationship work. There are many good things about it, but there are some issues. How can we make this relationship successful?

Learn to love unconditionally. That is, regard yourself or another in a positive manner without conditions. Honor, and appreciate someone, yourself or another, exactly the way they are. When you love unconditionally you accept another the way she is. You love all of her. You look past the appearances of imperfection and see the Christ, or Spirit in her. Unconditional love includes making sure your behavior reflects these things.

What if the other person has negative characteristics?

Positive qualities are expressions of love. So-called negative characteristics are requests for love. When a person does something that appears hurtful, it is a call for love.

How do I love a person when I feel like I'm being attacked?

You refuse to judge. You love her by not judging, rescuing, blaming, or criticizing. To help you do that, look within. Ask: "Why am I choosing to feel hurt or angry?" Listen for the answer. When you get it, do not judge or criticize yourself. Simply give thanks for the answer. You may want to tell your partner about your insight. You do not need to analyze it or justify it. Tell the simple truth. This kind of honesty will bring you closer together.

What you are saying is good, but I need help with the how you do it. How do I love someone unconditionally?

It is something you have already done.

I have?

Yes. Do you remember what it feels like to fall in love?

Of course!

When two people fall in love they create a new reality. They see perfection in each other. Faults seem unimportant. Positive traits are the points of focus. You think of each other as wonderful, loving people. You feel your connection and that feeling is joyous. You create a loving space for each other to step into. Feeling loved, you love yourself more. Feeling loved by the other person, you love her more.

Why doesn't it seem to last? Sometimes it lasts for a few days or a few months; in some relationships it goes away, is renewed, only to be lost again. I've never seen it last forever. I always thought I could meet someone, fall in love, and it would last forever. How do I make that falling in love feeling last?

After a time, in relationship, your issues come up. That is, you perceive that the other person is not as perfect as you thought. Also, you fear the other person will discover your imperfections. You were attracted to each other because you resonated with each other. You have issues that are either the same or that activate each other.

So, as the issues come up, I may become critical of the other person, or angry, or hurt?

That is true. As you know, it is not the other person causing those feelings within you. You must deal with discomfort when it comes up. In relationships people tend to either project their discomfort on the other person or hide it. This leads to an unhealthy relationship.

Sometimes it is very hard to work things out in my relationship. For example, whenever I get upset about something, I find it hard to express it to her. Whenever I do, she becomes defensive and upset. We get nowhere. I usually end up feeling worse after being honest about my thoughts and emotions. If I hold them in, I still don't feel good.

What is your experience when this happens?

Frustration. My emotions aren't important to her. She doesn't want to hear them. I feel in conflict, like I'm not supposed to have these feelings. It seems like my feelings are not respected.

You have always felt this way. You have always felt doubts and fears about expressing your emotions. You have always feared that your feelings were not important.

That's true.

This is one of the reasons you have created this situation with her. Her reactions activate these unresolved feelings in you. In Truth, you believe that your feelings are not important. Know that her presence in your life helps to show you what you believe about yourself.

That's how we resonate?

Yes, and there is more. You have developed beliefs about her. She reacted in certain ways the first few times you expressed your upset feelings. In your mind you took a photograph of her reactions and made that image your reality. The image you made of her is just that, an image. You do not see her. People are not fixed entities, frozen in time. They are bundles of potentiality. In your mind you have restricted her, this bundle of potentiality, to being defensive as well as disinterested in your pain. Believing as you do in her fixedness, you encourage her to act in a defensive, upset way. In other words, you have created an expectation in your relationship, and in your mind, she meets it. Whenever you communicate an emotion to her you expect her to react. You expect her to not care. Your hurtful reaction perpetuates the dynamic. You are in it together.

So, the more I blame her and feel dissatisfied with her reaction, the more it is perpetuated?

Yes. At the same time, your hurt feelings activate something in her. As a result she creates an image of you. All relationships work this way.

I feel like I've gotten myself into a trap, and I don't know how to get out of it.

The trap is of your own making, and it is an illusion. You act as if your partner needs to change in order for you to feel free to express. Were this true, then your partner would be your jailer. It is not true.

You hold the key to your freedom to express. Change your belief.

How?

Recognize that she does not cause your unhappy feelings. In prayer, express your intention to move to a higher level of thinking, to let go of this issue. When you find yourself in conflict, ask God to help you to perceive the situation differently.

I can do that. But, sometimes things happen so fast that the damage is already done before I get my head on straight. When I am in the thick of it I am convinced she is wrong. Then I feel hopeless because I can see she is convinced she is right. How do I remedy this situation?

Express your feelings in the highest way you can without worrying about her reaction. If she reacts, just let her. Instead of interpreting her reaction as a rejection of your feelings, see it as information she is giving you about her. In your confrontations there has been an intersecting of issues. By you coming to peace as quickly as you can, you also help her to do the same. It only takes one person to change the dynamic of a relationship. When you come to accept your feelings and hers you contribute to the resolution of both. It is your resistance that helps to maintain the issues and give them strength. Remember, what you focus on expands. Look for other things to focus on about her, such as, when she does listen.

This could be a big job.

Not if you truly intend to change. The reason you see this as a big job is that you are not sure you want to change. Part of you still wants her to change. Change your goal. Your goal has been that you would say something that would help <u>her</u> to change. That is an unattainable goal. <u>Wishing</u> for her to change will not make it happen. The result is frustration and anger for you. Change, instead, your belief. Elevate your need for her to change to a preference. It is certainly preferable that she would respond differently to your upset expressions, but it is not necessary. Now we are talking about unconditional love.

Unconditional love is not about waiting for someone else to love you in the way you think they should. It is taking the first step and loving another the way she is, and in this case, the way she appears to be. The way your partner appears to be to you is not who she is. Remember, she is a bundle of potentiality. You can help her to direct that potentiality in a loving direction by calling forth your own potential to be loving.

All behavioral expressions are energy. The energy is interpreted as positive or negative by you, the receiver. Stop interpreting the energy as something against you. See it as just energy. The energy is either loving or a call to be loved. If it is a call to be loved, then you can answer the call.

I am not sure how to answer the call.

First, answer it for yourself. Every time you feel your emotions are being treated as unimportant, part of you is sending out a call for love. Love yourself by expressing how you feel in the most loving way possible. Acceptance of your feelings is not determined by her reaction. It is determined by your interpretation. Choose to change your interpretation.

I would like to express my feelings in the highest way possible, but it will be difficult.

What makes it difficult?

I am afraid I won't be accepted, that I'll be judged.

If you are, what will happen then?

I'll be hurt, maybe angry, too.

Go deeper. It is not her disapproval you fear, or your anger.

I'm afraid that there is something bad about me, something unacceptable I don't want her to know about.

Say there <u>was</u> something unacceptable deep within you. Why should she not know about it?

She might leave. She might reject me and confirm my suspicions about myself.

You have been left before and you survived. You grew as a result. What is the worst that will happen if she leaves?

I'll feel sad, lonely for awhile. But, I know that when the grieving is done I'll be strong again. If I want, I'll find another.

You do not need to have her in order to be happy and fulfilled in this lifetime?

No, but I would like to have her.

That is perfectly fine. She helps you to be happy. Would you be happy if you could not have an honest relationship? Give her a chance to love you, to discover all sides of you. There may be times she has difficulty with some parts of you. You sometimes have difficulty with parts of her, but you have not left. You can handle the leaving if it ever happened. Knowing you can handle it, you are free to be yourself. Free to be honest. Free to offer love.

Let us look at the second fear. You are afraid there is something unacceptable deep inside you. You do not want to see it. You do not want anyone else to see it. The only thing there that you need to be concerned about is fear. Do not be afraid to look within and face your fear. When you can successfully confront your fear and see that it is a false image of you, you will gain great power and freedom. You will see that, deep within, you are truly beautiful and loving. No purer essence has been discovered by humanity than the pure essence of love that resides at the center of you. No matter what you have done, no matter how many sins you think you have committed, this pure essence is the real you, untouched by any evil. You do not see it because your fear is in the way. Your ego, which you have fed with fear thoughts, uses this fear to maintain control. The ego, though, is not your enemy. It is more like a child out of control. You must teach it by focusing on your pure essence, also called your Higher Self. Keep reminding yourself that you, as your Higher Self, exist.

If you truly want a beautiful partnership, keep reminding yourself that her Higher Self exists, too. See it in her every day. Give thanks for her presence in your life each morning when you wake up. When she does something that irritates you, or hurts you, deal with it honestly. Then as soon as you can, remind yourself that she is imperfectly perfect just as you are.

Forgive her quickly, and forgive yourself just as quickly. Often people hold on to grievances because they are angry at themselves. They are angry because they did not respond in a way acceptable to themselves. So instead of building up grudges, respond honestly. Deal with behaviors <u>when</u> they occur. You express something to her. She reacts. You accept her right to react. You express what you have to say in the highest most loving way that you can. Your goal was to express. It is accomplished. If your goal was to make a certain impression on her, then you have undoubtedly failed.

Let go of all need for her to change. Instead focus your energy on accepting her the way she is. Know that whenever you mentally analyze her and think you know why she has done something, you are probably mistaken. Learn to listen. This is how you truly listen: Ask, "Dear God, help me to see this situation through your eyes. I now let go of my outcome and I place it in your hands." Then forget what you know about her. Forget what you know about psychology, or interpersonal dynamics, or about people. Go back to zero and be totally open to learning. Do this for her and for you. Wipe your mental slate clean and start again. When you can empty your mind of all your preconceived ideas and knowledge you open yourself to learning. You will create a vacuum which will be filled by wisdom and guided by love.

What if we can not accept each other?

Do not get married. Long term relationships should be a conscious choice. If you can not accept each other then move on.

I'll keep thinking about this. My understanding is that the ability to love someone unconditionally in a close relationship is a matter of focus. When I have felt a deep love, I know that I was either focusing on positive aspects or feeling deep compassion for her feelings. When I change my focus to hurtful things or expectations that she is not meeting, I am departing from unconditional love.

True. In the particular situation where you feel not listened to, change the belief, "She does not care about my emotions," to "She is doing the very best she can to accept my emotions." Then make sure you accept them. Release your judgment of her behavior and listen to her.

In your interaction, first understand her emotions, then help her to understand yours. Whatever ability she has to hear you, accept that she is doing her best. You do not help her by accusing her of not listening. To love unconditionally you must stop waiting for her to change her ways first. That is a condition. Just offer love.

I wish we could talk over our disagreements in a reasonable way. But we can't seem to do it. We become so dysfunctional in this situation. Not wanting the dys-functionality, I hold back. I control my emotions.

Holding back is dysfunctional, too. Speaking up may be dysfunctional. What is the difference? Dysfunctional only means that this part of your relationship is not working. You will not get it to work by avoiding it. Talk to her. Go ahead and be dysfunctional if that is where you are right now. Stop worrying about whether or not you are dysfunctional. Speak your truth. Acknowledge your weaknesses. At the same time, do not expect her to be your therapist. It is not her job to fix you. That job is shared by you and God. If you need intensive psychological work respond with intensive prayer. Also, get help, either through a therapist or a trusted friend who knows how to listen.

You are right. She is not my therapist. Let's move on. I want to get back to this falling in love stuff. Is it possible for two people to fall in love and stay in love for a lifetime?

It begins with your intention. It may be that people fall in love at first, but staying in love is a decision they make. You must decide with all your heart that you want to love her. If you harbor feelings that there may be someone else out there who will love you better or who may evoke stronger feelings in you, then you do not want to love her. Also, if you harbor fears that she will leave you, then you are not being very loving to yourself or her. Make the decision to love her with all you have, then refuse to entertain the doubts, fears, and fantasies that contradict that love. Or, decide to part and love her from a distance, seeking another if you wish.

What if I decide to love her and she decides to move on?

Let go. Turn inward to God within you. Declare for yourself that you are always loved unconditionally, and you will be. You cannot be abandoned because God will not abandon you. If you want a loving, loyal, and intimate relationship with a life long partner, and that is what is best for you, you can have it. The Universe will provide this for you as long as you are willing to be loving, loyal, and intimate. As long as you have the positive expectation that your partner wants to be, and is, loving, loyal, and intimate with you, that partner will be attracted to you. Play your part and do not worry about her ability to play hers. Trust. If it is not in her best interest to play that role with you the Universe will arrange a more appropriate situation for each of you. Trust. Trust that you are in the right place with the right person, and follow your heart. Listen to the voice of love within you and your dreams of a life long love will come true. Listen to the voices of jealousy, suspicion, fear, and doubt, and those feelings will be played out in your relationship. What do you want?

I want this relationship to be a life long, loving partnership.

You have the intention to create a life long, loving relationship. Are you waiting for her to do or say something that will confirm this? Are you waiting for her to do or say something before you commit to loving her? You want her or you do not. The decision is within you. When you first met, you stated your intention. You told her you saw the potential for a long term relationship. Having stated your intention, you stepped back in order to allow her to determine her intentions. She expressed her similar intention.

If you truly want something, your thoughts, feelings, words, and actions must be in alignment with your desire. The Universe can only send you what you want. If you are sending out confusing signals, you will continue to get confusing results.

At one time you asked for this beautiful woman to come into your life. Next thing you knew, there she was. Then you found out she was human, and you discovered many of your own weaknesses, too. You began to doubt her and yourself. Let go and love. If you want it, the opportunity is here for you to love her so well that you will soon discover her humanity is only a role. In Truth, she is divine, and so are you. You came to this earth to discover your divinity through love. There is no other way, except to love. Of course, not everyone comes to share a life with another. Those souls who do not will learn their lessons of love in other ways. You have a deep desire to share your life with another. Follow that desire, for it is God given. God would not have put the desire in you were it not possible to fulfill it.

There are segments of you that long to heal. You see your companion as one with whom you long to be, yet you endeavor to change her. There are persons in life who present a way of inducing greater understanding of all that you may be. You know that you can change only what is within you, then you find peace. Attempting to change another will not bring you peace. It will, in fact, bring more conflict. Allow others to be as they will, for that is theirs until they choose another path. Take who you are and adjust yourself to see the perfection that exists in all others. In doing this you find peace.

Accept her as she is. Accept yourself as you are. Place your relationship in God's hands. Create the intention that you will accept the highest good possible. It will be so.

Bill's Journal

Maybe this isn't as hard as I thought. I need to be clear that what I want is a lifetime relationship, and then act in alignment with that desire. I can't be waiting for my partner to conform to my idea of who she should be. She is who she is, and that is why I came to love her in the first place. I don't have to handle all of this myself. I can ask for help through prayer. Maybe I don't have to worry about what to say or what to do. As we allow Spirit to guide us in our relationship, our issues are worked out. This doesn't mean we only have to talk to God and not really deal with each other. It means that by talking to God first, we will know what to say to each other. Also, I need to practice acceptance—acceptance of myself and of another person. We each are where we are. My fears are caused by my stuff, which is mine to work out. I can practice forgiveness of myself in order to clear away the negative thoughts and emotions I have.

Chapter 9
Defenselessness

My partner told me I am a very defensive person. She's as defensive as I am.

Are you defensive?

I guess I am defensive at times

You guess you are defensive at times? Are you or are you not?

Okay, I am defensive at times.

What is it that you are defending?

Myself.

Your Self needs no defending, because it is perfect. What are you defending?

If I'm not defending myself, then I don't know what I'm defending.

You are defending your view of yourself.

My view of myself?

You hold a view of yourself. Someone says something that challenges that view. You become upset and defend yourself.

I'm not sure what my view of myself is.

That is because it is always changing and is an incorrect view. Another word for "view of yourself" is "ego". Your ego is the ever changing, false view of you.

I don't know what I can do about this. Am I supposed to get rid of my ego?

You will release it from its role as the decision maker for you. You need not attack it, nor declare it your enemy. This will only give it more power over you.

Then how do I release it?

Change your view of yourself.

How?

You can change your view whenever you feel defensive. What does "feeling defensive" feel like to you?

I feel tension in my solar plexus. It swells up very fast. I get angry, and before I know it words come out of my mouth. It's like an automatic reaction.

You can take it off automatic and put it on manual drive. Be very aware of the "defensive feeling" you get. When it comes, stop. Close your mouth. Acknowledge that you have received the signal. Take a deep breath. Let it out. If appropriate, acknowledge to the other person that you feel defensive and angry. At the very least, acknowledge it to yourself. Give yourself permission to feel the way you do. Ask "What do I need to do right now to take care of the emotions I am feeling?" so that you can feel secure and loved. Next, do what you need to do.

I don't know if I'm strong enough or quick enough to do these things.

Do the best you can. It takes patience. Defensive reactions are based on false meanings you attach to events and false beliefs you hold about yourself. Your friend said you were a defensive person, and you reacted defensively to that statement. Why?

I don't like to see myself as defensive.

In truth, <u>you</u> are not defensive, but due to your false beliefs you behave defensively sometimes. Is that a fact?

Yes, it is.

Then what is there to be defensive about?

I don't think I'm supposed to be defensive. I think I should be above that.

You are learning not to be defensive and you are, through your own process of growth, learning to rise above it. Why not accept where you are?

I don't know.

In order to move up to the next step, a higher level of <u>defenselessness</u>, you must first accept where you are now. Once you accept where you are, you cease to be defensive. Your friend says "Bill you are being defensive." How could you respond?

Yes, I am defensive, and I'm angry, too.

Thus begins honest dialogue. When two people can acknowledge their respective weaknesses to each other, the relationship strengthens and love grows. It is arrogant to be defensive. The fact is, you do things that are less than loving, less than perfect, just like everyone else you know. Your behavior does not make you less than or better than others. Your behavior is an expression of your consciousness. Your defensive reactions are an attempt to make others believe you are better than you actually believe you are. Other people are the mirrors of what you think you are. You can break the mirror that holds your reflection, but it will not change how you think you look.

Use the mirrors to discover your false beliefs about yourself. Use the mirror presented by another in relationship with you to express honestly and grow. See beyond the appearance in the mirror to discover the Truth of what you really are, God's child, God's expression.

Defensive reactions are always from a position of weakness. You literally feel weaker after you defend yourself. Become defenseless and you will become strong. Become defenseless and you will become You. Every person who evokes an emotional reaction in you is a reflection of something unresolved in you. Being defensive (or offensive) toward an enemy "out there" is futile. The "enemy" is within. It is the collection of false thoughts and beliefs you hold. When you have the courage to look at these thoughts, and stand defenseless before them, they will lose their power over you. Your clear vision will pierce the heart of each false belief and it will die. The energy underlying the false belief will be resurrected as thought forms of love and truth.

I don't know if I can stop being defensive. I would like to, but it just seems to happen automatically.

Being defensive infers that you have been victimized. When you take full responsibility for your life, your thoughts, your feelings, your words, and your actions, you are no longer a victim. You become powerful. You have the ability to respond to whatever arises. You are powerless when you cannot respond effectively, because you are unwilling to let go of blame, hurt, fear or anger. A truly powerful person is simply one who knows how to respond effectively. This knowledge begins with your willingness to release your hurtful feelings.

You can only achieve this level of power by allowing Spirit within to guide you. Working with your personality alone, you would continually seek to make people or circumstances responsible for what happens to you. In Truth, God is the only Power in the Universe. By recognizing your oneness with God, you recognize your power. You cannot "hear" God's guidance if you are filled with anger and blaming.

When you are responsible, and recognize your oneness with God, you have nothing to defend. Whenever you feel that defensive feeling acknowledge it. You might say, "I am feeling defensive right now." This will weaken the feeling. Instead of reacting verbally, stop and think.

You might acknowledge how you are feeling as you said earlier. Another option is to become still, and allow the feeling to pass. After you feel more peaceful, you can respond from this place of peace.

Whatever you are feeling defensive about is a part of you that needs healing. Thank those feelings and let them pass. Ask for God's guidance. Each time you do this you will become more defenseless and more powerful.

Bill's Journal

I'm tired of being defensive. Why do I resist giving up being a victim? It seems so simple to respond from a place of peace. I do take responsibility quite a bit. It feels good when I have nothing to defend.

I know I can work out my relationship issues with my partner. We both want to be happy and to share our lives together. We are both committed to growing together. What about problems I experience with someone who doesn't want to work together? What about people I work with? What about someone who really doesn't seem to care? How do I deal with those people? There is this guy, Andy, I work with on a project who really ticks me off. How do I deal with a real asshole, like Andy? And, I know I'm supposed to be spiritual and not use terms like that, but that's how I feel. I think he's an asshole.

He's controlling; he operates from hidden agendas; he doesn't care about other people; and he's only concerned with getting what he wants.

You are not supposed to be spiritual. You already are spiritual, by your very nature. It is true that when you judge Andy you are not seeing spiritually or operating out of a high spiritual consciousness. People like Andy are letting you know that there are parts of you that need to be healed. In Truth, this person Andy is not an asshole. It would be more accurate and helpful to you if you would describe him as an angel disguised as an asshole.

It is difficult for me to picture Andy as an angel. I've never seen him do anything angelic.

Are you willing to play along and accept the premise, for the moment, that Andy is really an angel.

Okay, for the moment I will accept the premise.

The Andy's of the world are all angels disguised as assholes. Yet, who gave them their disguise? You did. Andy is only playing a role in your presence. It is you who believes that the role is real. Perhaps Andy does, too, but Andy is not your problem. Your perception is your problem.

Are you saying that the only reason Andy acts the way he does is because I perceive him that way?

Not quite. The only reason the situation you experience with Andy is in your life is due to your perception. Were you to perceive the world differently Andy would not be in your life, or he would act differently around you, or his actions would have no effect on you. You are getting ahead of us.

Okay, let's get back to this bit about the disguise you say I made.

Think about actors on television or in the movies. You see them in their respective roles. Being good at what they do, you believe each actor is his role. Remember that show you used to watch in the 1970's, about the bigoted father.

You mean "All in the Family"?

Yes. You read an article about the actor, Carroll O'Connor who played the role of Archie Bunker.

Yeah. The article said that people would see him in public and think he really was Archie. People who agreed with Archie's philosophy of life would express their appreciation of him. In reality, Carroll was nothing like Archie. He was Carroll, a man who didn't share Archie's bigoted ideas.

Yes. He was playing a role that he made. In the minds of the viewers, he was playing a role that they made. The viewers heard his words, saw his actions, and interpreted what he did so that he represented something to each and every viewer. To some he represented a man standing up for the rights of White people. He was a voice for the White people who felt that Black people and other groups were making too many gains at their expense. To others he represented the enemy—the old ideas that created racial inequity. To others he represented ignorance. There were many interpretations. Every interpretation was a disguise given this character. None of them were really Carroll. Archie did not exist. He was fiction.

He was a stereotype.

Stereotypes, in truth, are not real. They are representations. They become real to people who believe in them. The problem with a stereotype is that it prevents you from seeing those aspects of a person which lie outside the boundaries of the stereotype. Mr. O'Connor is a very convincing actor, but actors are not their roles.

Agreed, actors are not their roles.

When you accept the role as real you are fooling yourself.

Is that bad? I mean, movies and television would not be fun if we didn't accept the roles as real.

No, it is not bad, but when you leave the theater you realize that it was just a show, just a story played out by actors and actresses.

Of course I do. So, are you saying that Andy in my life is just a show?

Yes. You and he are playing out a drama. As long as you continue to express the anger and judgment toward Andy that you do, the drama will continue. If you manage to kick Andy out of your life without resolving your emotions and your judgment about the situation, another Andy will come into your life. Andy has come into your life for one reason.

And what is that?

To help you learn to love and heal the part of you that hurts when you have to deal with him. He is an angel to you, because he has come here to help you. Imagine that he really is an angel. Imagine that before you and he were born, your two souls came together and decided that he would come into your life at a particular time and act in such a way that you would judge to be like an asshole. If you knew this to be true, would it change the way you feel about him?

I suppose it would.

How would you change?

I would be more patient and forgiving. I would look for good things that he does. I would not complain about him behind his back. I would expect positive things from him. Sometimes, if I found his behavior to be irritating, I'd tell him to knock it off. Probably I would spend more time dealing with my own feelings, coming to peace with myself regarding him.

Then do these things. Expect only the best from him. Speak honestly to him, but only say those things you intuitively feel will contribute to your mutual highest good. Be at peace about him. You may also want to have a conversation with his Higher Self. In your conversation express your love and respect, and ask for assistance in dealing with him. Use common sense, too. Set limits if he behaves inappropriately.

All of this will make the situation change?

Yes, Andy may become more loving, at least toward you. Or, if he is not ready, he may just leave your life. At the very least, his actions will cease to affect you in a negative way.

Everyone who is in your life is there by invitation. Each person has something to teach you about yourself. Learn the lesson; give thanks for the opportunity and the person. Soon more and more people in your life will truly look like and act like angels to you. As you become peaceful and loving, the disguises fall away, and the angelic nature of each person appears. Your ability to see through the disguise influences others' ability to see through the disguise.

I feel a strong resistance to seeing this guy as an angel. I guess sometimes I just like to dislike someone. There is a kind of gratification in it. I can always say, I'm not as bad as that guy! I want to resolve this. It's time for me to go forward. If Andy is showing me a part of myself I don't like, well then, I want to make the change.

What is Andy teaching you?

Well, I don't think I'm an asshole. I mean, there have been times I have qualified for that title, but usually I treat people with respect. So, I'm not seeing myself in him.

What do you want from him?

I want him to treat me well—to give me respect. I want him to make my job easier.

What are your options when Andy acts negatively around you?

I can quietly put up with it. I can fight him. I can be compassionately honest with him and set boundaries.

Is there some resistance to setting boundaries?

Yes. Why should I have to do that? Why doesn't he just behave right?

You want Andy to take care of you. Instead, he is teaching you to take care of yourself. This is an important lesson for you. When you compassionately set boundaries you learn how to take care of yourself. At the same time you teach him appropriate behavior.

You are right. Instead of creating all of this drama about what a terrible person Andy is I should just deal with it. Thanks.

Bill's Journal

There is nothing to defend. There are no conflicts except the ones in my mind. There are no battles to fight unless I choose to invent them. There is strength and peace in defenselessness.

Chapter Ten:
Changing Negative Thoughts

Why do I think negative thoughts so much?

You think negative, fearful thoughts because you want the feelings they create. You want them because it is time for you to release the beliefs and attitudes that support them.

I feel like these thoughts have a life of their own. They come to me; they take me over; and even though I ask myself why I'm thinking them and push them out my mind; they are back within minutes. I am getting worried that these thoughts are going to attract conditions to me that could be very painful.

You have already created negative consequences through the suffering you experience whenever the negative thoughts are in charge, and through the tremendous joy and success you are missing due to these thoughts.

You know intuitively that you must evolve your thinking past these thoughts. These thoughts create painful feelings in your emotions and in your body. The question is, do you feel enough desire and intent to learn from these thoughts and release them, or do you need to actually experience a more intense physical manifestation of these thoughts and feelings in order to learn?

I want to release this negativity now. I don't want to wait for it to manifest as conditions in my life.

You have the power within you right now to do this. Use it. Declare with all the feeling you have that you are ready to evolve your thinking to a higher level. Release your negative thoughts to the Light of God. That is, imagine a spiritual light shining on these thoughts. See the thought dissolve in the Light. Respond to each negative thought in this way. Recognize each fearful thought for what it is.

What is it?

These thoughts are unhealthy. They create a hurtful experience which does not serve you.

I imagine painful experiences with other people. I create these stories where I am injured in some way. Then I imagine what I would say or do in the situations. It is like I am preparing myself in case these things happen.

Your thoughts are really not about any other people. They are about you. There are two reasons you think this way. First, you want to feel this hurt. Your second reason has to do with your ideas about love.

Why would I want to feel hurt?

You believe that you are not important to other people. How can one as insignificant and flawed as you be important to others? If you are unimportant, then of course others will treat you as unimportant. At the same time, you are unwilling to forgive yourself for unloving acts you have committed toward others. Instead you have chosen guilt. You cover your guilt with self righteous hurt. You create a desire to be hurt and to be a victim. If you are the victim of another person then you are right, and they are wrong.

I hate to admit it, but I think you're right. I can't believe what sick thoughts I have cultivated. I create this situation in my mind where another person hurts me and I feel small. I recognize that it's not me doing the hurting, it's them. That makes me feel better, or self righteous as you described it. I imagine myself telling this other person off, which makes me feel big. What am I doing to myself?

Emotionally, your experience is the same as if the dreaded event would have actually happened. Your rehearsals of dreaded emotional events actually help to create similar events in your relationships. You can clean this up through forgiveness. Forgive yourself for all of the times you think you hurt others. Forgive all of those who you think have hurt you. Many years ago you learned a visualization to help you to clean up this negativity.

You're right. I remember now.

Bill's Journal

The Forgiveness Visualization

Become relaxed. Sit in a position that allows you to feel comfortable for at least a half an hour. In your imagination go back to your childhood. Think about the first ten years of your life and the people who were around you. Ask yourself: "To whom do I believe I caused injury or pain?" As each person comes to mind, send them love, bless them, and apologize. Hear and see each of them telling you that you are forgiven. Thank each person and accept their forgiveness. Declare yourself forgiven. Next imagine all those who you think caused you pain or injury. Acknowledge something positive you learned from your experience with each of them. Thank each person. Imagine each person apologizing to you. Send them love and blessings and forgive them.

Next, follow the same process for the second ten years of your life. Repeat the procedure for the years from twenty until the present.

When you have finished, give thanks for all of these people and the lessons they have helped you to learn. Appreciate yourself for being able to do this visualization. A very powerful way to do this meditation is to do it with a partner. I did this once at a Tantric Yoga retreat. You can put the words on tape or say them. In order to do this, sit facing your partner. Look into each others' eyes throughout the meditation. Do not speak aloud about what is going on in your mind. You may choose to hold hands and/or have your knees touching. Often tears will flow during this process. Just allow it to happen. When you are finished you can talk about your experiences to each other if desired, but do not discuss the details. The purpose is to release hurtful feelings. Discussing them in detail may only strengthen their hold on you.

To follow up, thank God, and thank your Soul for all of the love you have received. Sit in silence for awhile, imagining that you are basking in God's Love. Quiet yourself and listen to the still, small voice within.

I remember doing this meditation many years ago. It was very powerful. The following night two people who I had left out of the visualization showed up in my dreams.

It is important to forgive yourself of the past. Let go of your regrets.

I do carry regrets over past actions.

You have worked those past events and your judgments of those events around and around in your mind. You have allowed yourself to become twisted and tight in your stomach area due to the emotions you have created over these past events.

Why do I do this to myself? The past is gone.

You are keeping the past in the present. You still have the mistaken idea that all bad deeds must be punished. Often you feel you do not deserve good things because of your past mistakes. You prevent yourself from receiving many blessings.

I have forgiven myself many times over for the past. It keeps coming back to me.

When you are through with it, it will stop troubling you. You must make the decision that you are done. You must release the fear that it will somehow come back to haunt you. Regarding past acts, whenever possible, apologize and seek to repair damage you have caused. Seek to feel a deep compassion for the other person. Know that the other person is responsible for taking care of his own feelings. This is not justification for poor behavior on your part. You have impact on other people and must take responsibility for it. Accepting responsibility does not mean that you feel guilty or that you must fix the other person. It means that you learn from the situation and change your behavior. You can also respond by letting each of your thoughts, feelings, words, and behaviors contribute toward his healing. This will help you to heal. Whatever you have done to harm another you have also done to yourself. Whatever you have done to help another you have also done to yourself. What you have sown, you will reap.

What about my guilt?

This guilt has no value. Compassion and understanding would be more appropriate. Guilt undermines love. It is destructive. If you hurt someone act to repair the damage. Learn from the experience. Choose differently in the future. Guilt prevents you from moving forward. Guilt tells you that you are unworthy. Your sense of unworthiness contributes nothing to the healing of another, nor does it serve you.

Change your focus. When the past comes up, ask yourself what you have learned. Focus on the lessons, and give thanks that you learned those lessons. Congratulate yourself that you made it through those situations. Remind yourself that you are who you are today because of those lessons. If you are no longer doing the hurtful behaviors you have no need to feel the guilt. It is over. Be grateful you have learned to act differently.

There is a fear inside me that I am a bad person due to mistakes I made. It is a very ugly feeling.

That ugly feeling underlies much of your negativity. It is not real. The history of the world is full of this sinner consciousness. Church leaders, political leaders, managers, parents, and educators have used this sinner mentality to control people. It has helped to control behavior, but the cost is great. The guilt, the shaming, and the blaming people have given and received has become a very strong, but false belief system. Know that it is not true.

Everything negative that you perceive in the world is false, but you have forgotten. Your job is to remember that you are an expression of God. Your negativity comes from your fear of remembering who you are. Part of you is afraid that you will lose something if you remember who you really are. Another part of you is afraid that you <u>are</u> that ugliness you feel inside. Of what value is this guilt? Of what value is your struggle? Of what value is your worry? You have derived learning from all of your experiences of guilt, struggle, and pain, but they have no value to offer you now, that you cannot surpass through their release.

Monitor your thinking and emotions. Call for help in letting go of your negativity, and it will surely come. Each time a regret or a negative fantasy comes up, remind yourself that your thoughts are prayers. Ask, "Is this what I want to be praying for? What do I really want?" You have the opportunity this very day to think happy thoughts, rather than repetitive negative thoughts. Today's negative thoughts are usually the very same ones you thought yesterday. Make a clear decision to begin anew with healthy thinking.

Bill's Journal

My mind is like a jar of dirty water that I keep shaking up. Over the years I have cleaned it up some. At one time I spent most of my day in a thought war. My thoughts were warring on me. I have gained more control. The water is not yet clear, but I feel better. For many years my thoughts were out of control. Today I have greater control and my life shows it.

You said that I want these thoughts. I torture myself with jealous fantasies. I see myself, in relationships, being left for another. I don't think forgiving myself will end this problem. This thinking is compulsive. It's a habit. I am worried my jealous thinking will make these imaginary conditions real. I have always imagined that the women in my life would leave me for another. My first two girlfriends did.

The experience is already real. The physical and emotional discomfort you experience through your fantasy is real, is it not?

It is. Why can't I stop it?

It is not that you cannot stop it. You know the thinking is unhealthy. You recognize you are doing it, yet you choose to continue. It is a choice. It is mental entertainment. It is drama. You have turned your mind into a soap opera. It is like going to a bad movie over and over again. You have addicted yourself to this drama in which you play the self righteously hurt hero—the hero with whom the imaginary audience sympathizes. Each time the bad movie begins, make a decision to turn it off. Let it go. Turn your thoughts toward more healthy matters.

As for your concern about creating the conditions you imagine, you do not have the power to create the specific hurtful situation you have imagined. You definitely have the power to create hurt for your self. If you continue in this trend, you may create a condition where your present partner will not want to be with you, and the relationship will change. She feels your negativity.

She has negative thoughts of her own about you, which you feel. You affect each other. When you feel insecure about each other, your respective negative thoughts increase. If either of you cannot resolve your negativity you will not be happy together. Although the details and the nature of your respective negative thoughts differ greatly, the result is the same. Unhappy thoughts about each other will, at some point, result in unhappy conditions.

I'd like to talk to her about these feelings, but I 'm afraid she won't accept me.

You can not control her reaction. Know that your love has the power to affect her in positive ways. Positive thoughts are much more powerful than negative ones. Trust in the power of love. You release your negative thoughts and become loving, without concern about her returning the love; without concern that she will in any way misuse your love, without any expectation except that she will be herself. Whenever you think of her or rehearse what you will say to her, visualize her face surrounded in light and love. See her responding with love. Do not put words in her mouth. Just create a positive expectation toward her. She will respond to you. Each moment you spend loving her, you help her to be more loving. Each moment you spend thinking negatively about her, you throw up roadblocks to creating love in your relationship. Put your confidence in love. She will feel safer and more open. Her willingness to express love to you will increase.

Am I manipulating her through love?

No. You are creating a loving space for her to step into. If she has any desire to be more loving or to be closer to you, she will step into it. No matter how much you love her, you do not have the power to make her love you. Express yourself honestly and see what happens.

How do I shift my negative thoughts and fantasies when they come up?

Be aware that your thoughts are creating discomfort. What you are thinking is not really happening. Determine if you have any evidence that what you are thinking could actually be happening. When you imagine your partner in an auto accident it does not mean that she is in an auto accident. Your imagining her having a secret rendezvous does not mean she is actually doing it. Since you are not with her you can assume bad things are happening or you can trust that everything is okay. You make the choice. Your choice determines what you will think, how you will feel, and the quality of your relationship. If you trust in the good, and something turns out to be not okay, you can deal with it then. Ask yourself how these negative thoughts benefit you. Make a decision to let go of these thoughts. Think healthy thoughts instead.

You have the power to manage your thinking. It just takes practice and desire. You must want to release the negativity.

Are you saying that if I do all of this my negative feelings will be released?

You are in a relationship. Would you like part of the purpose of this relationship to be that you assist each other to grow?

Yes, I would.

Then talk to her about your feelings. You do not have to provide every detail. Just say what you have been feeling. If it embarrasses you to reveal these feelings, then tell her that you feel embarrassed. You hurt yourself when you hide painful feelings from her. Ask for guidance, and go to her with an open mind and an open heart. If you can not do this then talk to a therapist first.

Jealous thoughts are a form of protection. You are preparing yourself for when a negative situation may happen. You are rehearsing so that you can feel secure when the dreaded event comes. You do not need to do this. If ever a situation would occur where you felt betrayed, you could deal with it in the moment. Acknowledge your feelings and act in accordance with your intuition. You never need to rehearse imaginary situations that you fear. You only need to listen within in the moment and you will know what to do to take care of yourself. Begin to trust yourself. A person who trusts himself, who is spiritually grounded, cannot be the victim in a relationship. Trust yourself to create reasonable boundaries. Trust your Creator to love you whether or not the person you are with is able to love you.

It is almost like there is this entity within me that taunts me with thoughts I don't want to think. It happens so easily. I can't be a victim of my own urges any more. I want to control my thoughts. Maybe it is that for so many years I have just let any thought that appears run rampant through my mind. I have to start being the gatekeeper on a constant basis. Whatever thought comes up, it's my decision. What do I want?

I talked to her. I was afraid of what her reaction might be. I was embarrassed that I felt jealous feelings. We had an honest talk. She revealed many things about herself that I did not know. I received reassurance of her love and friendship to me. After our talk, I see that my negative thoughts have no basis. They are leaving. I feel lighter, and I feel closer to her.

You did well. You did not attack her or allow your fantasies to convince you of anything. You simply expressed what had been going on in your mind. Sometimes negative thoughts fester in people because they have no outlet. The thoughts then become your reality. This happens when people do not communicate. They fill in the blanks with their own information based, quite often, on negative assumptions. It is most important to realize that you are creating the negativity with your thoughts. If you want to feel better, change your thoughts.

Okay, so now I understand why I have wanted negative thoughts. I wanted the drama and the self righteous feelings of being the victim. I wanted to punish myself for past mistakes. I wanted to protect myself from pain by making practice runs in my mind. You said there were two reasons why I think negatively. Tell me about the second one.

It is your belief about what love is between two people.

Wait a minute. I thought we already went through this.

I consider myself pretty insightful about love.

Are you ready for one more insight?

Okay. What is it?

You were taught about love as a child. How was love defined? How was being a good person defined?

I was taught that I should be unselfish. If I care about someone I do things for them—I help them.

In your relationships you knock yourself out helping and doing <u>for.</u> To you this proves that you love someone. What would be the flip side of this?

That if someone truly cares about me they will do that for me.

So to you, love is about doing what others want you to do. If they do not appreciate it, or if they do not do the same for you, they must not love you.

That sounds terrible. That's how I have been loving people?

Does it sound true?

Yes. Now I see why I have felt so much resentment in relationships. How can I approach this differently?

You need a new definition for love.

Tell me what love is.

When you love someone it means that you want what is in the highest good for yourself and for the other person. It means that you will not demand that another meets your expectations. Communicate your expectations and preferences and allow choice. It means that you accept another for who she is. You appreciate and support who she is right now. You delight in who she is. Love is respectful and kind, compassionately honest. Love is much more than wanting to be together. When you love someone you care deeply about her well being and her spirit. You would do nothing to harm her spirit. At the same time, you will not harm your own spirit. Love calls upon you to make choices which you know are in the best interest of another and yourself. Sometimes the choice may not be pleasing to either of you.

Explain more on this.

There were times in your past when the most loving thing you could have done for yourself and for another was to leave.

That's true. Sometimes the most loving thing to do was not to get started!

Love is often defined in terms of ownership, expectations, and personal gratification. See love as acceptance, appreciation, and desire for what is highest and best for each other. If you love in this way a partnership is possible.

I think a partnership is possible. I mean, everything isn't perfect, but we love each other. We want the same things in life—spiritual growth, travel, a peaceful home, a family, and a healthy, loving relationship. It feels like it's time to move forward. We both feel it. What do you think?

Trust yourself, Bill. Pay attention to your feelings. Act from love, not from fear.

Bill's Journal

We were married this summer, my friend and I. It was a beautiful wedding and a joyous occasion. For years I have desired a stable, loving relationship. Now it is here. Thank you, God.

Chapter 11
Fulfillment from Within

Bill's Journal

I have achieved my dream. We have been married for over a year. We just bought a beautiful home. Once, many years ago, I envisioned I would be doing work that I loved, earning a good income, happily married, and living in a beautiful home of my own. This is my reality now. For so many years I wondered if it would ever get here. Now I am here.

I have what I have always wanted, but I still have problems. Problems in relationships, problems at work, and with my physical environment. I feel bad that I haven't been focusing on God, lately. I pray, but I don't feel a spiritual focus to each day. As a result I'm struggling with a lot of things. How do I get closer to God? How do I get a spiritual focus in life? How do I become more joyful in my daily living?

I don't seem to be getting answers. I am so caught up in the events of my life that I don't seem to be able to get quiet enough to listen. I feel an urge to seek outside help. There was a spiritual reader (psychic) someone told me about. I have put off going for several months now. Perhaps it is time

Today I called the reader. I am having some doubts about this. You never know what they will say. I am told that this one is very blunt in his approach. I like blunt. Just tell me, and I'll deal with it. This is why I am going. People often go to psychic readers for fun and to be told wonderful things about themselves. I am hoping to hear what I need to hear. It may or may not be wonderful. I'm not desperate. I'm not suffering. I have so much to be grateful for. I do have problems that need to be solved. Perhaps he can help.

Three Days Later

Bills Journal

I am still recovering from my reading yesterday. My expectation was met: he was blunt. He fired off one thing after another. I'm a little shook up. No, I'm a lot shook up. I wanted to be shook up didn't I? I mean, why else would I go for a reading except that I wanted to shake loose from my mental moorings and move forward in my life.

I need to look at what he told me.

1. He said I was a healer and a clairvoyant. I need to get off my butt and start using these gifts. I need to be working in a center where people would come to me.

2. He said my marriage was unhappy and that we would be split in a year. We have moved away from love, he said.

3. He said I was not good for my partner in that I was blocking her spiritual growth.

4. He said two of the spirits around me were my earthly father and my maternal grandmother. My father apologized for his behavior toward me while he was on earth. Apology accepted, Dad.

5. He said massive changes would be taking place in my life in the next year or so. I would be moving to another area.

6. He said I was too hard on myself. I need have no regrets over the path my life has taken.

7. He said I was a good father to my children.

8. Everything he said about my past was right on the mark.

He was very specific. This gave him credibility. For example, he knew my father had died, the exact nature of my mother's personality, the specifics of my past love life, and more. He told me that I have a brother. I told him I didn't, but he was very insistent. I had given him no information about me. Since he knew my past and present so well, I have to give him some credibility for the future. Don't I?

What do I do with this?

First, get a perspective. Get a perspective on the reader and your spirit guides.

Okay. Well, I don't think I should believe everything a reader tells me, even if he is incredibly accurate. It is my life, not his. I've had readings in the past and everything didn't come true.

A reader gives you a probable future. Providing he is an accurate reader, based on your consciousness and the direction in which you are currently heading, the things he spoke of will come true. What does that tell you?

That if I make changes in my thinking or if I make different choices in life my future will change?

Yes. You have the gift of choice. Your future is not carved in stone, or there would be no free will. Spirit always respects free will. Look at the future the spirits speaking through your reader have painted for you. Is it what you want?

No, I don't, but the message was so specific, so definite. They told me my marriage would end, so I should prepare for that. I pressed the reader to tell me if I could change the trend. He admitted it was possible, but he was very doubtful it would change.

Spirit Guides see things differently than you do. It is as if they are hovering above time and can see where you are headed. Imagine if you were hovering high above an intersection. To the right you see a car traveling at 30 miles per hour. Up ahead you see a car traveling at the same speed. They are equidistant from the intersection. You see that they will collide if present speeds are maintained. This is how it is for your spirit guides. They can see your intentions and the speed at which you are approaching their natural conclusion. Consider this. Two of your spiritual speakers were your father and your grandmother. When they died each took along his and her respective consciousness. In other words, do not expect them to express a higher consciousness than when they were in body. They do not speak to you from a higher consciousness, only from a higher point of view. You may listen to and consider their advice, but you must make up your own mind. Better you would ask God directly for guidance. Your father and grandmother obviously love you, but they have opinions. God does not have an opinion. God knows.

Maybe I shouldn't bother with a reading.

A reading can be helpful if you use it to help you grow. Use the information to help you. Do not get caught up in the crystal ball effect. Do not put your trust in the reading; trust in God within you. Be your own reader. If you choose to get another psychic reading there are some things you need to consider. For example, you might ask why it is you want a reading. What is your intention?

Once you know why you are seeking this kind of help, choose your reader wisely. Not everyone who claims to be psychic operates with integrity. Psychic readers are people just like everyone else. They have opinions, faults, and problems of their own. Can they set aside their own opinions during your reading? Personal references work the best when seeking a reader. Calling up a psychic on the phone from a television ad is risky, extremely expensive, and for some, addictive. Many of these people are not sincere. They are being paid to tell you what you want to hear, and the longer they keep you on the line, the more they get paid. Good psychic readers charge about the same as a respectable therapist. Most will include a tape or a written account of the reading.

Psychic readers do not make things all better. They provide you with information, hopefully, accurate information. You still have to do the work. Readers will sometimes tell you of wonderful things that will happen someday. This does not excuse you from dealing with your current issues.

Beware of the "occult effect." A reader may tell you amazing things about you. It is almost like a magic show. People find this entertaining. A reading may help you to grow spiritually, to get closer to God, but it is nothing to be worshipped. Follow a reader's advice only if it feels right to you. Most wise readers will not give you advice. Seek advice within. Readers are not always able to separate their opinions from Truth. The level of guidance you receive is comparable to the level of spiritual growth achieved by the reader. In other words, if your reader is not tending to his own spiritual growth it is good reason to question the quality of the reading.

I think I followed most of those guidelines. The reader thinks I should just leave my marriage and get on with life. That was his opinion. It doesn't feel right to me. I want to look at this situation. This is an opportunity for me to learn something and to recommit to my marriage. He painted this picture of me leaving town and going off to become some great healer. That's what he did several years ago. He went to another psychic who told him he shouldn't be with his wife. They split up and he started the healing center that I went to. That's his biography. I am writing my own biography.

Bill, your future is not determined by the words of a psychic. It is not determined by what your spirit guides say. It is determined by your intentions. You developed intentions before you were born. You, that is, your Soul, created intentions for your growth in this lifetime. You, as a human on this earth have intentions. The reason your marriage is floundering is because the two of you have mixed intentions. In other words, you want to stay together and you also have doubts. According to your reading the doubts are beginning to win out. If you two split up, you will each go on to accomplish your respective Souls' intentions in another way. So, Bill, the question is: what is your intention regarding your marriage? What do you want?

I know that I am here to learn how to love. Learning about love is more important to me than achieving greatness in the spiritual field. How can I teach and heal if I don't have my own life together? How can I tell other people about love if I fail at it? I want to deal with this relationship. We chose each other. We decided to love each other. My intention is to learn how to love, and I want to do it here and now. It is here that I make my stand. If, by some chance, things don't work out, then it will not be a result of me not loving enough.

Your intention is clear and that is good. Whether or not your marriage continues, this intention will result in a loving relationship.

How do I hold my partner back spiritually? That is the last thing that I want to do. How does the way I love her hold her back?

Your thoughts affect her. With all of the fighting you two have been doing, you feel very self righteous and negative toward her.

Wait a minute. I thought we covered this.

You are correct. We have covered this. You gained insight into your negative thinking and your negative fantasies. Were you cured? Have you completely stopped thinking negatively?

Well, no. I'm just expressing my feelings.

It is not the expressing of your feelings that is the problem. It is the thoughts behind those expressions. Thoughts and intentions are powerful. If you think negatively toward someone you spend time with, they can feel it. You may hide the specific thoughts, but you can not hide the fears behind them.

Maybe you could help with one of our issues. This is one of the areas where my fears seem to take over. It is upsetting to me that she occasionally gets home late, but does not call and tell me. I worry about her.

It is the considerate thing to do.

There is more to it than that is there not? There is an issue of trust. You do not trust her.

You're right, I don't.

Has she ever given you any reason not to trust her?

At times she is secretive, but no. This is a pattern I've always had. My trust was broken many times in some of my past relationships. I guess I'm expecting it to happen again.

This is now, not then. This is your partner today, not some past relationship. You have choices to make. You have chosen not to trust. You asked God for a relationship where trust could be had. You married a woman who has been trustworthy for you, yet still, you do not trust.

I don't and I am weary of this. I realize I have done this in most of my relationships. I am afraid that if I don't know what she is doing at all times I'll lose her.

Many people fear abandonment in relationships. What most of you do not realize is that you not only fear abandonment, you are counting on it.

What do you mean?

Fearing abandonment is fearing commitment. You not only fear it will happen; you hope it will happen. If she leaves then you can tell yourself that you are not responsible. After all, she was the one who left. You tried, but it did not work out. You are so afraid of being abandoned that you facilitate abandonment. Once you are alone you do not have to fear it anymore. In the past you have attached yourself to women who were not intending to stay with you. Now you have found someone who makes a commitment. You treat her as if she wants to abandon you. This treatment encourages her to have doubts about being with you.

I don't want to play this game anymore. How can I overcome this issue?

Decide what you want. Do you want a loving partnership? Do you want to share your life with someone you trust?

Yes to both.

Then establish that as your intention. Pray for help. Ask that this be a holy relationship.

What is a holy relationship?

It is a spiritual relationship. You turn over your relationship and its future to God. You become willing to accept the outcome, whether it be staying together or parting. You stop adding up her imperfections and see the perfection in her. You practice unconditional love. If it is not in your best interests to stay together then Spirit will guide you elsewhere. Pray about this.

Prayer for Help

Holy Spirit, Holy Presence of God, I give thanks for this relationship, for this marriage. Thank you for bringing this beautiful soul into my life, for loving me through her. I give this relationship to you; I place it in your care. I invite you into this relationship, and I ask you to set the goal for our relationship. "What is this relationship for? " is now a question to be answered by you. This relationship is now a holy relationship. Therefore I recognize that my partner is Spirit, that she is a child of God, totally blameless. I let go of my judgments of her and accept the person I see before me as already whole. I trust that your Spirit will teach me to perceive her and myself as whole spiritual beings, healed. There is now a purpose for this relationship, one that I do not completely understand.

I know that it is Your purpose, therefore it is good. Thank you, God.

I talked with my wife about the reading. We prayed together. I felt a shift. I felt her relax when I told her about my reading and about my intent to let go of distrust. We prayed together that our relationship would be a holy relationship. To us this means that our relationship is in God's hands, and that we will seek to see the best in each other.

The reading that caused you much distress has become a blessing. It has helped you to see yourself more clearly. Discontent is the catalyst for positive change. In our eyes, you two are a holy relationship.

I feel closer to her now. We are communicating.

You are filled with love, however you will be tempted to judge and to doubt. Do not allow yourself to be taken over by judgmental thoughts. There may be difficult times to come. Trusting that God is at the center of your relationship will guide you through. Discipline in your thinking will allow you to see love rather than fear.

Bill's Journal

Learning to love is important to me. I know that sometimes relationships need to change, but I don't want to go through life exchanging one relationship for another whenever I get uncomfortable. If, in Truth, it would be better for the both of us to part company, I would let go with love. At the present I see no reason, so I will continue to love her and cherish our relationship. It is her intention to make this marriage a happy one. As long as both of us have the same intention we will grow in love.

I have not written for awhile. Things have been happening quickly. Two weeks after healing our relationship we conceived a child. This created both excitement and fear in me. Bringing a child into the world is a big responsibility. In spite of my fears I felt happy.

In the third month the baby was miscarried. A dark cloud hangs over our home. I am filled with sadness. My wife is filled with pain and disappointment. Each month becomes another disappointment as we seem unable to conceive again.

One Year Later

I feel tremendous pressure on me to do and be things I don't want to be. We are fighting again. I feel like I am fighting for the right to be myself.

Who is putting the pressure on you, Bill?

My wife. She complains to me. She seems to be disappointed in me so much of the time. I can't be everything she wants me to be. I can't say the "right" things and do the "right" things.

Bill, throughout your life a lot of energy has gone into filling other people. You have been deriving your sense of worth from what you do for other people. If your wife is happy, then you must be a good husband. If your children are happy, then you are a good father. If your clients are happy, then you are a good facilitator.

You come from a loving, giving place, but now in order to reap the benefits of love you need to give to yourself for your own joy and happiness. You can not fulfill other peoples' needs. Realization of this, in turn will support them in their own search for God, and for happiness within themselves. This offers each of you the opportunity to experience and practice self love. You need to be invested in filling your own cup.

Not theirs first, but yours first. Then the overflow will be there for all of you to enjoy. This is the difference between seeing peace and seeing lack.

Experience your wholeness and see wholeness in others. They are capable and whole with you or without you. Think of the freedom that seeing this offers you. You have yourself on a scale that measures only that which you give to others. You find you cannot fill another's needs, and so you feel lacking. Filling another's needs does not make you whole. You are already whole. You are running into repeat performances which have you saying "There is not enough of me to go around." You are confused by "their" needs. Find yourself free from this responsibility. Be as dedicated to experiencing love of self as that which you have been for others.

So, it's me that is putting on the pressure. I pressure myself to make her happy.

You are not helping her. She, too, must find her own happiness within. If you constantly try to drive away her discomfort, when will she learn to deal with it? You are angry with her for the pressure you feel. Yet, it is you who has decided your mission, not her. Your partner is looking for attentions that will help her to get full. Her needs are unmet by another (you or anyone else) and she feels fear. Can you allow her her reaction? Can you see it is in her best interest that you not disrupt her process? Her desire for fulfillment is deep. Her lack in this area is painful for her. Will you hold her hand through this? Will you offer compassion and caring without trying to fix or blame her? Be centered in who you are. Trust in the Spirit within you. Trust in your love. All will be well. You may compliment each other not necessarily as being of like mind, but as being of the One God. You may be united in Spirit though you are each seeing the world differently.

It seems that as I act more in accordance with my true desires she reacts more strongly to me.

Do not take it personally. Allow her to react as she will. When you are in distress turn within. Ask for help. Choose to see her in light, not in darkness. That she is traveling through a dark time does not mean that she is less than the great soul she is in Truth. See the greatness in her. Speak to her greatness, not to the pain. Send her love and light rather than blaming thoughts. This is your lesson, too. Love is not something you offer only when times are bright.

Bill's Journal

It seems my partner and I have created a situation where we are both being challenged to look within for our fulfillment. I cannot gain fulfillment by taking care of her. She cannot gain fulfillment through me. We must gain it for ourselves. We can love and support each other. As we achieve our respective feelings of fulfillment we can share with each other. Two whole people sharing their love and joy with each other is the goal.

Months Later

Bill's Journal

My life is good. I have enough money, and I see more coming. I am still married, and we're doing well. I love my work. I am very grateful. Now, I want peace. I want to feel the peace of God, to know it, and to extend it.

One moment I make the decision to be at peace and the next I am caught up in my worldly thoughts. I am at least two different people. Which one is me? Being both feels so contradictory. The more time I spend lost in my worldly thoughts of conflict, fear, competition, and worry, the more I seem to lose sight of my Soul. Is this what I want? My every day thinking indicates that, yes, I do want to be in conflict. If I didn't want this, wouldn't I just stop? If I truly wanted peace, wouldn't I have it?

I am disappointed in myself. I say I want to be more at peace, more spiritually aware, but it appears that I really want to be in conflict. I must want to struggle and to worry, because that is what I am doing. I see conflict in the world. I see people hurting each other for money or love. I'm not out there hurting people in the physical, but I think thoughts of conflict. In those thoughts I get hurt or I think of others in conflict with me. So, am I any different? I am different in that I have an awareness of what I am doing. Most people in conflict are not aware of what they do. I am aware that my thoughts not only affect me, they affect my relationships with others. This is why I feel disappointed—because I know better and yet I continue thinking the way I do.

How can I change what I want?

Bill, you are taking the first step by being honest with yourself. You have stopped pretending and decided to face your weaknesses. It is easy to act as if you are spiritual and continue to think unloving thoughts. You want to be real, to be and to act as you say you are. Your feelings are a signal that it is time to heal the conflicted parts of you and move to a higher level.

I would like to move to a higher level, but I keep getting in my own way. I find myself being defensive and scared. When I get into that mode I start hating myself.

Bill, the way to stop hating yourself is to face each of your issues honestly. Become aware of thoughts which are unhealthy. You do not need to let them direct your behavior.

The other day my wife questioned me about something I wanted to spend a sum of money on. I felt defensive. I wanted to avoid her questioning. This upset her. We ended up arguing. Yesterday the issue came up again. She could not understand why I was not discussing the issue with her and began to theorize. Her theories were not right and I reacted. Finally I realized that I was filled with fear. I truly was avoiding her and not wanting to discuss the situation. Looking deeper into myself I found a little "nest" of fears and hurts. The truth was that I felt I had moved too quickly in the situation, making financial promises without much thought of their effects. This reminded me of how I acted in the past when I fell on my face financially. I felt very foolish. The thought of being foolish or reckless with money was not bearable, so I buried it and rationalized my actions with defensiveness.

When you discovered these things how did you feel?

I looked ugly to myself. I felt disgusted. Suddenly everything I didn't like about myself came rushing in. I felt disgusted and disappointed with my negative thinking patterns that I can't seem to shake. I saw my impulsiveness, over sensitivity, insecurities, and my inability to know how I feel sometimes. I didn't like myself at all. I felt unworthy and I wanted to be alone. I felt very sorry for myself and at the same time critical of my self pity. I felt hurt and could not understand how anyone could love or appreciate me, because I didn't. I hated myself. I wanted to escape somewhere and be alone, outside of life.

I decided not to try to be positive, but to just feel the hatred and disgust. So I immersed myself in it for awhile. The next night I talked to my wife, honestly, about how I felt. I also explained that I was very unhappy with the defensiveness in our relationship—that I would like for us to be able to discuss feelings without defensiveness getting in the way. She was receptive. I felt better after telling her my feelings.

You fear exposing your true feelings to her. Begin to understand what it is you fear. Is it abandonment or rejection? Talk with her about the fears you feel. Take the risk and find out if she will abandon or reject you. Do you want to be in a relationship where you are not accepted? Do you want to live a life of hiding your feelings out of fear? The result of those choices is stress and unhappiness. So many souls go to work each day and pretend to be who they are not. They then return home to pretend some more. The self repression is unbearable and takes its toll in diseases in the body and pain in the emotions. If you are repressing you are missing out on the joy of living.

Turn within each day and ask for guidance. Ask Spirit to tell you what this day is for. Expect the Universe to provide you with what you need for that day. Give thanks each time you receive it. You do not need to become someone else to get love or money or approval. Be in constant communication with Spirit. Trust that God is expressing as you. Trust your Self, this holy Self that is the real you.

As for your faults, accept them. They are but guideposts along your path of growth. Instead of seeing them as defects in you, see them as markers you are passing along the way. Accept that they are part of your journey. Love yourself for having them, and for your ability to recognize them.

Ask God to help you see the true You. Express appreciation for the person you have become. Think back to the past and see the distance you have traveled. Appreciate your progress. Thank God for the help you have been given.

I have felt self hatred many times in the past. I usually wanted to escape from it or make it go away. I tried various techniques like affirmations, or thinking about something else, or making myself busy. This time I just let it happen, and it made a difference. Some of those self hateful feelings were resolved. I know I still have some of them, but I feel better.

In the past you would feel conflict, fear, and worry. Then you would play out those feelings in your life experiences. Your awareness has increased to the point where you know what is going on at the time it happens. You were hating yourself and you were aware of the hatred. You were both inside yourself and outside of yourself at the same time. As an insider you experienced what self hatred feels like. You made a clear decision to experience it. As an outsider you observed what you were feeling and perceived the futility of it.

You had the opportunity to move through the feelings to a higher level without having to play them out in your life. The road home, the road to joy, passes through your deepest fears. No person or situation, no psychic and no teacher can rescue you from this road. You are the traveler; it is your journey. We are always here to guide. Continue to call on us.

Bill's Journal

I have learned much this past year. My marriage was transformed. I am no longer fearful of loss. I don't worry about the future of our relationship. I love my wife and I love our relationship. I can't predict or control the future. I can only control my thoughts and actions right now. I continue to be myself, to express honestly and lovingly. I accept her for who she is and her right to express herself. Loving someone without fear is a new experience for me. I stopped worrying about her whereabouts. As a result we have no conflict in that area. When I stopped pressuring her to keep me informed, she began keeping me informed more often. Funny how that works. When you have to have something from someone, they are reluctant to give it. Now that it's okay if she doesn't call me, she calls me. I trust her, and that frees me. It frees me from stress and worry. It frees me from conflict and discomfort.

Another miracle happened this year. I asked my mother if I had a brother. She was shocked at my question, and admitted that it was true. Before she married my father she had given birth to a child. He was adopted out. This was a secret she carried for fifty years, and she had intended to keep it as a secret. She began telling her story to trusted friends and family. This turned out to be a very healing experience for her. At the urging of one of my sisters, she launched a search. Within a few weeks, her lost son "happened" to walk into the office of the county administrator who was working with my mother on the search. A reunion has taken place. Amazing how many good things came out of that reading—how many lives were affected.

It is true that many positive outcomes have emerged from your psychic reading. The reading by itself was simply information. The miracles in your life, the transformed marriage, the mother and son reunion, were the direct result of actions taken. You initiated the chain of events. You initiated conversations with your wife and made the decision to change your perception. She chose to stay committed to

your marriage. You initiated conversation with your mother. She chose to bring her secret into the light where healing could occur. All of you have made choices which have led to healing.

Life is decisions. In the the past you made many decisions out of fear. You have clarified your intentions and acted upon them. Life has come into focus for you. You are beginning to lead with your Soul.

Chapter 12
Leading With Your Soul

Sometimes I don't hear the Voice within me very well. Speak to me please.

Our presence is always here.

I believe that. I just can't hear you sometimes. A while back you said something about leading with my Soul. How do I lead with my Soul if I can't hear Its voice?

There are many reasons why you would not hear or sense guidance. How have you been feeling?

Okay, I guess.

"Okay" is not a feeling. Do you know how you have been feeling?

I haven't thought about it. Now that you ask, I think I've been a little stressed lately. I'm always on the run; I'm eating a lot. It seems like I'm always hungry. I guess I haven't taken care of myself very well.

We see pain and discomfort beneath your conscious surface.
You are avoiding these emotions.

I consider myself to be very aware of what is going on in me. I feel okay.

Then why are you always eating?

Maybe I'm just hungry. Let's say you're right. I'm avoiding some issues. What are they and why would I avoid them?

Your Soul desires to lovingly express Its own truth. Your fears rise up to prevent this expression. Your fears create the pain and discomfort. You avoid feeling the fear with your compulsive eating. The fear feels bad; the food appears to feel good. The constant rushing around and the experience of eating and drinking serve to dull your feelings. We say get back into your body. You operate as if you are outside of it. Be in your body. Take notice of how you are feeling at all times. Love your body. Give it the rest and the exercise it needs to maintain the level of energy you require. Put food and liquid into it that strengthen it, and avoid those things which weaken it. Allow yourself to feel life. Emotions are signs which can lead you deeper within. If you want to lead with your Soul pay attention to how you feel. Avoidance distances you from your Soul.

Do I have to give up treats?

God is treating you every time you eat or drink. It is interesting that you define only sugary food items as treats. Do not make sweets or high fat foods your regular fare. If you would have a craving for a particular sweet food, then eat it. Yet, do not turn it into a habit. Eat a well balanced diet. Treat your body well.

There are good things that I enjoy. I love a good glass of carrot beet juice.

Savor your food and drink. Often you shove it in, not really enjoying it. Eat less and enjoy more. Slow down. When you eat too much sugar and fat it does not just hurt your body, it blocks you from sensing. You eat and drink away your emotions. We say, deal with them. This is why many people feel worse when they first clean up their diet. Food and drink can be used to mask emotions. When the excess food and drink are removed the emotions are felt. Feel and release negative emotions that you may be cleansed. Let go of negative thoughts that your mind may become clear. A clear mind with a clean body can hear its own voice. You will also hear the Voice of God and the prompting of your Soul.

I have always struggled with this food thing. I can fast and I can overdo it. Why is it so hard just to maintain a reasonable and healthy diet?

You are constantly surrounded by food and food messages. This affects your thinking. You must make conscious choices throughout the day.

So, how healthy do I have to be?

Be as healthy as you would like to be. Listen to your body. Pause before you eat to think about what you are eating and to give thanks for your food. Ask before you choose to eat less than healthy foods: "Do I really want this?"

I would not mind cutting a few inches off this stomach.

Do not worry about your looks. Focus on the fine machine your body is. Give it the fuel it needs to operate well. Your body is a receiver for sensing the world around you and the world within you. When the receiver is not working well you lose awareness. This is why you have not heard our voice of late. We have not ceased communicating. You were unable to sense our message.

Let's say I allow myself to feel my fearful emotions. What fears will I have to face? You said I was avoiding. What am I avoiding?

You avoid your fears. You are avoiding life. Our concern is less with your dietary specifics than it is with your tendency to use food to avoid life. You allow fear to drive your behavior at times. You worry about money. You worry about pleasing your wife, your children, and other family members. Sometimes at work you still worry about pleasing your audience. You worry about being criticized for your work. Face this fear of being yourself. Follow your fears inward in order to find release.

We've already talked about this. You told me to stop trying to fill other people's cups, and to fill my own instead. Haven't I improved?

There are many levels of healing. You have improved. A guiding principle will help to continue healing and to bring your Soul to life. What do all of these driving forces: money, approval, and criticism, have in common?

They are outside of me. They're externals. I have no direct control over them.

If you allow these things to drive your behavior you must live in fear. You fear there will not be enough. The appearance of lack of money, the appearance of lack of approval will put you into fear. You, not wanting to experience the fear, create activity or eat extra food.

My guiding principle would be then to never allow fear to drive my behavior?

Let fear be a signal that drives you inward. Acknowledge that fearful perception is the problem. Choose to be driven by love; by Universal Truth; by strong values; by a desire for the highest good for all concerned; and by a faith in the Creative Intelligence of the Universe. These internal factors will serve you well. Universal Truth teaches you that what you give you will receive. This principle works whether or not you have faith in it. If you wish anything less than the highest good for another you wish it for yourself. Worry is faith in hurtful outcomes and serves to create hurtful experience. The soul comes to express love and to express faith in who it is. It desires to return to its own pure state. This expression is prevented when fear takes over.

If I allow money to drive my behavior, then I will only be at peace when there is "enough" money. I will choose money over people and perhaps over my own values whenever I feel lack. This makes me unstable. If I am driven by a faith that my needs will be met, then I am stable. If approval drives my behavior I will act in ways I think will help me to get it. This means that sometimes I will not act as myself. The guiding principle then is to be myself?

Money, approval, and situations come and go. Universal law and the love you have within you are constant. The guiding principle is to focus on internals. Remove your focus from that which you have little or no control. Fear is a signal that externals are driving you. Listen to the signal and go within. Face the fear and make a decision that it will not drive you. In any situation, intend for the highest good for all concerned. Let go of your worries and trust that which is within you. This brings you freedom from fear.

Your greatest fear is in relationships. Fearing others will disapprove, criticize, or condemn, fear leads you to attempt to control their behaviors. If you trust your own Soul; if you trust God; there is nothing to fear. You are free to look upon others with love. You are free to see the best in them. You are free to be yourself. Confront your fear and see that you need not allow it to control you. Leading with your Soul means to lead with love.

You have always had the ability to do this, but often you have forgotten. There are times, however, when you have remembered well. There are times when you have led from your Soul. We love your story about Marcy. In that situation you followed your fear inward and changed the situation from the inside out. Recall that story and you will have an idea what living from your Soul means.

It was many years ago when I was teaching middle school. A girl joined my class part way into the school year. Sometimes when we meet someone new we just don't like them. There's really no good reason; we just don't. That's how I felt about

Marcy. I didn't like her. I found her voice and her mannerisms irritating. I didn't want to deal with her. I wished I didn't have to deal with her.

Although I was quite young, I had enough maturity to know that it wasn't her fault that I didn't like her. I asked myself: "Why don't I like this child?" There was no logical answer. She had never done anything to hurt me. She was an innocent twelve year old. I knew that if I continued to dislike her she would become aware of my dislike. I did not want her to suffer because a teacher didn't like her. The problem was in my mind, not in her personality. So, yes, I followed my fear inward to my own irrational thoughts. I made a commitment to myself to see something good in her every day. I made a commitment to drop the expectation that she act differently for my benefit.

Each day I would notice something Marcy did right. If she was kind to another student, I made note of it. If she completed her assignments, I noted it. After a few weeks something began to happen to me. I started liking her. I started liking her a lot. I found her to be a delightful child. I came to enjoy her smile, her words, and her presence in my classroom. She became one of my favorite students.

I realized that when I don't like someone, it's not the other person who has the problem. It's me. I perceived incorrectly, and I learned to perceive her as the child of God that she was. I chose love, and she benefited from it. So did I.

It is a beautiful story and a beautiful example of choosing love. Know that every person you encounter is a soul, as you are. Your wife is a soul. Do you see her?

What do you mean? I know she is a soul. I know that she is an expression of God.

We see that you can go beyond an intellectual understanding of this. You know that what you focus on expands. When you interact with your wife, whether in thought or speech, what is your focus?

That depends on what is happening. Often I look at her and see great beauty. I am delighted by her laughter, her energy, and her love. When we are in conflict I focus on other things, like her stubbornness.

What is marriage to you now?

It's a holy relationship.

If you are in a holy relationship, what is your focus?

My focus is on her positive traits. I focus on what I love about her.

A holy relationship is a pairing of two souls whose intention is to grow and maintain their mutual awareness of divinity in each other. Bring your Soul more fully into your marriage. See your wife as the precious, highly respected entity that she is. Know that she does not stop being this precious soul when you argue. Even in the midst of anger and conflict see her soul. She is your teacher. When you focus on her spiritual greatness you bring more love and depth into your relationship. Loving thoughts create loving behavior. Loving thoughts create a loving marriage. At the same time grant the same level of love and respect to yourself. Refuse to compromise who you are. Make sure she knows who you are. Trust that you can both express more fully.

It's easy to get caught in the trap of focusing on the perceived negative traits of another person. Both of us are aware of this. Our relationship keeps getting better because we are learning to see each other more clearly.

This is good. Know that seeing each others' positive traits is a beginning, yet not the whole of it. Seek to develop compassion and understanding. Release judgment when you disagree. Maintain the awareness of her divine nature.
Refuse to let fear dictate your relationship. When you focus on what you think she should do or say you create fear. Lead from your Soul in this marriage. Do not be controlled by her opinion nor try to

control her with your opinion. Releasing the need for control will create more peace in your home. At any moment you can decide to love and appreciate your wife more deeply. The decision mobilizes your body and your emotions to align with the intention. Decide, also, to love yourself more deeply.

Follow the fear and it will tell you of your true intention in any situation. When you argue, your intention is to get your point across. You tell yourself that she must understand you. Thus, in this situation, her understanding becomes the god you worship. Your Soul's desire is to simply express. Speak honestly when you have pain, yet take ownership of the pain. You cannot give it to her to fix. When she speaks of pain you may not fix it. Listen with love and acceptance. This is how two souls nurture each other.

We have a lot of work to do, yet I can see my marriage getting stronger. I can see my wife and I loving and accepting each other more deeply. We are committed to this kind of love. Sometimes when we argue I forget momentarily, but I soon remember.

What about other relationships? I love my wife, but what about others? Do I have to love everyone to live from my Soul?

The feeling of love comes and goes depending on many things. The decision to love is always at hand. You may always choose. Know that as you learn to love others more completely you become more complete. Until that time, act as if you love others. Ask yourself: "How would I interact with this person if I truly loved and appreciated her? How would I interact if I truly cared about her life? "

If I truly loved and appreciated another person I would look for the good just like I did with Marcy. I would focus on her best qualities. I don't know if I can choose love all of the time.

When we say to choose love we are not saying to be nice all of the time. To love someone is to care about what happens to her. If you see someone acting in hurtful ways, tell her. Do not lecture. Just tell her as honestly and compassionately as you can. If she does not listen, do not try to change her. Just love her, and do what you need to do. You may need to create a distance socially, but you can still love her. Teach her how to treat you by the example of your behavior. Set limits and be very clear about what you will and will not do.

In other words, I shouldn't enable destructive behaviors?

Give people constructive feedback about their behavior. When their behavior is destructive, speak honestly and compassionately. At the same time, act as if they are beautiful souls, children of God. Treat them with respect.

Let me see if I've got this right. Someone acts out an inappropriate behavior. I can call them on it. Then I treat them with love and respect. I act as if they are not making these mistakes?

That is close. You are discerning but not judging. You use discernment in deciding whether to speak, and if you do speak, what to say. You use discernment to determine your level of involvement with this person. You do not condemn him.

For example, you had a business partner who lied to you. You told him that lying is not okay with you, and that you would stay in business with him only if he was willing to be truthful at all times. You received his commitment to be truthful. Soon after, he lied again. You reminded him of the commitment and told him that you were no longer interested in being a partner. At the same time, you treated him with great respect. You respected your Soul by respecting his. You allowed him to experience the consequences of his actions, knowing that that was how he would learn.

So, by taking care of myself and not rescuing him, I demonstrated respect for his soul. Shouldn't I forgive him?

Forgive him, yet do not continue to work with him. Respectfully dissolve the partnership, and send him on his way. You need not fix him. You can not. Forgiveness does not mean that you have to stay involved with a person. It just means that you act as if he never did anything to hurt you. Then you let him go with your blessings. You let him go because lying is an act that runs contrary to the way you have chosen to do business. It would be harmful both to you and to him for this situation to continue.

Okay, so choosing love means that I always look for the best in each person. If he acts inappropriately, I give him feedback and allow him to experience the consequences of his actions. I forgive. I choose to be or not to be involved with him based on whether or not continuing the relationship would be for the highest good for both of us.

Yes. By seeing the best in each person you tend to draw out the best in each person. You create an environment where others are encouraged to look at themselves rather than blame you for what happened. Seeing the best in others brings out the best in you.

It doesn't seem like I brought out the best in my partner. He still lied.

You brought out the best in you. You planted a seed in him for future change. You can not make someone change. You created the opportunity. In the long run, your act will lead to bringing out the best in him. It may not happen soon. It may not happen in this lifetime. Had you not dealt with him honestly, you would have contributed to his continued lying.

So, being nice to people sometimes brings out the worst in them?

When the niceness is pretending to accept inappropriate behavior, yes. Sometimes your honesty will appear to bring out the worst. People will get angry and deny responsibility. In truth, you have not brought out the worst. The worst was already there. Your action simply served as a catalyst to make it visible. Be true to yourself and you will always bring out the best in you. The best in you is your Soul.

What is my Soul?

Your Soul is the real you. Your essence. You, your Soul, is an expression of God. If God were the sun, then your Soul would be a ray of sunlight. God expresses Itself as your Soul.

Why don't I know that I am my Soul?

It is the nature of this earthly existence. Life is like sleeping. As you become more aware that you are your Soul, the dream (life) gets better. When you know that you are your Soul you begin to awaken.

Are you my Soul?

Yes, your Soul is here.

I have a question for my Soul. How do I get close to you?

Your Soul is as close as your breath. As close as your skin. Your Soul is within you and all around you. It is everywhere else, also.

How can that be?

Your Soul is not limited by time or space. For your Soul there is only here and now. You and your other personalities from other lifetimes are parts of the whole. All is connected; all is one. You believe you are separated by time and space. In spiritual reality, there is no time or space. Therefore, the growth your Soul experiences in this lifetime affects all of your personalities from all of your lifetimes.

Karma goes in both directions?

Yes. The good that you create benefits all of your lives, not just your so-called future lives.

That's a difficult one to understand.

The spiritual world is the only real world, and in that world there is no time. There is only now! Therefore, your Soul is playing out all of its lifetimes now! You must remember that time is only a measure based on celestial revolutions and the changing of the seasons. Time is not real! It is a grid you put over your experiences to measure them. Time is a tool you can utilize to experience the journey back to your Soul.

I want to join with my Soul now! I don't want to wait any longer. If time is not real, then I should be able to connect with my Soul right now. I shouldn't have to wait years or lifetimes.

You should not and you do not. Your waiting is by choice. You are afraid that you will lose something if you become one with your Soul right now. Let go of this fear and embrace your Soul. Say the word, mean it 100% and it is done.

I can say the word, but how do I get myself to mean it? Tell me what to do.

We can tell you, but it will not be different from what we have already told you. Perhaps you are more ready to hear it now. Perhaps we can say it in such a way that you understand.

I'm ready. What do I do first?

The first step is to realize that you experience yourself as in your body, but you are not your body. You are your Soul. Next, recognize that your Soul, through its Higher Self, is one with God. Knowing your oneness with God; knowing that God is all there is; recognize and trust that you are one with everyone and everything. You, in your present state of consciousness, have not come to this discovery yet. Until you do, practice trust. Trust God. Trust God more than you trust money, or jobs, or any appearances. No matter what you see, trust God. No matter what decision you have to make, ask God first. When you give your situations over to God, you are asking your Soul to step in and act as you. You are refusing to let your thoughts and behavior be guided by your personality.

When you trust God you know that God is all there is. You see God in all people, even those who you think are evil. You give thanks for every situation you encounter knowing it is for your benefit; that all negative effects are illusory; and that you are safe. Know that as a soul of God you cannot be hurt.

If you find that you are feeling fear, and unable to trust God, act as if you trust God. That is, ask yourself "What would I be thinking right now if I trusted God completely?" Begin to think it. Ask: "How would I stand or sit or walk if I knew God was guiding me right now? What facial expression would I hold if I totally trusted God?" Do these things. Ask: "What words would I be saying and with what kind of conviction would I be saying them if I trusted God?" Then say those words with confidence and conviction.

I would be play acting. It wouldn't be real.

You would be practicing and it would become real. Bill, you have no idea of the power you would feel and express were you to do these things. You have no idea of the total confidence with which you would proceed were you to act out this level of trust. You do not have to believe us. Do it. Do it for a day, or better, a week. See what you become. No greater joy have you experienced.

You will also experience resistance. Your personality may not want to give up control. It may create challenges that will tempt you to go back into your fearful thinking. If your intent is clear it will not matter. You will succeed.

It sounds simple.

It is. It is the easiest most difficult thing you will ever do. It is the higher path. There are many paths which you could choose. The path of totally trusting God now seems more strenuous, but the rewards are great. It is the road home to your Soul.

It is your analyzing which makes it difficult. You think you must figure everything out. Cease running the same thoughts over and over through your mind. For example, you hope money will come from this source or that one. You do not know, specifically, where the money will come from. Allow yourself to be in a place of not knowing. Be content to not know who will supply you. Let go of any need for money

to come from a specific place. Just know that God will provide. This is
the time to trust your feelings.

I'm not too sure about that. I let my feelings determine my life several years ago and things turned out to be a mess.

Now you let your head decide?

I think before I act.

When we say to trust your feelings we are not speaking of your fearful emotions. You trusted your fearful emotions and took action. You did not follow your fears inward. You experience internal feelings of joy, discomfort, or confidence. These feelings are intuitive. They are the signals you receive to guide you in your decision making. You have already used these feelings many times. We are asking you to use them <u>all</u> of the time.

All of the time? How can I do that?

By paying attention to how you feel at all times. Your point of reference for making decisions is always within you. You must make the distinction as to whether you base a decision on the inclination of your Soul or on your fears.

I'm not sure I understand. What is the inclination of my Soul?

Your Soul is inclined toward love, therefore make decisions based on love. Listen to the inner prompting of Spirit; listen to your values and beliefs; and seek the highest good for all concerned. When you go against your inner knowledge or your values and beliefs, you are in conflict. When you are in alignment with this inner self you may experience the disapproval, anger, and upset of others, but you will know you have acted in accordance with your Soul. You will express with integrity. We define integrity as truly being and acting as the person you are. You wish to be one with your Soul, therefore you will act as your Soul. When you do not, your Soul will let you know. Acting in ways not in alignment with your Soul is painful. You feel it in your body. For example, were you to take something that is not yours, you would feel discomfort in your body. This is the pain and stress of not acting with integrity. Often people ignore or suppress this stress, yet it is still there.

I understand the integrity part. I know that if I base my behavior on Soul related things like values, love, creativity, and respect, I feel strong. When I allow my fears to drive my behavior I feel the discomfort of acting without integrity. I feel weak. You said that I always need to look within. I'm confused about where my soul is? You said it is within me and around me. Please clarify that.

You are an eternal expression of God's love and spirit. Your Soul speaks from within your body, but your Soul is not inside you. You (your point of awareness) are within the cosmic expansiveness of your Soul. Your consciousness, at this moment is limited to this solitary human experience. You think yourself special, and you are not. You are your Soul, and your Soul is its Higher Self.

I don't get it. Where is my Soul? I want my Soul to answer me. Where are you?

I am.

Yes, I know you exist, but where are you?

I am. The Soul is. The Higher Self is. God is. In the Bible God tells Moses: "Tell the people, I Am sent you."

I know. God said his name was "I am that I am." Popeye said it, too.

Yes, Popeye was certainly a metaphysician.

"I am what I am and that's all that I am".

God is what God is and that is All that God is. You are God being you. You, as your Soul, and as your Higher Self, are everywhere present. You are connected to all that there is. There is no separation. You are in this earth life where all seems separate; where each moment is measured and marked as different from the next and the last; where limitation appears to be reality; that you may discover that none of this illusion is true. As you identify with Oneness; with ever present eternity; and with unlimited reality; you discover who you are. Your Soul is integrating its seemingly many parts that it may find its way home to the Higher Self.

So I guess the answer to my question about where you are is, "Here and now."

Yes, we are all here and now.

As a human I have been lost in this illusion of separation, time, and limitation. Why?

Fear prevents you from seeing. Love opens your eyes. Fear created the illusion that there was something wrong with Marcy. Love opened your eyes that you could truly see her. Fear keeps you closed off from hearing the prompting of your Soul, the voices of your teachers and angels, the Word of God.

Many no longer hear the prompting of the soul. For many years you did not. You ignored the Voice within. You became wrapped up in your fearful thoughts and emotions preventing yourself from hearing. In recent years you have accepted more loving thoughts while releasing more fearful thoughts. You began to listen. Often you receive guidance. Continue to choose loving thoughts and let go of fear. Continue to listen. In each and every situation in which you find yourself you can know what to do and what to say.

I'd like to know what to say more often. This is especially hard for me in one on one relationships. I tend to be more direct with groups of people in my work, and I often know what to say. I stand in front of a group and the right words just come to me. I seem to be able to get past the fear of alienating people and I speak my truth.

Yet, few people are alienated. When you are at work you speak from your heart. You are open and honest. You do not allow fear to drive your behavior. This is why people trust you. You make decisions based on the prompting of Spirit, your values and beliefs, and your desire to find the highest good for all. You will aspire to even greater heights of honesty and openness.

In personal relationships your progress has been slower, yet progress has been made. You have withheld your truth in fear of the reactions of others. Thus you have made yourself a target for manipulation. As we stated earlier, fill your own cup first. You cannot make other people full. Your well meaning gestures lead to greater pain in the long run when you protect people from the consequences of their own actions.

I sometimes find myself in a position of helping a person; it could be a family member, a personal friend, or a friend I've made at work. I can see the potential in each person, yet each is struggling. I avoid giving away money, but I provide ideas and opportunities.

Do they take advantage of the opportunities?

Sometimes. Sometimes I feel like I care more about their success than they do.

It is good to help others. You are not much help when you care more about their success than they do. You cannot make someone want to succeed. Quite often, you do great harm when you rescue people from the consequences of their actions. We are not saying you should be cruel, or offer opinions on what people should do. Do not take joy in another's suffering. Have compassion. Each person is in his present situation because there is something to learn. It is not your job to make another person feel better, only to love him. Sometimes people need to feel bad in order to motivate themselves to do great things.

You believe people have greatness to express. You recognize their intelligence, creativity, and skills. Each will find his own way to expressing his greatness. To save one from his choices only delays his progress more. It delays yours, too. You cannot play God and protect everyone. You must let them go. They will learn as you did—by their own experience. Love them. Believe in them. Express your Truth. Withhold your opinions on how you think they should live their lives. Help them when it is appropriate—that is, when you see that your "help" is for the highest good for them and for you. If you are not sure which way to help—ask. Pray. You will know what to do. You are great, as are your brothers and sisters of the Universe. You can not express that greatness if you are driven by fear—fear of disapproval, abandonment, judgment, rejection, or their "failure". This we say about your children, your relatives, your friends, and your clients.

Recognize that each person you interact with is a great soul. Speak to the greatness in them. Would you criticize a great soul? Would you feel sorry for a great soul? Would you prevent a great soul from doing his work by doing it for him? Would you rescue a great soul, and prevent him from discovering his greatness? Do not underestimate the great souls with which you associate. When you rescue someone you are sending a message that says: "You are not great and that is why I must take care of you." What is so often thought to be helpful is really crippling. Great souls must be accountable for their own actions in order to reinforce their greatness. This is true love.

You see a person is perfectly capable of earning money. Giving him money, in this instance, prevents him from experiencing a valuable lesson, therefore it is not for his highest good. Yes, the gift of money may make him feel better and you, too. Feeling better is temporary. Dear One, Love is a demanding way of life. It demands of you that you forego feeling better for the moment in order to do what is for the highest good. Speak the truth compassionately. Speak it from your heart with conviction. Do not feel sorry for people who are experiencing consequences to their choices. Place them in God's hands and offer what true help you can. Your faith and your love are the best gifts you can give. See each person surrounded in love and light. Behold the Christ in him. Behold the Buddha in him. Each is but a thought away from expressing greatness. Trust that this is true.

Do not work harder for another's success then he is willing to work for himself. Offer your help, then step back. You cannot save people; people must save themselves. You are becoming a spiritual teacher. This does not mean you save people. You teach by your words and your actions. You present learning opportunities to others. They choose to learn or not. Each lesson you present is also your lesson which others present to you.

Today you stand tall as a spiritual teacher. Years ago you could not have stood in this place. There were lessons to learn. No one rescued you. You received help when you needed it. Your trials made you stronger and brought you closer to God. You have come to understand yourself and grow closer to your Soul. This was your experience. Everyone needs their own experience. You must not protect your wife, your children, or anyone from their own life experience. Do not take away what is theirs in the name of helping. Listen to your Soul and you will know what and when to give. In the meantime, see what is highest and best in others.

Bill's Journal

I have had much to think about these past few days. As a parent, as a spouse, and as an adult child, I have so often wanted to help my children, my wife, and my parents. What is "help"? Love is a difficult path. True love means that I let go of my need to take care of another person. It means that I place them in God's hands and trust that all is well. I am learning to respect the greatness in others. Sometimes dissatisfaction and suffering are part of a person's path. They are what drives a person to grow and learn.

Bringing my Soul into life means meeting others soul to soul. It means I approach others with compassionate understanding, with honesty, and with respect. I do this for myself also. I can see the greatness in myself by knowing that God is in me (also around me and everywhere else). By respecting my body I create a clear channel for God to speak to me. Leading with my Soul means being truly helpful, both to myself and to others.

Leading with your Soul means understanding that being truly helpful to another is the same thing as being truly helpful to yourself. There is always a highest good for all to be had. It is not possible to truly help another without helping yourself. It is not possible to truly help yourself without helping others. True giving and receiving are the same. It is only your belief in separation that has you thinking your good is separate from that of another. When you understand true helpfulness; when you understand true giving; you find that it is effortless. It demands no sacrifice. True giving benefits both the giver and the receiver.

Okay. So I understand that leading with my Soul means living with integrity. It means loving myself and others. I feel like I am doing these things. Yet, it seems like I have been stuck. My financial situation, my work, and our quest for a baby all seem like they are on hold. As a matter of fact, I feel a little embarrassed. Last summer I gave a speech on intentions. In that speech I talked about how I had held the intention to prosper. I explained how I had managed to go from being practically destitute to being almost debt free. Since that time business has been slow. Some unexpected bills came up and now I 'm beginning to pile up some debt. Its only a few thousand dollars, but it is bothersome. Like I said, its embarrassing.

Why is it embarrassing?

I told a crowd of people how I had overcome those financial difficulties spiritually. I create my life. If things are not going too well, then I must have screwed up somewhere.

New age guilt.

What?

New age guilt. You create your life. Your thoughts create your life. So, if things are going poorly, you must have screwed up somewhere. Something is wrong with your thinking, right? Something must be wrong with you.

That's what you have told me. That's what all the books say.

Guilt is not an effective response to your situation. It prevents you from healing. Seek what learning you may find from the situation. What message are you telling to yourself? You are not aware of most of the messages that are buried in your consciousness. Thoughts and emotions from your childhood, thoughts and emotions from previous lives. They are all locked away in your subconscious mind. Yet, these thoughts and emotions you are not aware of are creating situations and experiences in your life. Each time you experience pain or discomfort, it is an opportunity to discover your deepest irrational thoughts.

How do I deal with this?

You already know how. Remember the experience of the back pain you wrote about in Chapter Five? You found thoughts and emotions that had been buried in your subconscious. You experienced healing in your counseling session when you were able to feel those emotions. You cried. You sobbed. You felt lighter.

So these circumstances are another opportunity for me to heal?

Yes. Being a spiritual person and praying a lot does not mean you will not experience challenges. Sometimes it means you will experience more challenges. Your Soul wants to heal. You can pray and affirm; you can take physical action, but if you do not heal the cause, the pain will come back. Seek healing. Ask God for healing. Express your willingness to face the cause of your discomfort. Then listen for guidance. Ask questions about the cause.

What is the cause of my present discomfort?

How do you feel about what is happening?

I feel frustrated.

Frustration is the gap between what you think you want and how it seems to be right now. Go deeper. When you think about or talk about money or work, what do you feel?

Inadequate. Like I didn't do a good job managing money and I didn't do a good job marketing my business.

You feel diminished when you speak about these things.

Yes, I feel small.

Where does this sense of being diminished come from?

When I ask the question I think of my father. I felt small in his presence. I thought I worked out all those father issues I had.

When you were a child you were open and vulnerable. You created the belief, based on your father's reactions to you, that you were not adequate. You felt small in his presence. You have proved yourself more than adequate in many areas of life, yet you have not healed the wound. Your present circumstances show this to you.

I feel very confident in my work. When I look at my whole life, the big picture, I feel like I'm not doing well.

Self improvement techniques are not enough. Through self improvement you became an excellent speaker. People find jobs, get rich, and accomplish earthly goals through self improvement. Without healing, symptoms shift to another area of life.

Now I know what is causing my circumstances. I know that this feeling of smallness is in my consciousness. What's next?

You have asked God for healing. Expect to be healed. At the same time, when the feeling comes up, let yourself experience it. Spend time alone with a willingness to move through it. Face it honestly. Step outside of it and look at it. The more you look at it, the more you are willing to be unafraid of it, the less power it will have over you. Be willing to feel worse before you feel better. Be not afraid of feeling this pain. You will be directed as to what you should do, if anything. You may be directed to a healer of some kind, as you were in Chapter Five. You may feel the urge to cry. If so, please do. Pay attention and continue to be willing. This will work out. Your Soul thanks you, because it desires this healing more than anything.

Bill's Journal

I've checked out several healers, but nothing seems to be what I need. One thing is working. Each time I feel that diminished feeling, that feeling that I'm not adequate, I stop what I'm doing. I challenge the idea of being small, and I tell myself that the feeling is not true. It's old stuff left over from childhood; it does not serve me. I assure myself that I am adequate, that I am a powerful man of God. I remind myself that I can do anything I intend to do. This helps. The inadequate feeling goes away and I feel confident. Each time I talk myself out of being diminished I grow larger in my self image. The key is not to allow the fearful emotion to drive my behavior.

I am willing to heal. You know, I'm a lot different than I was several years ago. My thinking is more positive. I don't allow negativity to overtake me. Relative to my past, my thinking is pretty healthy. I know I can become more healthy. What else do you want from me? What else does God want? I'm willing to think healthy thoughts. I'm willing to heal. I'm willing to teach.

You are thinking and feeling in more healthy ways; God wants <u>*you*</u>.

God wants me? Is this something new? Didn't God want me before?

God has always wanted you. She wants you to come home.
Surrender. In the past, you surrendered to your appetites. You surrendered to your fears. Much of that you have overcome. Now surrender to God. In other words, do not just trust God, go all the way. Allow your whole life to be in God's hands. Stop worrying about how much money you think you want, or what your career should look like. Place it all in God's hands.

I don't know if I am ready for that yet. I can let go and trust when I'm a speaker in front of a group, but to do it in my whole life? I'll think on it. It's like you're asking me to step off the edge of a cliff.

It is what your Soul desires. Become one with your Soul. In turn, your Soul can strengthen its connection with your Higher Self. Your Soul wants to go home.

Bill's Journal

I want to surrender to God and I don't. It is like I am two people inside. Maybe it's that word, surrender. Doesn't that mean, to give up? What would I be giving up? Fear, struggle, pain, trying to do it on my own? I can't just say it and mean it. I'm not ready. What will it take to make me ready? What important thing would I lose if I surrendered to God?

Surrender to Spirit involves no loss, unless you consider giving up fear a loss.

My wife and I have surrendered our desire for a child, yet nothing has happened.

Your child will come. We disagree that nothing has happened.

We've spent a lot of time and energy on fertility treatments without success. I've lost count of how many shots

I've given her. I never thought I'd be able to give anybody a shot. Psychic readers have told both of us we have a child coming. Where is the child?

You will be parents, yet something has already happened. We see that your relationship is successful. There is more love between you. There is greater intimacy and affection, greater respect. We see that each of you is stronger, more stable. You have both come through trying times with success. You are both able to be yourselves, and be together. This is success.

Yes, we are closer. Working toward a common goal has made us a better partnership. That's great, but what about the baby?

Trust, Bill. Trust. All is well.

I'm glad the child is coming, but it would be nice to have some details—like when she is coming. I can see I'm not going to get any details now. Okay, let's shift the subject. My progress in personal relationships has been slow, but sure. Let's talk about my work. Tell me how to do a better job of bringing my Soul to work.

Chapter Thirteen
Bringing Your Soul to Work

It seems that people are struggling in every work place that I visit. So many people seem to be dissatisfied, isolated, and fearful. Many are bored. I have a feeling that what the work place lacks, in general, is spirituality. People don't bring their souls to work. It seems that work is not the place to talk about spiritual matters. I think it's one of the places where our spirituality is most needed. How do I bring my Soul to work?

Know thyself. Know your strengths, your weaknesses, your needs, your deepest desires, your deepest fears. Be honest with yourself. You cannot bring your Soul to work if you do not know yourself. This you have done and continue to do.

Love yourself. Love yourself so much that you are willing to take care of yourself. Taking care of yourself means that you create a loving space for yourself at work. You enjoy what you do and you enjoy the people around you. You find joy in each task you perform. To do things only for money or because you "must" is not loving; it is empty. Come to work with the idea that you are there to make a contribution, to experience joy, and to create.

Be a radiating center of love and light at work. This means that you release attack thoughts and adopt thoughts that nurture and support yourself and others. Know that your Soul does not see itself as better than or less than anyone else. Search out those perceptions in yourself that have you feeling less than or better than. Both perceptions cause you to have attack thoughts. Less than and better than thoughts have you either attacking yourself or others. Ask yourself: "Am I here to attack or to heal?"

I know how I attack myself. I'm self critical. How is it that I attack others?

You try to "catch" them doing things wrong. You critique people, in your mind, when they are speaking in front of a group. There is a satisfaction you find in noticing the shortcomings of other speakers. This is an attack. Whether you say anything or not, it can be detrimental to that person. Your thoughts affect others. Do you wish to heal or do you wish to hurt?

I would rather heal.

When someone is faltering, send them supportive thoughts. Offer verbal support if it is appropriate. It is the nature of the soul to heal. It is the nature of the ego to attack and compete. Each thought you think is a choice between healing and hurting, between soul and ego, between love and fear. Be aware of your thoughts. Decide what kind of impact you want to have.

I am fortunate that I visit different workplaces. In each of them I find many people to be lonely, isolated, and fearful. I have felt these things before when I was in the corporate world. My solution was to get out and start my own business. It is easier to bring my Soul to work when I have my own business. But that is not a solution for everyone. How can I help others to bring their souls to work?

Simply by setting an example. Bring your Soul to work. Let them see your Soul.

It looks like Trust. Trust your Soul. Your Soul is an expression of God. It is Spirit. It is your Holy Self. It is the real you. Be the real you by trusting your Soul, trusting the guidance you receive. Your Soul is the link between you and your Higher Self. Your Higher Self is perfect. It is your "God Self". It has never forgotten what it is. Your Soul desires healing. Healing is the end to the sense of separation between you and your Higher Self. Your trust helps to open communication from Higher Self to Soul to you. In reality these three are One. Therefore, all of the wisdom you need is within you. Trust and you will know what to do, what to say, and how to solve problems.

I don't always know what to say and do. I can't solve every problem.

This is because your thinking gets in the way.

My thinking gets in the way?

Yes, your mind is so full of thoughts, often creating tension in your body. In this state you cannot know what to do. The information you need is available, but you are not. Trust is relaxing into the knowing that you will understand what to do and to say in the moment. Allow this deep understanding to rise to the surface.

How?

You already know what to do. Remember that your thoughts are creating your experience. Whether you feel tense, excited, frustrated, angry, guilty, or disappointed, it is only thought. Knowing it is only thought, you can realize that your emotions are but a passing thing. Seek the place in your mind and body where you feel more peaceful, more sane, then trust that your Soul will direct you. Your Soul is always in communication with God. Coming from this place of peace, you will make wise and loving decisions. "Be still and know that I am God."

Can the people I'm working with do this?

They can do this. They, too, have access to great wisdom within. Teach them how to act from their souls by doing it yourself.

It is hard to imagine some of the people I work with coming from a place of wisdom and peace rather than fear and anger.

This lack that you see is not in them. It is in you. You are presently unable to see them as they truly are. Instead you believe in the appearances you see—the appearances of fear and anger. You do not have to be frightened by someone's reactions in the moment. Their reactions are their thoughts made visible. See their wholeness instead. See God in each person. Let their thoughts and reactions pass by in your mind and see the sanity that is within them. Must you see loving behavior to believe that they are loving beings? If so, then you are loving them conditionally. Take away the conditions and your need to have them act "right", and regard them as children of God, unconditionally.

So, no matter how they act I should act with love, unconditional love?

No matter how they act, you <u>can</u> act with unconditional love. It is your choice. Listen to the wisdom within. Sometimes it will indicate that you say nothing. Other times it will indicate that you give information to someone about their behavior. What matters is your intent. If you wait until you can be in a peaceful place before you respond, your intent will be to heal. Remember, your words and actions either intend healing or hurting. If your intent is to fix someone, to get them back, to teach them a lesson, it will most often be interpreted as an attack.

People who are attacked usually defend themselves or attack back.

Yes. Know that you do not need to be in control. Let the collective inner wisdom of your souls be in control. Do not determine what outcomes should be. Let go of what you think should happen and allow what is best to happen. By you having faith in your own inner wisdom, and in the inner wisdom of others, you will influence the organization and help to lift it up. It only takes one person to begin this process. When you see people relating in healthy ways, ways that heal, acknowledge them. When someone tells you a problem, look for, identify, and acknowledge to him his healthy thoughts and behaviors. When your inner wisdom indicates, help him to see how his thoughts create his experience.

What you're really telling me is to stay above conflicts and pettiness. I should refrain from the game playing and negative politics, the gossip, and the back biting.

Be conscious of what you are helping to create. If you participate in gossip, then you are helping to create a climate where gossip thrives. Perhaps you refrain from gossip, yet you think negatively of other people. Recognize that your negative thoughts about others have an effect. Your thoughts affect your behavior and your speech. People will sense through your body language and tone of voice that you disapprove of them. Your decisions and actions will be influenced by your fearful thoughts. People will literally, sense your negative thoughts and feelings. Imagine the work place as an energy field. The energy field is created by the collective thoughts and feelings of all the individuals. Ask yourself: "What am I contributing to the energy field in this organization?" Can you not walk into a store, a school, or an office and feel the energy?

Yes, I can. There are some places I don't like to shop because I don't like the feeling I get when I am in there. As a facilitator I sense the feeling, or energy field of a group. I can tell when they are tired, agitated, excited, pensive, or just not happy to be there.

How do you deal with a group that is agitated?

I ask them what is going on. I acknowledge how they feel, and then I move on. If I am inspired to say something helpful I say it. If not, I just listen. Whatever is happening, I set a positive tone. I turn over the group process to Spirit, expressing my intention for the best outcome possible. But, I begin by accepting them where they are.

You see something else. When you look into each of those agitated faces you see something behind the face. You make an assumption.

My assumption is that they want to learn and grow. That they want to have a good experience.

You trust that God is in each person there. You find positive qualities in every person. By doing so, you draw out the positive qualities.

This is why I love my work, but everyone doesn't appreciate what I do. Even when I do everything right—I pray, meditate, respond in a loving manner, come well prepared, know my material—there are usually one or two people who don't appreciate my work.

No one is appreciated 100% of the time, no matter how good you are. Simply see that one person with love. Accept that person, recognizing that his comments are his thoughts in the moment. No one shows up 100% every day, including you. People have high expectations that are often not met. This causes frustration and anger. See the good in people every day. Forgive them when their thoughts prevent them from expressing it. Give them unconditional appreciation regardless of their behavior or mood. In this way you lift them up. Join in their mood, or attack it, and you support it. When you find that you have allowed yourself to become upset, recognize it. Accept yourself where you are. Let your upsetting thoughts pass and allow your Soul's thoughts to rise to the surface.

My Soul's thoughts?

Yes, the thoughts of the real you. Your thoughts of love. Your thoughts that create a peaceful, confident feeling. These thoughts, your Soul's thoughts, thoughts from God, are always available to you. It is important that you listen from this perspective. Listen without judging. When you judge you create separation. Your judgment says that this person is separate from you. You are not separate, you are one. All people are connected. Refuse to take low moods, unloving words, and fearful actions personally. They are merely expressions based on fearful thoughts. Lift up the situation with your loving thoughts. Acknowledge your connection to all that is good within another person.

What if I totally disagree with someone's destructive behavior?

Tell them. Tell them with great respect. Set limits as any healthy person would do. You are the creator of your day. Decide what kind of day you would want and turn it over to Spirit within you. Let go of all outcomes. If you feel you must have a particular outcome say to God: "This or something better than this. Thank you, God."

You're saying I need to set an intention for each day?

We are saying let your intention be Peace. Let your intention be love. Let your intention be joy. Then turn over the details to Spirit. Be at peace and you will know what to do. Creativity, wisdom, solutions to problems, and words to say will come to you. Begin each day with this prayer adapted from a similar prayer found in A Course In Miracles:

Holy Spirit, Holy Presence of God,
I am here to be truly helpful
I am here to represent You, the One Who has sent me.
I do not have to worry about what words to say
or what things to do, for You Who have sent me will guide me.
I am content to be where You wish me to be, for
I know that You go there with me.
I am healed as I allow You to teach me to heal.
Thank you, God.

My intention is to serve well. I turn the day over to God and let it happen. With all the things that happen in a day I don't know if I can keep this perspective up all day. I'm only human you know.

We know what you are. You are much more than human. We do not ask for perfection. We ask only that you live each day consciously. You will make mistakes. You will experience emotions. As soon as you recognize that you are in your emotions begin your return to sanity. Seek to be in your feelings, that great well of wisdom that bubbles up from within you. You will know what to do. Spirit, God, your Soul, and We are always communicating in you.

How do I know which is which?

It is all One. We do not experience separation as do you. We are constantly aware of our Oneness. You are One with us, too. You are part of an awesome team of teachers and leaders. Of course, we speak of ourselves. Trust that this is so. You are of God. Think and act from this place. See God in others, and you will help others to see God in themselves.

We will speak once again of the river of life. Beneath the surface of life a calm, quiet current runs, one that has been present throughout time. It's presence has not been known to you because of the chaos at the surface. When you see a river, you see the waves and peaks on top. If you would stand and look into its depths, you would find the peace of surrender in the depths of the river's being. Do not allow the surface tensions to destroy this peace for you. Once you are certain and confident that what you need will flow to you, you abide in the calm depths of the stream. Your calm example teaches others. Your unwillingness to allow fear of lack to create your behavior offers strength to others.

I'd just be happy to get them to work together without all the blaming and conflict.

They are where they are. It is not your job to fix your clients. A facilitator of the word has not the responsibility for seeing things out to the finish. Teach. Create experiences where they may learn. Express as lovingly and creatively as you are able. See their highest good and speak to it. Do this and you will be successful.

Bill's Journal

There are a few guidelines I have learned about bringing my Soul to work. When I talk about bringing my Soul, I'm not discussing religion. I don't need to tell people my particular belief system, I just need to live my belief system. I think that in the past, I left my spirituality at the door when I went to work. I was driven by deadlines, management approval, money concerns, and job security issues. When I enter the workplace I should also enter as my Soul. This includes the following practices:

- Trust myself. Trust the prompting of my Soul. God is in me and speaks through me. I need to listen.
- Love myself and others. This means I look for the highest good in myself and others. I refrain from criticizing and fixing others and instead look to their wholeness, their innate goodness. This doesn't mean I let people walk all over me. Love isn't always nice. Sometimes love means setting clear limits with someone.
- Recognize when I am in my emotions. Find the inner space of peace and confidence before I solve a problem. Praying could help here.
- Create the kind of day I want. I can set my intention for the day, then align my thoughts and behaviors with that intention. I will speak and act from the deep well of peace that flows from within me.

If I do these things then I'll have successfully brought my Soul to work.

What about creativity? What about that incredible feeling people get when they are working together well? How can I help myself and others to reach this level?

People as individuals and as groups go through stages of growth. As you become aware of the stage they are in, you can be helpful to them.

What are these stages?

The first stage is characterized by dependency and duty.

What do you call that stage?

How about Stage One?

I was hoping for something more creative but that will do. Go on please.

In this stage the individual is dependent on the words, behaviors, and moods of others. If the boss is having a good day, I am having a good day. If the boss has a bad day, then my day is terrible. In this stage people blame one another for problems. Responsibility for change is almost always perceived as outside of one's self. People tend to gossip, defend themselves, protect turf, hide, rescue, sabotage, attack, and fight each other. There is usually much stress in this stage. The world seems to be made up of victims and perpetrators. There is very little freedom or creativity because people are expected to follow orders.

Yes, I know that stage well, both from my experience and from what I see every day.

The Stage Two is characterized by independence. In this stage we realize that we are responsible for our own moods and that we are not to blame for how other people feel. People often separate themselves from one another and act on their own in this stage. Attacking, blaming, and defensiveness are still evident, but people are more likely to take charge of their own situations and attempt to move forward. At some point during this stage, people begin to take personal responsibility. People in this stage resist taking orders and often choose to act on their own.

They are not really working together yet. That comes in the next stage.

Stage Three is characterized by synergy. In this stage people realize that they need each other because they are connected. Everyone's behavior affects everyone else in some way. Having this knowledge people are more willing to communicate honestly, to sit down and work out their disagreements. They also see a need to establish a common direction, values, and goals. People are willing to accept each other and whatever differences they may express. A synergistic organization or group is created through a conscious effort by a critical mass of people to coordinate, cooperate, and seek out the highest good possible.

Synergy becomes co-creation. Co-creation, Stage Four, results in innovation and exceptional performance. People use disagreement to create high quality solutions. Decisions are based on intuition, universal principles, and values. People who are co-creating are working in sync. Where you leave off and where I begin are both clear and ambiguous. As individuals we have clear boundaries. We respect one another. We each take personal responsibility for our respective lives. Yet, while we are in the process, working on a project, playing the game, or solving a problem, the boundaries between you and me become ambiguous. We are as one. Where two or more people are focused and acting in unison Spirit is there, too. In this situation people will let go of the ego and trust—trust each other and trust the process. This is equivalent to trusting God, although the words may not be said.

I've been there. I played on a basketball team. We beat a team that had ten times the talent we did. We were so much in sync; we were so focused that we won the game. It was incredible. Why is it so rare? I mean, most people have experienced co-creation in a group at least once. Why not all of the time?

The stages can be experienced both as an individual and within a group. Individuals are influenced by the groups they join. A synergistic person can be influenced by a dependent group resulting in dependent thinking by that individual. Or, a synergistic person can teach a dependent group and help them to evolve to a higher stage. People often become part of groups that tend to match their respective levels of

216 *evolution. You have gone through these stages. You have moved back and forth between the stages. Step back from your life and you can see where you spend most of your time.*

Synergy. I am usually conscious of the synergy of people in a group. I fall back into dependency and independence now and then, but I usually realize it and move forward. Often I am hired by Stage Two groups who see an opportunity to create synergy. There are often a number of people still in the dependent stage who resist change efforts, but it is exciting to work with groups and with individuals who want to grow. My biggest concern is with my personal creative pursuits. I seem to struggle. Why am I not experiencing more time in the co-creative stage?

You do not feel the trust that is necessary for this stage. When you facilitate a group you are sometimes in the co-creative stage. At this time you trust the inner wisdom of the group; you trust the process. Your faith in their wisdom draws out their wisdom. They begin to have faith in their abilities. As their faith increases they let go of fear and the need to control. This creates a space for the Creative Intelligence of the Universe, or God, to come through. It matters not whether they are aware of this.

The co-creative state is a very natural state. When you see the world through dependent eyes you become a victim. When you see the world through independent eyes you think you are doing it alone. Often you can achieve much, yet it takes great effort. This is true with your writing. Although you discuss your writing with us, you still think you are doing this alone. This causes you to struggle. With eyes that see synergy, you see the world as willing to help you. Things come more easily to you because you expect to receive what you need. You expect people to be helpful, so you attract helpful people. As a co-creator you are in touch with your Divine Self, your Higher Self. No one personality creates great works alone. Also, Bill, you are resistant to the co-creative state. This is due to fear. It is difficult to create when fear is driving you.

I want to get past the fear and achieve the co-creative state more often.

You can not <u>achieve</u> the co-creative state. It happens. You achieve the synergistic state. As a member of a group, you understand the basics for effective communication. You recognize your interdependence with others. You practice a win-win philosophy in conflict, in negotiation, and at all times. You hold and express loving intentions. As an individual, you abandon yourself to the flow of creativity. You are in synergy with the Universe. Co-creation, like any other miracle, cannot be <u>made</u> to happen. You set the stage. You take full responsibility for your thoughts and actions. Abandon yourself to the moment — whether you are in an athletic contest, a project, a work of art or music—trust in a power greater than you and let it happen.

I have several projects going, some with other people and some alone. It sounds like I have to do the preparation. I must get myself into a mindset of expecting to receive what I need. Obviously, I also need a clear intention and purposeful action. I've prepared; I'm focused; I've taken purposeful action. Why isn't creativity pouring out of me?

There are two fears you hold. The first is your need to control outcomes. You design an outcome that you want and predetermine how you will get there. This prevents you from seeing a better way.

Okay, I admit that I tend to try to control outcomes. I'm working on that. How do I get myself out of the way?

Embrace ambiguity. Ambiguity is opportunity for creativity. Allow yourself to not know the outcome and be comfortable with that. We have discussed this before. Create a vision and move forward. Do what is before you to do. The Universe will take care of the details.

I have to resist my urge to be manager of the Universe. That job is too big for me, but I still try to be in control. What is the second fear?

That you will succeed. That you will be great. What if you wrote a great book? What if you wrote a beautiful musical? What if you had an incredible marriage? What if you were constantly in touch with the voice of God?

I don't understand why I fear greatness.

It feels safer to stay where you are. There is always the fear that you will be shot down. It is always safer to be just another member of the group. When you speak your truth, you stand out. When you stand out people may attack you. Then there is the freedom issue. You always want to keep your options open. Commitment to any thing long term feels confining to you.

So, you think I'm afraid of being criticized.

Are you?

I don't like being shot down. I like being complimented and applauded.

When you go into a workplace you speak your truth. You tell people they are responsible for their own thoughts, feelings, and behaviors. We hear your prayer for assistance. We hear you speak boldly yet with compassion. We hear you compassionately confronting people when they are dishonest. You do not seem to be afraid of being criticized.

I'm not, because I am speaking the truth. I often feel guided in what I am doing. I know that there is no way to disprove what I am saying. Truth is Truth. The workplace feels pretty safe to me, but I want to expand my work. I want to do public workshops and speak at churches. I want to write and be published.

You feel safe in the Truth. You feel safe knowing you are guided. If it is your desire to write books and speak to groups on spiritual matters it is no different. Continue to ask for assistance. Continue to trust. Continue to speak boldly the Truth. Be yourself.

So I guess I have no excuse now for not shifting my work into more spiritual areas. When can I start?

When you are ready. What about the freedom issue?

I like my life. I have freedom to do as I please with the kind of of work I do. There is freedom in my marriage.

We will ask you a question. Think about the four stages of growth: dependency—independence—synergy—co-creation. In which stage do you think you are most free? And secondly, what is it that all souls want to be free of?

Well, obviously I am most free in the co-creative stage. I am free to be who I am. What do I want to be free of? Words like "obligation", "confinement", "should", "have to", "lack", "pain", "suffering" come to mind.

What causes all of these conditions?

Fear. And that's the answer to the second question. I want to be free of fear. How do I get free of a fear of greatness?

Set your vision and move forward. Do what is before you to do. Trust that you will be given what you need.

Bill's Journal

All of us are capable of expressing greatness, because God is expressing through us. To become more creative as an individual I need to let go of my desire to control outcomes. I need to relax and just be myself. I also need to work. These words don't type themselves. Creativity is not going to just fall out of the sky and into my brain. I set my vision, I move forward, doing what is before me to do. I trust that I will be given what I need. I've done this before.

Once I had a vision to create a musical/visual program for Mother's Day at a church I attended. I didn't know how to do it, but I was focused. I didn't know who would work with me. My passion and faith were so strong that I had no doubt it would be performed. People just started showing up! Talented musicians and support people joined me to create a spectacular program. It was an act of co-creation that was enjoyed by over 300 people. It was amazing how everything fell into place. Are there more great works waiting to express through me?

Okay, let's get back to the group thing. When you started talking about freedom from fear I thought how fear keeps people in the lower stages. The dependency stage is extremely fearful. What can I do to help people move through this stage? How can I help myself move out of dependency and independence? Sometimes when I am upset I find myself blaming. I know blaming isn't helpful, but my emotions are so strong I don't know what to do.

In Stage One people are not in tune with their souls. It is survival time. You think you are doing battle with outside forces, but the real battlefield is in your mind and body. You believe you are interacting with another person, but you are actually interacting with your assumptions about that person. You interpret the situation according to your own mental model of the world, and you think it is real. It is but your misguided interpretation.

How can I demonstrate this dynamic?

Show them. Know for yourself, how the dynamic works. All interactions begin with perception. You perceive a person in a way that aligns with your assumptions, beliefs, and stereotypes. Your behavior emerges from your perception.
We will map out this interaction. Let us take a sample situation where you are working with another who is making mistakes. She is unable to meet standards set for the job. It looks like this:

Event: A person comes to your attention. You, at the same time, come to her attention

Step 1: You create assumptions and beliefs about a person. These assumptions may be based on stereotypes, past experience, or what was taught to you

Step 2: You create and use offensive or defensive behaviors. Your past learning has taught you this person poses a threat. Out of fear, you create behaviors to protect yourself. Self protective behaviors may include remaining aloof, complaining to other people, defensiveness, arguing and many more.

Step 6: You see her behavior

You

Her

Step 3: She observes your behavior and senses your discomfort.

Step 5: She creates and uses offensive or defensive behaviors. Her past learning has taught her that you pose a threat. Out of fear, she creates behaviors to protect herself. Self protective behaviors may include remaining aloof, complaining to other people, defensiveness, arguing and many more.

Step 4: She interprets your behavior based on her own assumptions and beliefs. These assumptions may be based on stereotypes, past experience, or what was taught to her

And around and around it goes. I see how this works: I think someone is not competent (1). In order to protect myself I withhold information, talk down to her, and criticize her (2). I think what I am doing is okay, because I must protect myself. She sees my behaviors and feels their impact (3). She interprets my behavior and decides that I am arrogant, a know-it-all, and rude (4). So she protects herself by hiding from me, defending her actions, and complaining to others (5). I see her doing these things (6) which serve to convince me I was right—she is incompetent (7).

We come full circle, and around and around we go. It seems like we form opinions of each other and look for evidence, or invent evidence, to substantiate our belief. We perpetuate conflict.

Often it appears more important to be right, then to communicate honestly.

Okay, I see the value of becoming aware of this dynamic. Now what?

Identify to yourself the assumptions and beliefs you have about this person.

I believe she is incompetent, unintelligent, and defensive.

Recognize that these beliefs mean nothing. They are not her; they are your beliefs about her. They do not matter.

What does matter?

Her behavior; her performance. Address her specific behaviors. Incompetence is a judgment. Find those specific behaviors that do not meet expectations. Teach her what she needs to know. Do what you can to help her succeed without doing it for her. Give her the opportunity to learn and succeed. If she does not succeed, let it be of her own choosing. She may not have the ability and/or knowledge; or she may decide the job is not for her. When you establish negative expectations toward

another you are likely to have them met. Establish positive expectations;
see the greatness in her.

What if she really is incompetent? What if she just can't get it?

Help her to find her true place. There is perfect work for her. It may or may not be in that particular organization.

So, if I set aside my judgments and deal with her behaviors, her performance, and speak to her honestly and compassionately, I should be okay. Also, I should communicate in a caring manner and make expectations very clear. Is that it?

Use unconditional positive regard. Love. You must suspend judgment and assume that she is a child of God. You must assume goodness in her whether you can see it or not. Look for the goodness.

Okay. If I don't see any good in her I have to act as if I do. I need to assume it. What else?

There is one more thing. Look at the words you have used to describe her. They do not describe her but they do say something about you. Which of those words upsets you? Fill in the blank. It really bugs me when people are_____?

...When people are incompetent.

Why is that? Why does the appearance of incompetence bother you?

Okay, I see where this is going. It's because I fear her incompetence will make me look bad. And maybe I fear being seen as incompetent myself.

Worrying about how you look is less important then who you are. Who are you? Are you one who heals or are you one who hurts? Make the choice. If you are one who heals, another person's lack of skill or knowledge is an opportunity for you to teach, to help. Do what you can to help.

I don't think that just because I am bothered by someone's behavior it means I fear it in myself. In the past I used to get real ticked off at forceful, demanding people. I wasn't forceful and demanding.

You were upset because they did not give you what you thought you wanted. Be honest. What did you want from that overpowering dictator of a boss you once had?

I wanted his respect.

And what else?

Okay, okay, I wanted him to take care of me, to protect me.

Instead he put you in a situation where you had a choice between submitting or standing up for yourself. What did he teach you?

He taught me about standing up for myself. He taught me that I could; I didn't have to be afraid of people in authority. Now I enjoy working with people like that, because they are direct. I don't have to guess what they want. I can be direct and to the point with them. They respect me for that.

For most people, the immediate reaction tends to be fight or flight. You attack or you defend. You hide or you run away. These behaviors arise from your sense of injustice. You fight because you believe an injustice has been done to you. Or, you run and hide believing injustice has been done. You have confused your interpretation of the fact with the fact itself. In the example with the woman who made mistakes, what were the facts?

She was not meeting job expectations.

That is the visible fact. Now let us add the Truth. She is a child of God, as you are. Relate to her as if she were a revered spiritual being. Communicate as if you are a revered spiritual being. This is the Truth in action.

In the work place of today much energy and intent is directed toward catching people doing wrong. This creates a fearful environment. Let your intent be to assist others in achieving their highest good. This will help an organization and its members to grow and prosper.

The actions of others trigger responses within you. The human tendency is to project your discomfort on to the other person. Deal with inappropriate behaviors directly. Do not attack; do not defend; do not rescue or enable. Be grateful this discomfort has arisen. Now is your chance to discover what you are doing in your mind to create your thoughts and emotions. Remember that other people reflect back to you what you think of yourself. Look into this mirror and ask to know what you are thinking and feeling. Everyone brings their "stuff" to work and to relationships. Conflict and discomfort are opportunities to discover what stuff gets in the way of you being the holy child of God you were meant to be.

Where does the stuff come from? I mean, do I learn it or am I born with it? It is the old argument—is it heredity or environment?

Both. You come into this life with a body and a personality engineered to to help you learn what you want to learn. Your Soul chose for you what you would be born into—your family, your socio-economic status, your body, your mental abilities, your talents, everything. You have exactly what you need to live a successful, joy filled life. Your childhood learning reinforces the tendencies you brought into life. You may think your parent caused you to feel under confident. He reinforced that thought/feeling. You were born with the predisposition toward under confidence. You were given a situation to help you develop that confidence—for example—to learn to look within for validation rather than to other people. Be grateful for everyone in your life, for you are learning well. Teach and learn not to project on to other people that which is yours to heal.

Whew! We've covered a lot of ground. Is that it?

There is one more very important thing. Focus on what is being done well. Positive reinforcement in the form of appreciation, compliments, and acknowledgment for specific accomplishments is very important. These activities create positive energy. It is more important to tell people what they are doing right than to tell them what they are doing wrong. People perform better, feel better, and enjoy their work more when this positive energy is created. It draws out the best in them and makes it easier to bring their souls to work.

Bill's Journal

It seems that the way to bring my Soul to work is to do the following things:
- practice positive communication skills;
- create intentions to assist myself and others to reach the highest good possible;
- express the greatness in myself;
- help others express the greatness in themselves;
- deal with inappropriate behaviors directly; and
- offer people appreciation, compliments, and acknowledgment for work well done. This helps to bring out the best in each person.

Positive, high intentions and the resulting thoughts and behaviors will set the stage for me to enter the co-creative state with other people. In the co-creative state God is expressing through us. I am at my peak performance. When two or more can express from this state of awareness a relationship can be co-creative. When most of the people in an organization can express from this state of awareness, an organization can be co-creative. I want to know more about co-creation possibilities in my own life.

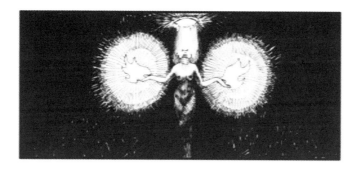

Chapter Fourteen:
Co-creation

You are a co-creator with God.

What does it mean to co-create with God?

It means that you allow God to work through you. You are in the flow. Imagine your mind to be a computer. Divine Mind downloads thoughts into your mind. The appropriate thoughts come at the appropriate time teaching you what to think, what to say, and what to do. Things fall into place. You move beyond faith into knowing. You feel an incredible sense of confidence, of knowing. As an individual you feel connected to what you are doing and the ability to do it. In a group setting you feel connected to each other and to what you are doing together.

How do I choose to be a co-creator with God?

Focus on the situation and allow your passion for it to arise. Again, you let go of your need to control specific outcomes. You perceive yourself, other persons, and situations with total love. You refuse to be caught up in the illusions of pain, disease, injury, or conflict. You may, of yourself, see no possible solution, no possible way, but you move forward with complete confidence assuming the situation is healed or completed. To co-create is to be in the flow. The energy of God flows to you and through you.

This is easier said than done. I'm no miracle worker, you know.

A co-creator is a miracle worker. Any belief in lack or disease is an illusion. You can dissolve any illusion when you employ the Truth. Beneath hatred there is love. Conflict is but a veil that hides the urge for peace. The sea may be raging violently, yet beneath the surface, lies a calmness that cannot be disturbed. Seek this place in any situation where the illusion of pain, conflict, or impossibility seems to be the reality.

It is very hard to look at a real situation and not see the pain and suffering, not to see the impossibility of the situation. My beliefs are rooted so deeply that I have little chance of seeing in this way. If someone is lying before me with broken bones how can I see them as whole? How can I heal them?

You can not. Bill's personality can heal nothing. God heals. You must get out of the way.

How can I get out of the way?

This you already know. Look at your thoughts. Recognize that your thoughts are creating your experience. Remind yourself that God is within you, within your thoughts. Let these God centered thoughts come forth. Ask God what to do. You will know. You have already co-created with God in your work. Whenever you have let go and allowed yourself to be guided by Spirit you have co-created. You have co-created miracles. You have helped people to see themselves in new light. You have helped people to see their relationships in more loving and effective ways. These people saw their respective situations as impossible. These were miracles. There is no limit in size or type for creating miracles. They are all the same. A person changes his mind. When the mind is changed the situation changes.

The only difference between your miracles and other miracles lies in your perception. You perceive the healing of broken bones as impossible. Yet there are many healers who have helped people with broken bodies to be whole again. Sometimes it took a minute; sometimes it took several months. Impossible situations are those which are seen and believed as impossible.

You haven't really said that I can heal broken bones. You said I would know what to do.

Yes, you would know what to do. Everyone is not in physical form to do everything. There are those who have the gift of hands on healing. They are in this life to use that gift in service to God. That is not your gift to express at this time. This does not mean that you will never facilitate healing in this way. You have other gifts. Better you would spend your time expressing your gifts than trying to heal bodies.

Your definition of a miracle is something that you think is impossible for you to do. You then say to yourself: "I can not work miracles." You are an instrument for miracles. You speak words that help people to heal. You write poetry and music that help people to perceive the world differently. A miracle is only a change in perception.

That's all?

That is all. When you perceive differently you experience differently. Very confident miracle workers can see for others. The one who heals the broken bones can see for the injured one that he is whole. The miracle worker creates a loving space for the "injured one." In that space of love the injured becomes whole — he becomes what he is in Reality. The bone is healed if that is what is best for that person. But the miracle worker does not decide that outcome. The miracle worker sees the person in pain. Moving his own thoughts aside, he turns within to God. Listening within, he takes action. He has no concern for the specific outcome. His only concern is that he is a pure channel for God's love. He knows only that his laying on of hands will help healing to come. He knows not what that healing will look like.

Is it any different when you speak to a group? You say the words you feel compelled to speak. But, you do not designate what effect they will have on the people in your audience. When you write a poem you write from your heart. The words seem to flow out onto the paper. You do not designate what effect the words will have on the eventual readers. When you speak to people do you not believe in them? Do you not see God in them? Your vision, your belief in them as children of God, your respect for them—all of this helps them to see those qualities in themselves.

I never thought of myself a miracle worker.

You are a co-creator with God. You are blessed with certain gifts. You prevent yourself from using these gifts when you place conditions on them.

What do you mean?

You believe you are not qualified. "Who am I to speak words of spirit and healing to people? Who am I to write spiritual insights? I have not healed anyone. Where is my credibility?" You prevent yourself from being all that you can be now with these thoughts. Do you still fear greatness?

I have a hard time seeing myself as great.

You very easily see yourself as great. You imagine writing books and having them published. You imagine writing a musical. You imagine shifting your focus from leadership in organizations to spiritual leadership. You imagine it. You have the knowledge and ability to carry it out. Why are you not doing it?

I don't know.

Tell the truth.

Well, it's a great responsibility to be a spiritual teacher on the level you just mentioned. I don't know if I am ready.

You are ready when you move through your fear of greatness. Millions of people have great talent they never tap. You stall around saying "maybe, some day." That day is now, because some day never comes. Now is the acceptable moment. Is it your intention to express the greatness of God that is available to you?

I guess, but why me? Everybody can't be a spiritual teacher.

Everyone is a spiritual teacher. All that you say and do serves to teach others. The question is not <u>whether</u> or not you will teach. The question is <u>what</u> you will teach. Who you are teaches much more than words that you say. A plumber or a carpenter can be a great spiritual teacher. A cashier can be a minister. Each person you meet is someone to whom you may minister and teach. It is not a requirement that a person make speeches or write books to be a great spiritual teacher. You choose to be a teacher of the word by speaking, consulting, and writing. You already know why you wish do this.

I do it because it's fun. I do it because I feel compelled to teach and to write. It's fun helping people to grow. I love to teach. I want to creatively express my gifts, but I don't see why I keep holding back.

Were you to express greatness, people might challenge you. If you are public with your gifts then you have to live up to them. The spiritual teacher is expected to lead a spiritual life. When you put yourself in the public eye you will be criticized. People will question and critique your ideas. This you have already experienced in your work as a teacher and a speaker.

I think I handle criticism pretty well.

You do handle it well, because you let us help you. You turn over your speeches and your facilitating to God. When people question you, you respond with confidence. You only feel fearful and defensive when you allow your ego to run things.

I'm glad you guys are there when I'm working.

We are always with you. When you pray to God for help, God sends us, your teachers and guides. Did you think we would abandon you if you moved to a higher level?

I never really thought about it. I think I can handle the pressures of expressing more greatness, especially if I know you are helping me. Are there any other barriers I am putting up to prevent myself from expressing greatness?

If you express greatness now it will not coincide with the view you have always had of yourself, the ever changing false view of your ego. This is the view that greatness belongs only to certain others. You are always telling other people how great they can be. You believe in their greatness. Believe in your own.

How do I move beyond the excuse making and lack of confidence, the fear of greatness?

Decide and do. Ask God for help. Listen for the answers. Move your consciousness down into your heart area and listen. What does your heart say?

Sometimes it doesn't say anything. I meditate but nothing comes.

That is a condition you have established: "I can not meditate." Since you can not meditate, well, then you must not be very spiritual. You do meditate. You will continue to get better at it as you continue to practice. What does your heart say?

In my heart I feel an urge to write, to stretch out and express my ideas and beliefs. This would bring me joy.

So be it. You will receive what you need.

I have a good life. I have a loving wife, family and friends. I have a home and work that I love. I have money. It would be easy to settle in, except I don't think God will let me. My Soul won't let me. This is a time of transition. My work is changing. I am feeling a dissatisfaction with much of what I am doing. It is time to move on to new frontiers, to meet new challenges. It is time to co-create, to allow miracles to be created through me.

The way I understand it is that a miracle is a change in perception. A present condition supported by a present belief is disputed by Truth. Truth then manifests as a new condition. It is easy for me to see this in the world of relationships between people. When I look at another person differently the relationship changes. It's still hard for me to compare routine "miracles" with what I see to be real miracles. I change my perception and a problem is solved. How does that compare with say, raising someone from the dead?

In the New Testament, Jesus demonstrated this. One of the most dramatic miracles was the raising of Lazarus. What people saw was that Lazarus' bodily functions ceased to work. His sisters perceived him as dead, gone from their lives. It was a terrible thing to them. They grieved his passing, expecting not to see him again. They were sad, hurt, and perhaps angry that God had taken him. In their minds, he was separated from them. No more could he enjoy life. No more could they enjoy him. There was now an emptiness in their lives.

Jesus knew there was no such thing as death. He knew that one cannot lose someone. He knew this could not be terrible, because Lazarus did not die. Knowing the beliefs of others to be an illusion, Jesus saw through them with his faith in the Truth. He gave thanks for Life and Lazarus arose from his grave.

The veil of illusion was removed so that the Truth could be seen. The appearance of death was based on a belief in dying and separation. The Truth is that life is eternal. Death is an illusion that we have chosen. Jesus dispelled the illusion.

You talk of it as if it were an ordinary thing.

For Jesus it was an ordinary thing. One of his gifts was the ability to heal the sick and raise the dead. But remember, he, of himself, did not decide that Lazarus should live. He saw the Truth. He asked God for help. He proclaimed the words that came to him. He did not wake up that day and say, "I think I will raise Lazarus from the dead today. Something like that would impress people for all time." Now let us talk about one of your miracles.

One of mine?

Yes. What about that young man who spoke to you about how your class had affected him?

He said that my talk about perception had helped him. He didn't fight with his wife nearly as much as he used to. He said he felt better at home and his marriage relationship was improved.

A change in perception followed by a change in conditions. It is no less a miracle than any other.

It is not the same as raising the dead.

Perhaps you helped to raise a dead marriage. There is no order of difficulty in miracles. One is no more difficult for God than another, therefore no one miracle is more important than another. Miracles are miracles. God is. The perception of levels of difficulty or of importance is yours.

You have the power to change events in your own life. See through your beliefs with the Truth. Miracles, which are simply examples of the Truth becoming manifest, will occur in your life.

Does that mean that if I am ill I can become well by disputing my belief in my illness and replacing it with the Truth?

You can not be ill. You experience the illusion of illness. If you are ill, there is a need you are expressing. The need may be for attention, love, rest, sympathy, struggle, guilt, self punishment, or another reason. The need may be to correct an incorrect belief. These beliefs include your sense of separation from God, your undeservingness of love, your unwillingness to forgive your self or another, or the collective belief that people must get sick. The Truth is that as spirit you can never be sick. As a child of God you deserve love. You are a spiritual being having a human experience. You are God expressing as you. You are the Christ. You are the Buddha.

Then illness is an opportunity. It is an opportunity to see Truth. If I'm sick I should be able to reclaim my health.

The illusion of illness is an opportunity to change your perception. Illness is not a punishment. Illness is sometimes a wakeup call, telling you to cease a certain lifestyle. For some it is an opportunity to rest they would not otherwise take. For some, illness is part of their soul's purpose. The soul takes on the experience of illness to learn or to teach others. Therefore, your goal is to change your perception which will, in turn, change your experience. The miracle is the experience of peace which you feel whether or not your physical symptoms disappear. A miracle is like waking up. You realize that your trouble was only a dream you believed was real. Now you see the Truth. A miracle is the perceiving of the Truth.

So, any situation in my life that I don't like is a result of irrational and incorrect beliefs that I hold. If I can find the belief and challenge it, replace it with Truth, then my situation will change?

You will experience healing and you will know that you are healed. Do not focus on the specific physical outcomes.

So if I'm creating miracles I am co-creating ?

Co-creation depends on which part of your mind you are thinking with. If you think with your analytical mind, the part that calculates and figures, you are not co-creating. But you are creating. Thinking is creating, and you are always thinking. Every thought becomes form in some way. When you co-create you are in the flow. You get out of your own way and let thoughts that are creative, inspirational, and new come through your mind. Co-creation does not apply only to problems and illness. Co-creation brings new ideas and new creations. You are co-creating this book. You co-create the talks you give at churches. You co-create the workshops you develop for organizations. You have co-created music.

We have talked about a lot of things here. It would help me if you would summarize the keys to co-creation.

First, recognize that God works through you. With God's guidance, clarify your intentions and speak them. Co-creation begins with a vision. The vision is fueled by passion—a passion to express. Sometimes it is an idea that, at first, seems vaguely possible. Cultivate the vision. Focus on the feelings of joy, love, peace, or wholeness that will result. See the ultimate benefit for you and for others. When you co-created your music program you envisioned the seats full of people, all enjoying and being deeply touched by your program. You declared you wanted 80% of the people shedding tears. Your vision miraculously manifested. Your passion attracted other people with passion. Your combined energy drew the people and the things necessary to complete your vision.

You placed your vision in God's hands and set about doing the work. God is energy and you are part of that energy. The energy, through the process of co-creation, becomes form.

You're right. It was an amazing creation.

What would you like to co-create now? What are your intentions?

I have a few things: First, I want to write, publish, and sell my book. I want it to be the highest expression possible. I want to be able to sit down and read it and be pleased with it. I want to offer it to others who may find it interesting. I had many misconceptions about spiritual growth. When I started this writing six years ago, I wanted to show that the spiritual growth process was not a quick fix. I wanted to show that it was an ongoing process.

Focus on the expression. Focus on the feelings you will have when you see your completed project before you. Focus on the joy you will feel knowing that people are benefiting from your work. Do not worry about how the details will be completed. Follow your passion, and ask for help. Write each day whether or not you think the writing is good.

That leads me to my second intention. I want financial security. I want to know that there is always enough and more. Beyond that, I want the feeling of abundance in life. I want to feel the confidence that there is no need to struggle, but that I am always able to receive.

You have made much progress in this area. You need not worry about money or material things. God is providing. Remind yourself daily that God is your unfailing source of supply; that money comes quickly as you need it.

Third, my wife and I want to have a baby. We have tried for a few years now. We want to conceive and birth a healthy child.

Do what is before you to do. Hold your vision, yet be willing to accept a different outcome if that is what is best for you.

But, will this miracle happen?

We do not reveal specific futures to you. Some things are best not known. There is learning for you and your wife in this process— learning which we would not desire to take from you.

It is so difficult to pray and work for something so desired as this baby. We have been to doctors, and we have been to spiritual healers, yet we still do not have a baby.

You and your loved one have learned much through your experiences with doctors and healers. Whether a child is born or not, you have both grown from this. Place your desire in God's hands and do what is before you to do. Take those steps, whether medical or spiritual, which you feel drawn to do. All will be well.

I think now is the acceptable time for this baby.

Be patient. Remember, you cannot make this happen. Let go. Do you have another intention?

I want to feel closer to God.

You are already close to God. When you breathe, you breathe God. When you think, God's thoughts are gently pushing on the walls of your resistance. When you are with people, God looks out at you through their eyes. When you love, you become aware of God's presence. You can not become any closer to God than you already are.

Then my intention is to become aware of my closeness to God.

Chapter Fifteen
Getting Closer To God

Strange things are happening. I want to get closer to God, but things seem to be getting a little crazy in my life. Deals are falling through at work, and checks are coming late. Emotions are close to the surface. What's going on with me?

"Seek ye first the kingdom of heaven" is a thought that offers great wisdom, and this commitment will have you feeling the beauty and prosperity you desire. Do not think of that which you need, but see that your learning has come through your experience. You are receiving the lessons of this lifetime. Is it to be without its periods of confusion and discontent? You are learning to trust and grow through each situation with which you are met. You are receiving what you need.

I do trust that God is providing. Each day I search for ways to be closer to God. Why must I still experience insecurity?

Your search has run into obstacles. Diversions have appeared along your way, constantly reaffirming your need to choose love. Did you think that once you achieved your dreams all would be perfect? Did you think that you would arrive?

Know that God will supply the wealth that you demand on all levels of existence. See that you supply the willingness. Are you willing to release patterns of agitation when things do not go as you expect? There are always opportunities to choose. You perceive your life as lacking, therefore you experience it as lacking.

So, I need to stop getting upset when things don't go right for me. Is that it?

When checks are late; when clients delay in calling you, you need not feel irritation. Allow yourself the freedom to see that what faces you now is life. Without care, abandon yourself and your needs to God. Allow His presence to guide. Strive for greater union. Do not worry about business you do not receive. What is yours is yours; what is not is of no concern.

In times when things seem unknown, this is when you turn within and ask. Trust these times will keep coming back until you stay centered in trust knowing that all is well.

You are telling me, once more, to let go and let God handle things.

Completely! State your intentions, your desires, and your dreams. Share your heart, all that matters, with the Infinite One. God will hear your prayers. Describe all that you feel. Do not hesitate to explore that which you deem unnecessary, such as negative feelings or judgments. Do not allow your mind to edit your thoughts and feelings. Give all of your thoughts over to God's care.

I try to pray and meditate. Many times I ask questions but I don't always get the answers I need.

An endless stream of thoughts hardly allows for a response. See that you take a break. Cleanse yourself before prayer or meditation by verbalizing all of your fears and worries. Then see, as the quiet comes, what will be told to you. With a sense of knowing you will press on to engage in your day. Direct all questions within. Be still and quiet. Be calm, and know that all answers are there to be had.

So, as long as I confide in God within, and trust that I will be answered, everything should be okay?

Take each day as an opportunity to renew your life's commitment to grow with the One who desires only that your being recognizes His Presence all about you. See your day expand in glory by achieving states of knowing that there is no absence of the treasure that is given you. God exists and His Truth will be provided and be present throughout an eternity. Walk forth in confidence and calm knowing that we are with you now and always.

Bill's Journal

Okay, two things need to happen when I feel troubled or unsure:
1.   I need to trust, knowing that God is within me and all around me.
2. I need to turn within for the answers.
I thought I already knew this stuff. If I'm getting agitated at my circumstances, then I am not trusting God. Instead of allowing myself to get agitated I can choose to trust.

How do I really trust God?

Do you believe there is a God?

Yes.

Do you love God?

Yes.

How did you arrive at this place of believing in and loving God?

I don't know. It just happened.

Yes, exactly. You have spent years praying, thinking, and reading about God. You have spent years learning about yourself and coming to an understanding that you are made in God's image—that you are God's child. You have spent so much time talking to God and thinking about God, that thoughts of doubt regarding God's existence have little chance of survival in your mind.

Bill, you have built a relationship with God. Communication and trust have taken you to this place, this understanding you have of God. Continue to communicate. Once, years ago, you felt no love for God, nor could you make yourself love God. Now you do. You planted the seeds of love through your prayers and contemplation; love blossomed. Your love and your trust will grow beyond your present imagining.

I would like that, but I have one question regarding doubt. How do I know this relationship with God is real? I have no doubt there is a Creative Intelligence. How do I know I really have a relationship with this Intelligence? What is the difference between me hearing the Voice of God and some religious fanatic who says God ordered him to kill someone? I saw a preacher on television who said God spoke to him while he was praying the other night. These people probably feel just as strongly as I do about their respective relationships with God, yet each of us has a completely different idea about God's communication. We each think God speaks to us. How do I know it isn't just my voice? How do I know you guys are real? Maybe I'm fooling myself. Maybe I'm just imagining you.

I think that if you repeat something enough it becomes rooted in your mind. After a certain amount of repetition you start to believe it. That's why people have some success with affirmations. I can tell myself over and over again that God is here; that I have a relationship with God; and that God is speaking to me. Does that make it true?

I could repeat to myself that I'm the smartest guy in the world. I could possibly have myself believing I'm the smartest guy in the world. That doesn't make me the smartest guy in the world. What I'm asking is: what is the truth and what is illusion? I heard the preacher say God spoke to him, but I don't believe God speaks that way. His version of God threatened people with dire consequences.

I read about a fanatic who thinks he's going to heaven because he killed several people, but I don't believe him. Do these guys really have a relationship with God? Are they in touch with the truth or am I? I like this feeling of being close to God, but I don't want to be fooling myself.

God speaks to everyone, yet the content is framed by one's own mental arrangement. The Voice of God is the voice of love. There is no difference between your true voice and the Voice of God. Listen to the voice within and ask: Does this voice lead me to peace? Does this voice lead me to joy? God is continually willing to express through you.

If you believe you are close to God, then you are close to God. This does not mean your vision is clear. Everyone is close to God, because there is no difference between "everyone" and God. To express your closeness is to open a door of possibility. Each of you has given God a form, but the form is not God. God is formless. To be more accurate, God is both form and formless. God is All There Is. The point here is that God is not restricted to a form. God is all form. The preacher, the fanatic, and you each have a passion for God. Your deep love helps you to feel close to God. At the same time, your judgment of each other serves to distance you from God.

When you are close to another person, when you love someone deeply, you often see what you are conditioned to see. You see the image of the person which you have created, not the person who God created. This is true of seeing God. You see the God you want to see. To be closer to God; to see God more clearly; see God in both the preacher and the fanatic.

How?

Humans have a saying about seeing the glass half empty or half full. We say, you can focus on those behaviors of people which seem to indicate God is not present, or you can focus on behaviors which indicate God is present. See where God is present. This will bring you closer to knowing God.

I should ignore the fact that the fanatic is killing people?

We ask you to ignore nothing. A child of God is killing his brothers and sisters. How can you help? We will explore this later. You spoke of difficulties in your own life. There will always be challenges in life. You may choose to see each challenge with love and trust, or you may see it with fear. When confronted with a challenge, turn within. Pray. Talk with God. Tell God your troubles and your fears. Let it all come out. Then ask for help. Be completely willing to follow God's will. God's will is your happiness; it is your answer.

I am willing, but I can't seem to get past the clutter in my head.

Why do you wander in your thoughts during meditation and prayer? Do not answer this question too quickly. Pause and let your mind be still a moment.

Maybe it's because I don't want to hear God's Voice.

Why do you not wish to hear the Voice of God?

I don't want to hear God's Voice because I'm afraid to know what God has to say to me.

Why are you afraid to know?

I am afraid to know because I'm afraid to be too closely connected to God.

Why would you not want to be closely connected to God?

I am afraid to be too closely connected because I would lose my identity. It would be the end of me .

You have your answer, Dear One. And you are partially right. It would not be the end of you, but it would be the end of your present view of yourself. At the same time, you would find your true Self.

But I don't want to give up who I am.

I am me. I am Bill. If I connect with God I might lose myself. I don't want to do that.

Growing closer to God is an evolutionary process, a series of transformations. In each transformation you become more. More accurately, you <u>realize</u> you are more. You do not lose who you have been. Be who you are and realize that you are much more. Rise above who you think you are and become more. When you become more you include what you have already been. Turn within to the Voice of God and hear it joyfully. It will not take away who you are. It will only help you to add to your awareness of who you are. There is so much more to you than meets your senses. You are not your body. You are not your collection of small and worrisome thoughts. You are a spiritual being, an expression of all that is divine. You are as we are.

How can I be the same as you?

There are no levels of importance in the Universe, only levels of growth and learning. You are essentially no different than Jesus or the Buddha. Did not Jesus ask " Is it not written in your law, I said, you are gods?" (John 10:23). Did he not say that the disciples would do even greater works than he? Humans tend to make other humans greater than themselves. You do this with great prophets and sadly, with celebrities. Jesus was not only the great exception; he was the great example. Do you think that he was the son of God and you are not?

I am a child of God, too.

Then perhaps you would choose to act as one. As a child of God you are created in God's image. God is love. God is creative. God is not confined to a body. Your purpose in life is to become more God-like. To do this you must let God in. You are afraid to lose yourself in God. You have it turned around. With meditation and prayer you do not lose yourself in God; you find yourself in God. You find out who you really are. You have experienced but a small portion of the joy, love, and peace that God is. There is much more, beyond your present imagining. Let go of your fear and turn within. Give over all of your concerns and trust completely in God. Your present circumstances are an opportunity for you to trust, to know that God is providing for you.

How does that help me with the ambiguity in my life right now? Everything seems to be up in the air.

Can you choose love? Each moment in your life you make choices. You choose between love and fear. There is no other choice. Things seem unsure. You can love and accept your situation or you can fear it. Take time and contemplate the effects that may be created in your life were you to choose love. If you would love unconditionally, what effect would love have on the situation? How would you be affected? How would your love affect others?

I don't know the answers.

We do not ask you to answer. Only to contemplate. Only to love. See what happens.

What would it be like to love unconditionally? If I loved my insecure situation unconditionally, what effect would that have on my life? How would I feel and what would I think? The first question that comes to me is what is there about it to love?

Can you not love the opportunity? You are now in a position where you have the opportunity to place your trust in God, not in your business clients. You can love that you are truly learning to trust the Universe to supply you with whatever you need. You are learning to turn inward rather than outward for the fulfillment you seek. You need not worry. You are cultivating a sense of confidence. This will make you stronger.

I don't know the details of how things will work out. I feel out of control!

You will remember that many things you have experienced
began with you having only an idea and faith.

That is true. When I made a commitment to my business, calls came from unexpected directions. Most of my business came not as a direct result of my efforts. But it is hard not knowing.

You trust that God is already providing for you. It is not that God will provide someday. God is providing all that you need now.

I thought I was beyond this. I went through years of financial struggle and lack. For several years now I have done very well. In the past year I have been able to invest some money. Now my income has dropped over the past few months. I feel like I just traveled in one big circle, back to where I started.

It is not a circle, but a spiral upward. You will notice that your present situation is not the same as that which happened previously. Today you worry that you will drain your savings, that you will not be able to take trips. In the past you struggled to pay your bills, and you had no savings. Years before you found yourself deep in debt with no home of your own. You have come back to a place of feeling lack yet you are on a higher level. This is growth. This is life. You will circle around to higher and higher levels.

Your basic needs are met. You experience now an opportunity to go deeper, to trust more completely, to cease your dependence on external factors. In spite of what you think you see, be at peace. Be confident that you are in God's care. You have come to a place that is almost peace, that is almost trust. Take the next step without benefit of the knowledge of when and where your income will flow. Let it flow from God. Know that all that you seek is flowing from God. All that you require flows through your mind into physical existence. See your life as full, and so it will be. Let go of worry, for it adds nothing to your life.

Meditate each day. Address your fearful thoughts by speaking them and releasing them. Give them over to God. Empty your self each day of negative thoughts and emotions in this way. Be mindful of your thinking and feeling. Take care of all that you have control over and give to God all that of which you have no control. Give over your troubles in prayer. Acknowledge your many blessings in prayer. Listen to God in meditation.

How will meditation help me? I feel like I am wasting my time sitting there wandering in my thoughts. Is there a technique that will work?

There are many techniques for meditation. Choose one that works for you.

Help me on this one, please. I've tried many things and they didn't work. I want to hear God's Voice in meditation, but I'm still having trouble.

We will make a suggestion. Sit comfortably. Speak to God. Tell God all that worries you. Empty your thoughts and concerns by pouring them out to God. If you still feel tense, do a progressive relaxation on your body. That is, beginning with your feet, tighten muscle areas then relax them. Move through your entire body. Spend extra time on those parts that seem particularly tense. When your body is relaxed, begin breathing deeply, pushing your diaphragm out on the in breath; pushing it in on the out breath. Focus on your breathing completely. For some, a mantra is effective. Choose a word or short phrase that has meaning for you and say it over and over again mentally. For many a visualization works. Visualize yourself in a beautiful place. The important thing is that you are totally relaxed. If you find yourself thinking about other things, bless those thoughts, let them go, and come back to your meditation.

Bill's Journal

It is so hard for me to meditate. My mind abhors a vacuum. The moment I empty it of thoughts more thoughts come rushing in.

Things appear unclear in your life. Ambiguity is opportunity. Take this opportunity to get to know God better. Take this opportunity to turn within for your support rather than looking outward to the world. The world does not have what you need.

Chapter Sixteen
I Am Here To Be Truly Helpful

For the Beloved One

My Heart yearns
for you.

I think of you always,
wanting you near,
 to be
touched by you,
to feel you inside me,
to know your warmth.

Closer than hands and feet,
more intimate than breathing
have I needed you.

I have sought you
among the faces in the city,
in both library and tavern,
in churches
and in the marketplace,

sought you in the
arms of lovers,
searched for your countenance
in both victory and defeat,
amongst the crowd
and in solitude.

In loneliness
my soul cries out for you.

This morning I seek you
in field and forest,
in the faces of nature.
Drunk with her
extravagance I am
reminded of your beauty,
your grace, your love.

Rays of sun light
bring thoughts of your radiance,
and I can wait no longer.
We are meant to be as One.

In the shade of a tree
upon an overlook,
suspended over brilliant blue waters
I rest.

Awakened, my heart increases its
rhythm as I see you
approaching.
At last I have found you.
Joy overflows my being
as You embrace me.
I am held yet
I am free.
My life is for you my Beloved One.
I give to you what has been given me.
and I am at peace.

I lay my head upon your
breast. So begins
my happy dream.

Your poem is beautiful.

Thank you.

It is written from your Soul. People think souls travel through lifetimes searching for love in the form of their soul mates. It is God that you seek. You desire intimacy with your Creator. You are drawn to your Creator by a powerful love.

I do love God. I feel a deep joy when I think about God. I feel joy not only for the awareness of God in me that I have gained, but for what is still to come. There is much more. Once I wondered if there really was a God. Recently I asked you how to be closer to God. I have meditated every day. I didn't meditate very well, but I meditated. I spent time contemplating God. Contemplation seems to work best for me. Now I feel a deeper love.

No one can make himself love God. You made the effort to seek God in your life. You meditated and contemplated God. You intentionally thought loving thoughts toward God. As a result, God has shown up in the form of this deep love you feel. Love begins as a verb. It is a way of thinking and behaving. You thought and behaved in a loving manner toward God. Love, the noun, the feeling, follows.

Bill's Journal

Nothing much has happened in recent days in my external world. Today I spent time with my son who was struggling with many aspects of life. His energy was heavy; he was in a low mood. I have felt incredibly joyous all day. I have felt an indescribably good feeling in the area of my heart. I am happy. This happiness is related to nothing in particular going on in my life. If I died right now I'd die happy. I feel great! Thank you, God. I began my day in prayer. I asked that I may be truly helpful to my son and to anyone I might encounter. I asked Spirit to guide me. My day has been productive in getting tasks done, maintaining a sense of peace and joy, and relating in a positive way to my son. I didn't try to make him feel better. I was there to listen, and I knew he would work things out. I just emanated joy. I'm not sure what happened to me, but I am glad it happened.

You opened your heart. When one opens one's heart love flows in. It is like punching a hole in a dam. Water rushes in and fills the area behind the dam. You opened your heart and love rushed in, filling you. Your cup was filled so much it overflowed. You were radiating love all day, and you still are. We share your joy.

I feel great joy. But the world is not a joyous place for most people. There is much suffering. How do I reconcile my joy with the reality of the world? I'm not going off to the mountains to live in solitude. I want to live in peace and contribute to the peace of others.

The world is not a joyous place because people choose to make it what it is. By your choosing peace consistently you help others to choose the same. You cannot make people choose peace.

I know. I can't even make people in my own family choose peace.

When you choose peace, Bill, you influence others. You cannot make family members appreciate each other, yet you can be appreciative yourself. Each thought you send out has either love or fear as its intention. Each word that you speak has either love or fear as its intention. In love, you do not try to fix other people. A spiritual teacher is not here to fix others, but only to love them.

But how do I love someone who is being very critical of another?

You speak from your heart. You understand that another person is speaking from hurtful thoughts. Speak from a higher place, a place of peace. If you attack another person she will only defend herself. Seek to understand her hurt and her need to project it onto another. Be at peace and you will know what to say. You can ask God for help. Ask, "Dear God, what would you have me say that would be helpful to all concerned in this situation?"

What if I can't think of anything to say? Or, what if I can think only angry thoughts?

Then say nothing until peaceful thoughts come.

Bill's Journal

I have given much thought to this idea of coming from a place of peace when I speak to others. It wasn't long until I had an opportunity to practice.

I was talking to my mother on the phone. She was angry at one of my sisters, so she began analyzing and criticizing. My muscles began to get tense. My shoulders, arms, chest, and stomach muscles all began to contract. It was like I was getting ready to pounce. I felt angry and was about to tell my mother I was tired of hearing her criticism. Then I stopped and recognized what was happening. My anger and tension were caused by my thoughts, not by my mother. I let go of my angry thoughts and became more peaceful. I listened within for something helpful to say. I empathized with her feeling. I have children, too. Yes, I have felt disappointment, too. She began to sound lighter. She was hurt because my sister had not returned her phone call. I responded that it was not the lack of a telephone call that had made her feel hurt, but her expectation. I explained how I had learned to change my expectations because my children don't always call me as much as I would like. I asked her to take better care of herself by not allowing unmet expectations to sour her relationship with my sister. She agreed that she was creating her own misery. By the time we had hung up both of us were feeling lighter.

Just when I was feeling pretty good about my ability to be at peace I had words with my wife. I can't remember what the problem was. We were both angry. I could not find a place of peace, so I stopped talking. She did, too. We were okay with each other later. I wish I could have known what to say and do in the middle of the argument. I kept telling myself I was creating my own discomfort and anger, not her. I still couldn't get past my anger and frustration.

I'm disappointed in myself. Why couldn't I get past my anger with my wife?

You did get past it. You stopped fighting. You recognized you were not capable of being loving or peaceful at that moment, so you did the most loving thing possible for you at that moment. Whoever is more sane is responsible for ending the conflict. This time it was you. You cannot expect yourself to be where you are not. There will be times when your angry thoughts and emotions seem to get the best of you. As long as you recognize that you do not have to act on them you will do fine. Continue to practice and you will find peace in the midst of conflict more often and more quickly.

You are a spiritual teacher. To be a spiritual teacher it is not enough to be public about your beliefs and convictions. You must live the life of which you speak. This you do. You are not afraid to admit your shortcomings when you speak and write. Others, then, learn with you. You know that you are not above or below them, but the same. In this similarity people see their own possibilities. If you appeared perfect, people would not relate to you. They would place you on a pedestal or run from you. If you who has these very human fallibilities, temptations, and emotions can choose peace—if you can accept your mistakes and move forward—if you can use your errors as lessons for living—if you can continue to walk closely with God without regard to how well things are going, then can not they?

I believe everyone can. If they want to.

Never think that you have have arrived. Your spiritual growth is dynamic. It is your learning, your continual dealing with your human fallibilities that provide you with opportunities and material to teach. People learn from your experience as you learn through it—as you have learned from the experience of others.

When I teach I find myself looked to as a leader. I feel such a big responsibility here. People approach me and ask for advice; they want to know what I think they should do. If I am to lead I want to lead well. What should I keep in mind to do this?

Remember that you are here to be truly helpful. This means that when you teach, your communication has the purpose of being helpful both to you and to those who would listen. Teach love both to yourself and to others. That is, make sure the intention behind your words is loving. Treat no one as an enemy, but as a friend. Speak your truth compassionately, respectfully, and with love. Your criticism is not helpful. Words intended to hurt or punish will not help.

You are responsible for what you think, not just for what you do. Thinking is the basis of feeling and action. When you feel angry or frustrated, see yourself in an honest respectful way. Instead of saying "I am angry at this person." say "I have created the experience of anger in myself. My thinking is the cause of this." If you are so angry you cannot see the thoughts that cause anger, know that they are present. Recognize that the person with whom you feel anger may be acting out of fear. Your anger comes from fear. You are unable to meet each others' expectations. As you can not manage the person's behavior, perhaps you would manage your expectations. Have compassion for him and for yourself. Ask God: "Help me to see this situation from a perspective of love." Then let go of your blaming thoughts. Your experience of anger will pass and you will begin to feel loving as loving thoughts enter your mind.

We must emphasize responsibility for you particularly in the area of your own self. You are more critical of self than you are of others. Your expectations of self border on the impossible. See the trouble you make for yourself with your thoughts. When you sat down to write today you felt discouragement within minutes. Think about this. It was not the writing, not the task at hand which discouraged you. Take responsibility for your thoughts.

I have myself feeling very discouraged about this writing. My thinking causes this. I think that I have nothing of real value to say. Then I think I must put the writing aside until I feel more inspired. Next I begin to rationalize, to excuse myself for not writing.

Soon you are doing something you find easier to do. Thus your progress is quite slow and the completion of your writing is sometime in the future. The future never arrives. Is it not easy to see the great accomplishments you will make as sometime in the future? Is it not easy to see yourself as a spiritual teacher some day, as an effective meditator some day, as a being of great wisdom and love some day? We do not say this to push you. You desire greatness yet you desire it not. What is your intention? What thoughts do you entertain? If it is your intention to express the greatness in you then why hold back? You are called but do you choose to answer?

I want to feel inspired. I want the words to flow on to the paper. When they don't, I get discouraged.

You do not "get" discouraged. You discourage yourself. Your statement of discouragement separates you from the inspiration you desire. You are not making a statement of fact; you are establishing the fact. Yet it is not the truth. Thought is creative; therefore your thoughts of discouragement are but a self fulfilling prophesy. What is "discourage" except to lose or take away courage? Choose to encourage yourself instead. Realize it is only thought which creates your discouragement. Let those thoughts go. Revisit your intention making sure it is what you truly want. Ask God for help and give thanks for it. Move forward with confidence. You need not struggle unless you wish to struggle. Nothing prevents you from moving forward but you. You have the power to choose. You are not powerless. All true power is of God, and you are of God, too. Accept your power and do not allow yourself to diminish it with "discouraging thoughts". Face your thoughts and respond to them. Take away their power and recognize that the Spirit within you has the real power. Ask: "How can I feel encouraged right now?" You can only feel encouraged by encouraging thoughts.

I have faced those discouraging thoughts, and I now recognize that they are only thoughts. I now feel more excited about this writing. I feel motivated. Tell me what else I must do as a spiritual teacher.

You are here to represent Spirit who has sent you. You are created from Spirit therefore represent Spirit in all that you think, say, and do. Do only the will of God. Do and say only that which will promote God's will.

What if God's will and my will are different?

They are never different. God's will is your will. Yet sometimes when you are in fear, you think your will is different. Fearful thoughts and emotions lead to actions not of God's will. When you take responsibility for your thoughts and feelings you become peaceful. When you are peaceful you hear God's will and become most glad to do it.

You do not have to worry about what words to say or what things to do for Spirit will guide you. Be at peace. Respond to the Voice within. You will know what to say when in front of a group. You will know what to write when sitting with your paper or your computer. Do not worry about it. Do what is before you to do and do it gladly. You may not know where it will take you, but that does not matter.

If I do the will of God then what will happen?

You will be healed. You will be whole. You will be complete. Your life will be miraculous.

Over the past several years I have set goals for myself and made great effort to achieve them. If I am to do God's will then it seems that setting goals is unnecessary.

It is your intention that matters. Make sure your intentions are loving. Be willing to follow the Voice of God within and you will have little need for external goals. Be content to be where Spirit wishes you to be.

A goal is specific, measurable, realistic, and falls within a timeframe. For example, my goal might be to increase my business and my income by 20% this year. Are you saying this is not a good thing to do?

No, the practice of writing and achieving goals is neither good nor bad. We are suggesting that you do something different. Give your year over to God. Let it be your intention to let go of trying to control your business and income. Follow your heart in your work; do what is before you to do; and expect that God will provide. Say that you are content to be wherever God wishes you to be and mean it. Listen, pay attention, and act upon your guidance. Allow "goals" to rise up from deep within your heart.

It is similar when you facilitate a group process. You do not know exactly what the group should do. You do not try to get them to take any specific action. You listen. You usually know what to say and do to help the group grow and learn. Do this now in your own life. Throw out external goals. Your work is to learn to identify with your Soul, not your personality. The Soul knows It always has what It needs. The personality thinks it must plot and plan.

It has always been important for me to set goals that I may reach and stretch myself to attain them.

God will make sure you do plenty of reaching and stretching, but nothing will be put before you that you cannot achieve. Ideas will come to you, and some of them may seem to be impossible. You want to write a musical.

Yes, I've already written most of it, but I don't think I have the ability to complete it. I'm not really a musician or a composer.

One day the idea for a musical came to you. Songs started pouring out of you, and you sang them joyously. This opportunity came to you from within you. If you have the intention, there is no reason not to complete this work. What you need will be given you. Set aside your doubts. Do not limit yourself by setting goals and time lines. Do not try to envision what will happen. Simply let the vision take form of its own. You are a channel for great works. Your little human brain is not the creator. Most people have potential far beyond their human imagining. You know this. As a teacher you have worked to draw out the greatness in your students. Now see the greatness in yourself.

Are you telling me I can be whatever I want to be?

You can be whatever you <u>truly</u> want to be. What you truly want to be is what you are. You want to be yourself. You probably will not become a professional basketball player. You will not become the CEO of a multi billion dollar corporation. These positions do not come from your heart. All desires that are truly from the heart are capable of being achieved. Desires of the ego may become manifest, but will not bring you true happiness. Were your desire to write a musical be only for the financial and the recognition rewards you would not succeed. In part, because we would not help you. We are not caring about those things. If you compose the musical for the love of the expression, for the beauty of it, then we will assist you. Move forward into your projects, and approach them with love, intention, and discipline. Trust that you will be led to where you need to go. You are content to be where God wishes you to be.

Where does God wish me to be right now? I have so many ideas for projects that I don't know where to start.

Start where you want to start. Which project sounds like the most fun, the most joyous?

I am eager to complete the musical, but I don't know if anything will happen with it. I have no idea how to get a musical out to the public.

Reach deeply into your heart. Discover the desires of your Soul. You feel a passion for this musical. You feel a desire to create this story. Make it your intention. Begin working. What you need will come to you. The ideas and the people you need will come when you are ready. Refrain from sending your mind out to the future; be here now. Do what is before you. Ask Spirit to tell you what is to come of each day. Place God first and all else that you need will be added.

You are already where God wishes you to be. You are teaching what you need to learn. This is true of all spiritual teachers. For years you have taught communication skills. Why, do you think you were attracted to teaching those skills?

In my younger days I was not a very good communicator. I could stand in front of a group and communicate, but I had trouble in relationships with people.

You have learned to communicate well by teaching it. Is it not a beautiful process? You have learned to deal with conflict by helping others with their conflicts.

Conflict isn't fun anymore. In the past I would have the satisfaction of thinking I was right and the other person was wrong. I could enjoy some good old self righteous anger. Now, whenever I am in conflict my words come back to me. It's not as much fun being "right" anymore. But I do like it that I don't have to suffer the fallout from excessive anger anymore.

You are healing that part of you which could not deal with conflict. You are healed as you allow Spirit to teach you to heal. Your message has expanded and will continue to change as you change. A spiritual teacher teaches what he most needs to learn. This contributes to your healing as well as to the healing of those you touch. As your communication ability continues to grow you will have less of a need to teach it.

So this is why I am starting to speak at churches?

Yes. You are now learning to identify yourself with Spirit. In the past you had much resistance to publicly affiliating yourself to matters of the Spirit.

I'm getting into more challenging subject matter.

You are learning to speak the truth with authority.

There are many teachers from a variety of backgrounds, religions, and philosophies of life. I enjoy this diversity. Yet there are major differences between these teachers. Some are Christian and insist that all must believe in Jesus. Some are Muslim and believe that only Muslims are on the true path. Some are Jewish and see themselves as The Chosen People with their own special covenant with God. Some are pagan and seek God in the spirits of nature. How do I deal with these seemingly wide differences?

Know what you believe. Know it so well that you can speak it articulately. God, the Spirit within you, will guide you. Do not resist the beliefs of others. Listen to them and understand who they are. Find your common ground and emphasize it.

Throughout human history people of different beliefs have fought each other, have sought to have their respective belief systems prevail. You need not become a part of the conflict. In truth there is no conflict. Each person is where he should be. For the Christian, Jesus' teachings are the way. This is good. For the Muslim, Mohammed's teachings are the way. This is good. Do not worry about another person's relationship with God. That is between God and that person. There are many paths to God. You can not know what is best for another. You can not say that one should be Christian, Jewish, or Muslim. If you would judge another's spiritual path then you would play God.

You need not agree with the beliefs of another religion; only respect them. See the good that another does and give thanks. The division of religions is a human phenomenon. In the world of the Spirit, the real world, there is no religion. Spirit recognizes Spirit. See Spirit in each and every person you meet. Each is experiencing what is personally needed by that person.

In your world the belief in separation plays itself out in religion. If you want to be truly helpful meet each person where he is. Do not try to change his religion or his relationship to the Creator. Help him to strengthen his relationship with God. Meanwhile, continue to strengthen your own relationship with God.

I have chosen to follow the words of many teachers, yet I am drawn to the teachings of Jesus, both in the Course in Miracles and in the Bible. But I am troubled by the Bible because there are so many mistakes and insertions.

Worry not. Yes there are mistakes and insertions in the Bible. Yet, there is plenty of Truth to be found. Seek Truth.

I am seeking truth. Religion and scripture are not the major sources of my growth. My own experience in life teaches me more. You guys speaking in my head teach me. It's not even meditation that teaches me, because I don't hear God's Voice when I meditate. At least not yet. Contemplation seems to be my way. When I contemplate thoughts I hear you guys talk to me. You answer my thoughts with your wisdom. You have instructed me to be truly helpful to myself and others. To do this well, I need to love myself deeply. I know that my ability to radiate that kind of love is what will help me to teach well. You have said that as I help others to heal, I will heal. My teaching has contributed to my healing. My spiritual growth has been a long, slow process. It depends on my ability to reflect upon my thoughts, feelings, and behaviors. I want to do a little reflection on my belief system.

The area of religion in the world needs healing. I need to be able to articulate my beliefs and accept the beliefs of others. I need some help in this area.

We see that you read many books in this area. Your books stimulate thought. Let us contemplate what you have read and experienced.

Chapter Seventeen
From Religion to Spirituality

Bill's Journal

I was raised in a Christian home. I attended Church and Sunday School nearly every Sunday throughout my childhood. As a young man I rejected my Christian roots, and I began seeking other ways. I read books on every religion. I visited gurus, but I found nothing I wanted to make my own. I left Jesus behind, judging him by the acts and the words of his followers. Christianity as I knew it dismissed all other religions as not valid. It said Jesus was the only way. My explorations had shown me that there was much beauty and value in the various religious traditions. After spending time with my mentor, Marian, I gradually began to look at Jesus with new eyes. When I started reading the Course in Miracles, Jesus became real to me. In the last several years I have conducted my own search for the real Jesus.

I read that Jesus was born in Palestine in the year 7 B.C.E (Before the Common Era). Herod the Great ruled the country along with the Romans. The name *Jesus* is Greek for Yeshua or Yehoshua, which means "Jehovah Saves". Who was Jesus? People have argued this for 2000 years. Millions of people have died for their opinion. Was he human or divine? Was he the great example or the great exception? I recall, many years ago, being told I would suffer in hell because of my opinion of Jesus. I thought my opinion of him was very positive.

What have you discovered about Jesus?

There are many theories about Jesus. Some say Jesus never really existed. There were many prophets in those days. Jesus could be just a composite of all of them. The great historian, Josephus, who lived at the time of Jesus, mentions Jesus in his narrative, but only in one paragraph. It is interesting that Jesus only gets one paragraph out of thousands of pages of history written by one of his contemporaries.

As a child, I was taught that Jesus was the only Son of God. He was born of the Virgin Mary; healed the sick, raised the dead, and created many miracles. He was crucified, died and was buried; rose from the dead; made appearances to many disciples; and ascended into heaven to sit at the right hand of God. I was taught that I should believe in him as Savior if I wanted to be saved. I was also taught that he suffered in order that my sins would be taken away. If I believe that, I can have eternal life. If I don't, I am damned to hell. This theory has always been confusing to me. My sins are taken away because he suffered on the cross. I think my sins are taken away by me changing my thoughts and behavior. I must save myself.

It's kind of like the baptism thing. If you don't get baptized you go to hell, because you are responsible for all the sins that were committed before you were born. I can't imagine a loving Father throwing innocent babies in hell just because they weren't baptized. Nor can I believe a loving Father would throw good people in hell because they aren't Christians. For that matter, I can't imagine a loving Father throwing anyone into hell. I have never believed in the concept of original sin or that only Christians are saved. To me this is very arrogant. We are all made in God's image. These theories sound like God being made in our very human image.

A recent book describes Jesus as an illiterate carpenter who was an eloquent speaker. Another theory states that Jesus was just a human, like you and me. He was born of Mary and Joseph, a simple carpenter's son. He was a teacher who challenged the authorities of his day. He taught about love and morality. He was crucified and his disciples took the body, claiming he was resurrected. Other versions of this say his death was faked and he continued to live and teach for awhile.

One of the most fascinating theories I've found was in a book called *Bloodline of the Holy Grail*, by Laurence Gardner. Gardner said that Jesus was an Essene as were Mary and Joseph, John the Baptist, and Mary Magdalene. Essenes lived a contemplative, nearly celibate life. Essenes married but only slept with their partners one month out of the year (December) in order to procreate. Research indicates Mary and Joseph broke the rule and were together in June. Jesus was born in March. The Essene elders granted them their blessing because of who Jesus was—heir to the throne of King David. Jesus was well educated as he grew up. When he began his ministry he married Mary Magdalene. He spent the years of his ministry teaching and healing, as did many Essenes during his time. Jesus was crucified while Mary was carrying their child. Jesus was revived (resurrected?) and continued to teach with a lower profile. Mary gave birth to their daughter, Tamar. Later they had two more children, Jesus and Joseph. Mary eventually went to Gaul and died there at age 63. Jesus followed Thomas (the disciple) to India, where he died in Kashmir. A tomb still marks his grave today. Jesus' bloodline continued through his son Joseph.

I must admit an attraction to this last theory a lot. I don't agree with all of it, but it makes a lot of sense. We always assume Jesus had no wife. Where in the Bible does it say that?

Evidence can be found to support or refute every theory I've read. Who do we believe? The Bible is full of contradictions and mistranslations. For example, only Matthew and Luke tell the birth story and state that Mary was a virgin. Mark and John make no mention of Mary's status. Yet Jesus is referred to as being from the line of David because Joseph was a direct descendent of that line. Matthew goes through 42 generations from David to Joseph, then he says that Mary was a virgin. If Joseph was not the father, why does Matthew talk about his ancestors? In the original text Mary is described as an "almah" which translates as "young woman". The Aramaic word for virgin was "bethulah". This means the early Christians mistranslated "young woman" as "virgin". It can get really confusing when you start studying this stuff. The arguments continue today: Was Mary a virgin or not? Was Jesus human or was he divine? Maybe he was both. What do you think?

The problem does not lie in determining all of the facts. It is in determining the Truth. This is not a matter of who is right and who is wrong. It is the mental arrangement, or world view, from which all of these arguments emerge that we would address.

What mental arrangement is that?

It is the world view that says you are but mortal beings, sinful and human. That you have a soul which must earn its right to be close to God. God represents perfection, all knowingness, and is separate from you. You are down here, and God is up there (in Heaven). Therefore, if Jesus is the only begotten Son of God, then he is separate from you - the great exception, as you called him. If Jesus is only human, then he is separate from God like you—but he represents the great example of what a human can be.

That sounds about right.

What if you would change your view from a belief in separation to "there is no separation."? You are one with God therefore Jesus is one with God, and vice versa. This is the Truth. Armed with this Truth, when the fundamentalist says Jesus is the Son of God, the Christ, you can respond, "Yes, he is (and so are you and I)." When the Unitarian says Jesus was a human, you can say "Yes, he was (and much more than that, as are we.)"

So, Jesus is the great exception in that he is one of the rare persons who walked this planet knowing his divinity. He was the great example in that we can all do what he has done. He is not our parent, but our older brother. If we are like Jesus, then we are very powerful beings.

You may find verses in the Bible to support these Truths.

I have found verses.

Bill's Journal

Many verses from the New Testament and from gospels outside the New Testament suggest we are much more than human.

• Is it not written in your law, I said, you are Gods? (John 10:34)

• Ask and it shall be given to you; seek and you shall find; knock and it shall be opened to you. For whoever asks, receives; and he who seeks finds; and to him who knocks, the door is opened. (Matthew 7:7)

• Truly I say to you, Whoever should say to this mountain, Be moved and fall into the sea, and does not doubt in his heart, but believes what he says will be done, it will be done to him. Therefore I say to you, Anything that you pray for and ask, believe that you will receive it, and it will be done for you. (Mark 11:21).

• Truly I say to you. He who believes in me shall do the works which I do, and even greater than these things he shall do, . . . (John 14:12)

• Rather the kingdom is inside you and it is outside you. When you know yourselves, then you will be known, and you will understand that you are children of the living father. But if you do not know yourselves, then you dwell in poverty,

and you are poverty. (Gospel of Thomas)

• Peace be with you. Receive my peace to yourselves. Beware that no one lead you astray saying "Lo here, or lo there!" For the Son of Man is within you. Follow after him. Those who seek him will find him. (Gospel of Mary)

Who a person believes Jesus is emerges from who that person believes she is. The Catholics see a Catholic Jesus. The empirical scientific people see a man who created no miracles. The Fundamentalists see a Fundamental Jesus. Who you think you are determines who you think Jesus is. If you are a sinful being who is trying to be good, then Jesus is the divine, only Son of God. If you are a child of God, made in God's image, then you and Jesus share the Christ. He asks that you discover it within you as he did.

It is good that you study; that you learn about Jesus. Your study will be most valuable if you focus on Truth rather than facts. You argue that Mary was not a virgin. This may or may not be a fact. You have found writings that support both points of view. We can explain this best by adapting a Zen saying. "Before I began my path to enlightenment, Jesus was Divine and Mary was the Blessed Virgin. After I began my path to enlightenment, Jesus was no longer Divine and Mary was no longer the Blessed Virgin. When I became enlightened, I saw Jesus as Divine and Mary as the Blessed Virgin. "

I get it. Thank you. That third part was not about the physical. In Truth, Jesus is Divine and Mary is Pure.

I was talking with my wife yesterday. She said that almost all versions of Jesus have something in common. Most believe that Jesus taught about loving God, loving each other, and forgiving. Whether you are a Fundamentalist or New Ager, Protestant or Catholic, scholar or simple practitioner, there is a common ground here.

Seek this common ground always. Where you agree is more important than where you disagree. Attachment to point of view creates the illusion of separation. Common ground creates unity. Live your truth, yet acknowledge that others have a piece of the Truth also. Know who you are. Know what you believe. Often people are threatened by other religious beliefs because they do not understand their own. A deep understanding of the teachings of Jesus is contradictory to religious elitism. Be able and willing to articulate your beliefs and more importantly, to live them. Be willing to listen deeply to the beliefs of others.

I know what I believe. I am the Christ, a holy child of God, and so is everyone else. I am God expressing as me. I am seeking to remember my divine identity.

You have spoken the Truth. You and all souls have the Christ within you. The Christ is your template. It is what you were created to be. Jesus became Himself, the perfect being you are all meant to be. All are equal to Jesus. Let Him, or let another great teacher be your example. Or, if you prefer, seek on your own. The real Jesus is the one who lives in your heart. You need not know all of the details of his life, nor must you convince others of the right way to see Jesus. There is truth in all points of view. There is value in all teachings. You cannot say a person should believe differently then he does. Share your Jesus with whoever shows an interest. Give love and respect to those who have a very different Jesus in their heart. Give love and respect, also, to those who have Mohammed, Buddha, Krishna, Moses, or Lao Tsu in their hearts. For each who comes to this planet has his respective path. It is arrogant to think you know what another's path should be. Teach the Buddhist to be a better Buddhist. Teach the Jew to be a better Jew; the Muslim to be a better Muslim. Whatever you teach, teach love.

For many years I was not into Jesus. I think studying the Course in Miracles helped me to see him differently. In the Course Jesus presents himself as my elder brother and guide, not as the one and only son of God. The Jesus I understand was not a victim, persecuted and crucified. Much of the Christian world sees him this way, but I don't think he saw himself that way. He transcended the situation by refusing to take offense and by offering complete forgiveness. There are no bad guys in the Easter story. It is a story of a soul who chose to express God even while people were attempting to kill him. It is a story that demonstrates that evil has no real power.

Jesus did not sacrifice anything, nor did he die for me. He does not punish so-called sinners, nor does he command everyone to obey only him. He does not blame or punish anyone because he does not teach blaming. Jesus found and became the Christ within, and I can do the same. So can anyone else should they have the intention.

We accept your belief, yet do not become too attached to your belief. Believe with all of your heart. Attachment prevents you from learning. Always be willing to let go of your beliefs in the face of new awareness. Ask why you believe as you do. For example, your cosmology includes a loving presence that surrounds and inhabits all people. You see Jesus as one who rose above human illusions to realize his identity. You see yourself as having this same potential. Do you believe these things because you know them to be true? Or, do you think it's true just because you believe it? Do you believe these things because you want them to be true? Do you believe these things because you have always believed them?

Are you trying to create doubt in me?

We are asking you to assess your thinking. We ask that you dive deep into your mind to contemplate that which you claim to believe. Be willing not to believe. Open yourself to insight and inspiration. How can you learn and grow spiritually if you already know it all? Be open, else you are only practicing a religion rather than practicing spirituality.

Is there something wrong in practicing a religion?

No. Be aware that religion serves two very different purposes: one which promotes spiritual growth and one which discourages spiritual growth.

How does it promote spiritual growth?

Like minded people may gather together to love and support one another. People are taught information from scripture and other spiritual writings. Lessons are learned which help people to grow closer to God. Spiritual growth is greatly accelerated when attempted in community with others. The love and support of others is invaluable to you. At the same time, the stress of relationships challenges you to practice spiritual principles. Loving your neighbor is easy when you have no neighbors. Loving neighbors who have their own opinions and personality traits teaches you what love truly means. Religion can provide useful guidelines for life. The "rules" of a religion provide discipline and structure for thinking and behavior.

How does religion discourage?

When people seek answers only outside of themselves. To promote the Bible, religious teachers, or doctrine as unquestioned authority deters people from searching within. As we have said, religion is often about control. To grow spiritually one must question all sources of information. Take information from these sources within and ask if it rings true. Ask for meaning and insight. Let guidance come to you.

Spiritual growing is an inside job. External sources are valuable. but as we have said before, do not mistake the finger for the moon. Do not mistake the form for the essence. Do not worship the rules. Refuse to worship your ideas. Worship only God, the Creative Intelligence of the Universe.

How do I worship only God?

Be willing, each time you enter meditation or contemplation, to suspend all beliefs, all preconceptions, and all opinions. Be the empty cup that God may fill with wisdom. Remember the Taoist saying which states: "Those who know do not speak; and those who speak do not know." True knowing in the deepest part of your Soul can not be spoken. It is knowing beyond words. It is understanding that cannot be communicated through speech. The most powerful spiritual beings on your planet need say very little. Their presence speaks for them. Love radiates from them.

I want to live and teach the truths I have learned about life, about the Christ, spirituality, forgiveness, and love.

You teach who you are. Speak what you know, and listen to others. The teaching process is an exchange. If you are not learning when you teach, then you are not teaching well. Teaching and learning are one and the same.

You have suggested that I not judge others, and that no one can tell another what his spiritual beliefs should be. You have encouraged me to always seek the common ground. I can do this. I pretty much know what I believe and I can articulate it. Most of the time I can respect the beliefs of others, yet it is difficult at times. I am irritated when people tell me their way is the only way. I hear a lot of this from fundamentalists and evangelists. I can accept that their beliefs may be the only way for them.

Why does it irritate you?

It is the arrogant attitude that they have all the answers. Often they know very little. They quote Bible verses they don't understand. There is a general disrespect and outright dismissal of other spiritual paths. I can't have a real dialogue with someone who already knows it all. Not every Christian is like this, but many are.

Literal translation and application of the Bible bothers me. I'm fine with people using the Bible to guide their lives. I'm not okay with hitting people over the head with the Bible because their lifestyle is different. People pick out certain verses and apply them while ignoring others. Many condemn gay people because of a verse in the Bible. The Bible also says if a man is jealous toward his wife, he can make her drink a "water of bitterness" which will make her sick. If she doesn't get sick, then a priest pronounces her innocent. However, if she does get sick, she is cursed. It says children who dishonor their parents can be stoned to death. I Corinthians says it is shameful for a woman to speak in church. I don't see too many people following these verses. People pick verses in order to exclude people and lifestyles they don't like. I think there is much of value in the Bible, but I don't see it as the inerrant word of God.

You are irritated by what you perceive to be spiritual arrogance. You want them to accept other beliefs including yours.

Yes.

Teach what you would desire of them. Accept them where they are. You have no control over their understanding of the Bible or acceptance of you. Refrain from attacking another for his beliefs, no matter how immature his beliefs may seem to you. If your intention is to convince a person of your way of thinking, or to diminish his way of thinking, you will create conflict. Make it your intention to fully understand his view. See deeply into his soul. Listen with your heart and you will understand him. You will know what to say. Make sure you do not practice spiritual arrogance. As you said earlier, no one can tell another what he should believe. This does not prevent you from speaking your truth. Speak your truth with confidence, yet be open to new ideas. Most importantly, live your beliefs in all that you say and do. You teach best when you teach with integrity.

Bill's Journal

This past weekend I discussed religion with a friend who is an evangelist. He believes everyone must accept Jesus as their savior or suffer in hell. He also believes in the inerrancy of Biblical scripture. I listened to him, and I expressed my beliefs. Neither of us convinced the other, yet both of us enjoyed the conversation. The benefit for me was that my beliefs and my ability to communicate them were strengthened.

I think his beliefs are erroneous, yet I can see how they have value for him. I can also see that his cosmology is the basis of his life. If I could destroy that it would create tremendous instability in his life. He is a good man. His values are strong and he treats other people with respect. It was not my intention to change him, but I did enjoy a good, healthy exchange of ideas.

My friend's view of life and death is very black and white. Mine isn't. I believe in reincarnation, and that we are each spirit. I believe my soul took on this body and identity to learn and grow. When I die my soul will still be alive. I'm not so afraid of death as I used to be. At the same time, I'm not ready to die, because I'm not done here yet. There is much for me to experience and learn. But to be honest, I don't really know what happens when I die. Where do I go? Am I reborn again quickly or do I spend some time in the spirit world? Will I find myself hovering over my body and my loved ones? My focus has been on this life, not the next. Yet, I still wonder.

So. what does happen when I die?

Nothing.

What do you mean nothing?

Nothing happens because you are. You always are. Remember the saying "God is a verb"?

Yes, Bertrand Russell I think.

You are also a verb. You are a verb who thinks he is a noun. You are an is who thinks he is an it. You are a spirit who thinks he is a body. You are always in a state of being. When you understand this concept fully you will think as a verb. When you think as a verb you become a miracle worker. You will move beyond the limitations in which your world believes. You will move beyond petty religious squabbling. You will move beyond any desire for conflict. You will move beyond good and evil.

Will I understand this one day?

You will, because you are.

What is the most important thing I could do right now to grow in this direction?

Learn to love yourself.

I'm working on that. What about good and evil? How do I move beyond that? If good and evil aren't real, then what is? Isn't God good? And isn't evil the opposite of good?

These are good questions. Perhaps you would contemplate good and evil for awhile; then we will talk.

Chapter Eighteen
Deliver Us From Evil

What is evil?

Evil is the absence of God.

I thought that God is everywhere. If God is everywhere, then how can there be an absence of God?

There can not. There is nothing outside of God. Nothing exists that is not within God. You have free will. You may behave as though there is no God, and you may choose to behave without care toward another. You can separate yourself from God in your thinking only. In the world of Spirit, the real world, there is no such thing as evil. There is only God. God is all there is. There is one power, one thought, one basis for all creation. This is God. God has no opposite. How can something all encompassing be opposed by something evil? Or, to use one of your earth sayings: "Which part of God is __all__ there is do you not understand?"

Then I don't understand evil.

Evil is in your experience that you may know Good. Just as fear is present that you may know love. Feeling lack is present that you may understand abundance. Pain and sorrow appear that you may know joy. Conflict is present that you may know peace. Neither evil nor fear, nor lack, sorrow nor pain, nor conflict are real. They are experiences you have created to know that which is real—God, love, peace, joy, abundance.

So what does it mean in the Lord's Prayer when we say: "Deliver us from evil?"

It means to deliver us from illusions. It means, "Help us to see that which is real and to release that which is not." When you condemn someone as evil you are supporting evil. You give it recognition as real, which it is not. When you recognize it as real you create it. The appropriate and effective response to the illusion of evil is love. Think, feel, speak, and act in love toward one whom you would call evil.

So when I ask to be delivered from evil I am really asking to be taught how to love?

Yes. Deliver me from this illusion of evil. Deliver me from this fear which causes me to condemn my brother or sister as evil. Teach me to see the soul which is the essence of this person. Teach me to find this person's soul that I may be of assistance to him in finding it for himself. Teach me to see what he cannot see that I may help him to see it.

Imagine a seemingly "evil" person surrounded by love. Imagine a seemingly "evil" person spoken to with the highest respect, with the greatest affection, and yet held accountable for his actions.

How is an evil person held accountable?

The Law of Cause and Effect is always operating. Therefore, people are punished by their sins, not for them. You need not punish others for their acts. Your role is to love them.

It is difficult to love someone who does evil things. For example, some dictators like Saddam Hussein, seem to be evil to me. He uses his people for personal gain. How can I love this person who hurts people for his own gain?

Know that the face of Saddam which you see is not real. It is a facade. It is his political persona. It is also your image of him. Images are not real. As we have said before, images you create are based on assumptions, beliefs, and stereotypes you hold. Beneath the political persona, beneath your many assumptions is the soul of Saddam, as glorious and beautiful as your own Soul. He is as much a part of God as you are. You and Saddam are one. To hate him, to judge him, to condemn him is to do these things to yourself. You may be saddened or disturbed by his actions, but to respond with anything less than love is to be in agreement with what he does.

But I don't agree with what he does. I don't like dictators who lie and have people killed to support their own ambitions.

We are not saying to agree with his tactics. We offer only that you may choose to respond with love. Forgive him. See him in your mind with love and send that love to him by way of thought. These thoughts are uplifting thoughts. They will lift you and will lift up the world. There is no separation in your world. All is One. Your thoughts affect the whole. You may choose to lift the whole by adding your loving thoughts or you may choose to help bring it down by your thoughts of upset and condemnation. Disagree with him honestly and openly if you choose, but do not condemn.

Jesus disagreed with the political powers of his time, yet he did not hate them. When they crucified him he did not offer self righteous or hateful words. He did not see himself as a victim of evil. He saw himself as a son of God. As the Christ, he said, "O Father, forgive them, for they know not what they are doing."(Luke 23:34) In your modern world there have been many examples of loving souls who have refused to hate or condemn, but who have stood for the Truth . Martin Luther King Jr., Mohandas Gandhi, Aung Sang Suu Kyi, the Dalai Lama to name a few. Each of these brave and loving souls have faced the evil acts of men with the love and strength of God.

Do not fall into the trap of being <u>against</u>. To be against is to support and give power to. Instead be <u>for</u>. Be <u>for</u> love, peace, and joy.

Be for the expression of Godliness on earth. To be for this is to actively seek it, and to know that even if you can not see it, it is there. Those souls who we have named who are still in body, Aung Sang Suu Kyi and the Dalai Lama, bravely speak the Truth. They stand for peace, for the opportunity for all to live and be free. They do much to raise the consciousness of the souls of earth.

So, I can criticize Saddam's acts but I should not condemn him?

Speak the Truth. Speak it from a place of compassion and understanding. Do not condemn yet do not make excuses for him. Know that most people usually do not see themselves as evil or wrong. A man throws a bomb into a restaurant killing several people. You see him as a terrorist. He sees himself as a freedom fighter. Another flies bombing missions in war, yet comes home to be an astronaut, and a fine citizen. You see him as an American hero. To the survivors of his bombings, he may be seen as evil.

How do you see each of these persons?

As children of God. As souls who have taken on human form in order to better understand their spirituality and the Oneness in Spirit that they share with all. We do not judge them as right or wrong. We love them as we love you. We see their beauty and we seek only that they would see it for themselves. People do things that hurt others because they believe they lack for something. They believe they must do "evil" things in order to get what they think they must have. The Truth is that each already has all that is needed.

But we don't think we have what we need, so we lie, steal, kill, or manipulate others to get what we need. I read a book that theorized there are five basic human needs: survival, love and belonging, freedom, power, and fun (Choice Theory, by William Glasser). Wouldn't so called evil acts be inappropriate ways to meet these needs?

We would call them unloving acts. Unloving acts are based on fear. Read what Aung San Suu Kyi has written about fear.

I have been reading her work. She says: "Fearlessness may be a gift, but perhaps more precious is the courage acquired through endeavor, courage that comes from cultivating the habit of refusing to let fear dictate one's actions, courage that could only be described as 'grace under pressure'—grace which is renewed repeatedly in the face of harsh, unremitting pressure." (Aung San Suu Kyi, *Freedom From Fear and Other Writings*, Penguin Books, 1991)

You help to engage the Saddams of the world by refusing to let fear dictate what you do. You may feel fear, but it is your choice as to how you act. By consciously refusing to be motivated by fear, and by calling upon Spirit to guide you and help you, you experience grace under pressure. As you practice this you become more adept at engaging fear and evil—more adept at becoming the presence of love. Evil is an absence of love. You cannot eliminate an absence with another absence. In other words, you cannot fight hate with hate, or evil with evil. That which is expressed attracts and perpetuates that which is like itself. Hate creates more hate. Evil creates more evil. Means and ends are the same. Practice grace under pressure and you become grace.

I think I understand what you are saying. But I see a world full of troubles. Children are living in poverty. Crime is everywhere. Violence is all over the world. Our government seems unconcerned with remedying these problems. Is it enough for me to just practice loving thoughts and loving responses in my own life? Should I ignore the world and its politics and live a spiritual life?

Were you to live your life and practice only loving thoughts and responses you would leave your world a more loving place than you found it. You are a teacher. Teach. Be who you are. Ask God how you can be helpful, and listen for the answer. Not everyone need be politically active. But being spiritual does not exclude activism. Every field of endeavor needs spiritually aware people at work. Check within.

What do you want to do?

I am a teacher, not a politician. I will teach, counsel, and write. I don't want to run for office, but I think I should vote. I would like to support candidates who speak for love and peace. I would also like to send letters to leaders encouraging them to seek the highest good for all concerned. I can pray, too.

Realize that you and each person alive are creating this world. It is a reflection of your collective consciousness. Do not abdicate the running of the world to politicians. Take responsibility. Speak the Truth with love and compassion. Think the Truth always. Let your life be a continuous prayer. Pray for people who appear to be evil. In prayer, talk to their souls. Ask them what you can do to help. Acknowledge their holy presence. Your prayer will serve to draw out their holiness. Behave toward people who appear to be evil as if they are beautiful souls, because they are. Hold them accountable for their actions, but do not judge them. As the Bible states: "Do unto others as you would have them do unto you." Add to this: "Think unto others, believe unto others, and speak unto others as you would have them do so to you."

I'm still having trouble understanding evil. Are you saying there is no evil in the world, or are you just saying evil isn't real?

Evil is real to the extent that you experience it as real. It has as much power over you as you are willing to give it. The quickest way to diffuse evil is to refuse to acknowledge it. You do this best by refusing to be its victim. A victim is led by fear. Fear gives evil credibility. People follow evil persons because they are afraid. They are afraid of losing— losing life, health, love, money, relationships, self importance, or possessions. Or, they are afraid of not getting that which they think they must have.

I have another quote from Aung San Suu Kyi that goes with what you are saying. "It is not power that corrupts, but fear. Fear of losing power corrupts those who wield it, and fear of the scourge of power corrupts those who are subject to it."

So evil comes from a sense of lack. Fearing lack, we act in fearful ways: ways which support evil.

Yet, in Truth, there is no evil in God's Universe. Evil is an illusion. Anything that is not love is an illusion. Learning to love, you rise above the illusions. Have you ever realized that you were dreaming while in the midst of a dream?

Yes, I have.

How did you feel? What did you think?

I lost all fear. I thought: "This is just a dream. Nothing can hurt me, because I will wake up." When I was a child I taught myself to wake up when I was being chased by monsters. Once, instead of waking, I faced the monster and it disappeared. I felt invincible.

You are invincible because you are spirit. You are sharing a dream with everyone else on the planet. It can be a happy dream or an unhappy dream. It can be a dream filled with love or a dream filled with evil. Once you become aware that this life is but a dream you become powerful. You begin to see that the rules that people employ to guide their lives are supported by perceptions. Wrong and right change with the times and the circumstances. You have the illusion that good and evil are somewhere etched in stone, yet, in truth, you are making it up as you go along. You interpret scripture and the words of prophets to suit your perceived needs. Knowing these things you are free to act with love, to state the Truth, to use the power given you to help others.
You are all on this planet Earth living this thing called physical life that you may learn and grow, and experience it together. Everything that happens is an experience. If you must designate between good and evil, then call it good. Whatever is happening call it good. The word "good" is derived from "God". Whatever the experience may be, whether painful or pleasurable, God is with you. When you see someone experiencing suffering, have compassion. Have compassion for the people who suffered in concentration camps, for the slaves so mistreated in America, for the groups of people who are today being mistreated

and killed. But also have compassion for the perpetrators and the captors. Remember, what you do to another you do to yourself. To condemn them is to join them in their illusion of evil. To love them is to lift them up that they may see. All souls are on the road home, and all souls will arrive. The question is when and how much more suffering will they create before they arrive.

It is your illusion that there is a battle between good and evil out in the world. You think you stand for good, thus your anger is justified. Justifiable anger leads to revenge and attack. After a time, who remembers who began it all. Anger and rage lead to the doing of evil. You must not become what you fight, but you do become it. Are your bombs more holy than theirs? Are your barbed words more blessed than your enemy's? The battle between good and evil takes place within you. All external battles are projections of your own conflicts.

Do not support the illusion of evil. Do not condemn it, yet do not ignore it. Do not fear it and do not attack it. Refuse to be its victim. Speak the Truth, lovingly, compassionately and with great strength. Trust in God. Act in accordance with the Voice of God within you and live with an understanding of the Laws of the Universe. What you sow you shall reap.

Bill's Journal

I think back to my spiritual teacher, Marian. On my second visit to her I asked for a past life reading. I wanted to know what effect other lives were having on this one. She gave me a reading using a pendulum and an alphabet. The pendulum would point out letters to her. The pendulum was directed by her spiritual source. And so, my past life was revealed to me letter by letter. Even she didn't know the content until we looked at the letters and divided it into words. It said: "You are a prospective teacher of the new age. (Pride/desire) filled ugly servants of self must be clean himself. He opened himself to a mountain of trouble when he served dark force as a magician in the court of pharaoh in Moses('s) time. His brilliant brain was a prisoner of a hot trust in the power of Lucifer. He grew horns since he could make a rod become a snake (and) ground people into dust with fear of his power. He has paid. Lots of lifetimes he has spent regretting his pride. His work is to teach universal truth, conscious that one spends many lives undoing the pollution of pride. He will teach well because "Got to reap what one sows" has meaning for him. So be it. "

The "I" which you have known in this lifetime is but one personality, one aspect of your Soul. You are more than your personality. Another personality expressed by your Soul was the magician in Egypt. Your Soul created "Bill", and Bill's potential as a teacher to help balance its expression. The magician used people to feed his insatiable need for power, and to express his anger at feeling unloved. Bill is here to serve people, understanding that his power is God given and that he is always loved.

You and nearly every soul that walks this planet have played all the roles: the hero, the magician, the tyrant, the victim, the priest/ priestess, the wealthy landowner, the poverty stricken peasant. How is it that you can judge another without judging yourself? Love others; give thanks for their presence, for the opportunity they provide to help you find your Self.

So, if I take this reading seriously, I was evil.

You were living an illusion. You thought you were all powerful. When the personality of a soul intentionally causes pain for others, that soul experiences loss. It is a loss of part of itself. It is the soul's nature to be loving. In your "evil" life you went against your Soul's true nature. In order to reclaim itself, your Soul created many personalities over many lifetimes to experience the pain that was caused by the magician. Through these experiences you have been learning to overcome pride and the fear that created it. With this lifetime, where you find yourself teaching and helping others, you now create balance for your Soul. You are learning the value of true power, the power of God expressing through you and as you. As a magician you exercised ego power.

But where did the fear and pride come from?

From old wounds. You were hurt. Rather than healing, you chose to cover them up with ego power. You were hurt, but you would not be hurt again. You would be, instead, the one who causes hurt. You would gain so much power and control over people and situations that they could not possibly hurt you. You gained and expressed the power of faith, but you used it to serve your fearful ego.

Then maybe we should change the words of the prayer to "Deliver us from ego."

Negative ego and evil are the same. They are the illusion of separation from God. God is all there is. Therefore, there can be no separation in Truth.

So if there is no evil, there is no devil.

The devil is your ego. The conception of the devil is a way of externalizing evil. The devil is the collective ego of this planet. It is the collective belief that there can be sin and separation. This "devil" is imaginary and has only the power you give it. True power is of God.

Sometimes I can feel this true power you speak about. But I feel some fear when it comes to assuming it.

You need not fear it. You are worried that you will again misuse it. You had the true power in that ancient lifetime. You chose to use it in service to your ego. As a result, you fell from Grace. You fear to fall again. Worry not. You have learned well. As your guardians we will not allow you to have more than you can handle. This is our commitment to your Soul. We see who you are in this lifetime, how far you have come, and we are pleased. Be at peace.

Was I really that magician? I mean, the whole idea seems a little far out.

Do not worry about the facts. It is the Truth that matters. In Truth, you are seeking to overcome pride and fear, to help others rather than to use them. Past life information is valuable if it helps you to understand where you are now. We see no value in being caught up in past life identities or experiences. This would serve as a distraction. Focus your thoughts and energy on the here and now.

Okay. Just so I understand things. Evil is the absence of God. Since God is ever present, there can be no evil.

There is evil in your consciousness. This evil is created by humanity. God is Love and Light. Evil is a lack of Love and Light. There are dark places within all of you. Old wounds festering and hurting. These wounds are accompanied and aggravated by resentment, bitterness, anger, rage, hatred, and other negative thoughts. These thoughts and feelings lie in the dark places of your consciousness. You spend your lives running and hiding from this darkness, pretending it does not exist. Much of your spiritual literature is positive and does not deal with this darkness. To find the spiritual reality of pure Love and Light, where there is no evil, one must first face the illusions of evil created within. The human experience has convinced all of you that evil is real. Therefore, in your present state of consciousness, evil is real. It is real to you, but you do not want to engage it.

You try to escape it by accusing others of it. Fingers are pointed. Blame is assigned. With every finger that is pointed, with every condemnation expressed, evil grows stronger.

How do we weaken it?

You acknowledge it within yourself. Stop avoiding it. Stop pretending it is not yours. The Hitlers', Stalins', and Saddams' of the world are manifestations of group consciousness. Fear created these leaders. Fear maintained their regimes. As with all things, begin with you. Acknowledge and face your dark places with love and courage. Bring that which is dark into the Light.

I guess we have been doing that in all of our talks.

Yes we have.

Every time I try to project fault onto someone else, you put it back in my lap. This helps me to grow. It seems like I still have a long way to go.

As long as you still have reactions that include anger, resentment, self righteousness, and guilt—you have work to do. Resist not evil. Become defenseless and allow God to heal. Stop defending actions you have taken. Stop condemning the actions of others.

I realize that I must confront evil within myself. But, is there ever a time when we should try to stop evil in the world?

When thought leads to action, and action is meant to hurt others, do your best to stop it. Speak your truth. Allow your <u>presence</u> (of Love and Light) to engage the <u>absence</u> (of Love and Light). Do whatever you are guided to do. Become a pure channel for the Love and the Light of God. Allow yourself to be used for the good of all. Do not attack evil with self righteous indignation, as that will only serve to reinforce it. Be a light unto the world. Let love radiate from you into every situation that is less than loving. Face people who cause harm with courage and compassion. Courage in that you refuse to be led by fear. Compassion in that you see the loving soul behind the fearful image—that you see the pain a person is causing to herself.

My experience is that when I approach a person who is doing harmful things with courage and compassion, they don't always change their behavior. As a matter of fact, they seem to act worse. This happened recently in a consulting project.

It is true your client reacted negatively, yet in the big picture, the situation changed for the better. Your love and courage did have an impact.

Bill's Journal

I was asked to coach the manager of an organization. This manager ruled by fear, often embarrassing employees publicly, verbally attacking them, and threatening them. The negative behaviors were well documented. I worked with the manager and her boss to help the manager make the behavioral changes necessary to create a positive, productive work place.

I worked to reinforce the healthy parts of this person. At the same time I was very clear about unhealthy behaviors that needed to be changed. We worked to change negative mental models to healthy positive ones. I assisted the employees to help them learn how to stand up for themselves. I knew we were getting to the place where it was going to get better or fall apart. It fell apart. The manager took legal action, claiming harassment. She only pretended to work with me while she plotted and planned her strategy. She wanted to be able to come back to work and no longer be "harassed" by her boss. An interim manager was put in her place.

The old manager will not be going back to that facility. She was released from employment. The employees have now experienced a healthy climate and are unwilling to return to an unhealthy one. It is sad to me that the manager chose not to change her ways. Yet that is her choice. My goal was that I would help to facilitate the highest good for all concerned at this facility. Although it doesn't look the way I thought it would look, it is the highest good. The work place has become positive and productive. The manager is on her healing path. To leave her in there would only have perpetuated her "evil" behaviors.

I thought that the old manager had the potential to change. Maybe I was naive.

She did have the potential to change, yet she chose not to utilize it. You refused to accept anything less than positive, healthy behaviors. You created a situation where she had to make the choice between self reflection or continuing her harmful behaviors. She chose not to reflect on her attitudes and behaviors. Do not invest yourself in the choices people make. You prayed and you approached the situation with skill and positive intention. The results were positive for that workplace. Some people help an organization to improve by leaving it. She chose her path. You must let go. She is no longer in a position where she can do harm to the employees. Your work is finished there.

Well, I guess I can't save everybody.

You can not save anybody. You can only be yourself, offer love in all that you say and do, and provide them with information. Your client makes the choice.

Alright, it's time to move on. We've talked about religion, and we've talked about evil. We talked about getting closer to God, co-creation, and being truly helpful. It's time to take inventory and take the next step.

Chapter Nineteen
The Leap

Bill's Journal

I am not the same person who began this writing seven years ago. Parts of me have died, new parts have been born. I no longer think the same way. In past years I would spend my days in negative thoughts, plotting and planning for fearful outcomes. I condemned myself for every mistake. I thought God was withholding prosperity from me. Today I think thoughts of love. I am able to step back from my thinking and reframe negative thoughts. I am able to look upon my life, no matter what is happening, and call it good.

You are the same person, yet you are more.

More what?

You are more aware. You have acquired more wisdom; you express more love; you enjoy greater prosperity.

This is true. My life reflects all of this. Seven years ago I believed I lacked all that I have now. I have so much to be grateful for. Now, I want more. I want my life to be more. I can't stop here.

What is it that you would like?

Greater monetary income, so I can travel more. I'd like to be completely debt free. In my work, I want to reach more people through writing, speaking, and producing projects. I want to be more creative. At home, I want to move to the next level in my marriage relationship. My wife and I have tried to have a child without success. We would like to realize that success.

You are not telling us what you want. Speak to us of how you want to feel. More money will help you to feel how? Growth in your work will help you to feel how? A baby will help you and your wife to feel how?

I want the feeling of being completely in the flow— ideas, connections, people come to me in divine order. I would feel a sense of the Divine flowing to me and through me. I would feel great joy in this. I would feel a sense of greatness flowing through me —like I am part of a great purpose. I would feel truly prosperous—all of my needs and desires met—lacking in nothing. In my marriage I would feel a sense of new birth— greater heights of loving and being loved.

Your intention is to be in the flow. Your intention is that God's love, God's joy, God's peace, and God's abundance would flow through you and to you in your work and personal life.

Yes.

This you already have. The flow is unceasing and ever available to you. Your intention, Dear One, is to live it; to express it; to be it; to feel it more fully. Let your attention be more on these feelings rather than on the specific situations that you would have. Think the thoughts which would lend toward these feelings. Books published; musicals written; babies born; crowds gathered to hear; great amounts of money received. These things may or may not be the means by which you express your greatness. Let the Universe determine that. Seek to do God's will in everything. Seek to think, feel, speak, and act with this sense of greatness you desire each day of your life.

Focus on the feelings of greatness you intend to express. Acknowledge and face that which is anything less than great. Know that you are great, as are all souls. You will have moments; you will have days that feel less than great. Such is the human experience. Be not discouraged, for help is always available. Enter the silence and call upon God. Call upon us. We are here.

It is hard to pretend I don't want money when I do. Money makes me feel prosperous. How do I focus on the feeling of being prosperous without thinking about money?

You are again focusing on the things you want. Years ago you were affirming to get money. Now you are more secure than you have ever been. You want more. You believe more means more money. Would you be able to feel truly prosperous if more money does not come?

I would feel more pressure.

The pressure would come from your expectations. If you believe you must have more money you are creating a false god. Remember the Bible story about the rich man who asked what he must do to enter the Kingdom of Heaven?

He was told to go and sell all that he had and follow Jesus. The guy couldn't do it.

It is not bad to have great amounts of money. A spiritual life is not possible if you are attached to having money. What if God's answer to your request is decreased expenses? Would you not feel more prosperous if your expenses decreased?

Yes, I would feel more prosperous.

You who want to receive more, give. Give more money to your church and to organizations that are doing good works. Give more of yourself to life. Spend less time in front of the TV and more time in creative expression. Why spend your time lost in fictitious adventure when you can make your own adventure? Live and give.

Do not try to limit God, because you cannot. Allow what is best to come to you. Let the Universe decide what is best. Go ahead and express your preferences, but let it be known that you would accept this (your preference) or something better than this (God's preference). This is true for all your dreams.

You and your wife are attached to having a baby. Being attached you feel great disappointment and sometimes, anger, that things have not worked out as you thought they should.

This is what I don't understand. We have had faith. We have done the necessary physical things to create life including fertility treatments. There is no known medical reason preventing this birth.

Let go. Do what you must do to conceive and give birth. Acknowledge the disappointment and anger. We have heard your intention this month: To conceive a healthy child naturally, or something better than this. Now ask: Are there any thoughts within us that prevent this intention from completion?

Are there any thoughts which prevent us from manifesting this intention?

Your ego has put you here. You have adopted beliefs that have you thinking "I'll do whatever it takes to get this baby." Added to this you have yourself thinking "No matter what, I'm going to make this marriage work." These thoughts are creating your present circumstances. "Whatever it takes" and "No matter what" are manifesting for you. The Universe is answering these requests with "How about the chaos of radical fertility treatments?" Or "How about some increased financial pressure to test this marriage?"

The Universe is doing this to me?

You are doing this to yourself.

Why? Why is this happening? Having a baby is something good. Being loyal to my partner is also good. Why would the Universe throw obstacles at me?

The Universe is not throwing them. You are drawing these experiences. It is because you are exercising your will—your ego's will.

Isn't it God's will that I stay married?

It is God's will that you and your partner grow closer to God. If being married is the best way for you to do that, then yes, it is God's will. If being married serves to distance you from God, then we would say no. The point is, you need to be open to what God has to give you. Let go of your "no matter what's", your "whatever it takes'", and all of your "have to's". You are learning the lesson of aligning your will with God's will. This is a wonderful opportunity for you.

What else do I have to let go of?

Everything. If you want joy; if you want peace, if you want spiritual growth, let go of everything.

Everything?

This is what letting go and trusting God means. We are asking you to take it all the way this time. Let go of your marriage. You cannot force a marriage to work. Love and be loving. Support each other. Be yourself totally, and expect her to be nothing less than herself. For a marriage to work you must risk divorce every day. Once again place your relationship in God's hands. Make it a holy relationship. Let God make your relationship whatever it is truly meant to be. Whatever the result, you will both be happy. You can not be less than happy when you have surrendered to God's will. Surrender your marriage to God. Surrender the birth of your child to God. You can want it. You can speak your intention for it. Just do not think you must have it. Be willing to do without it if that is God's will.

Doesn't that take away from the strength of our intention?

No. It adds strength. When you must have something you make that thing your god. Let God be God, your Source. Speak your intention with confidence. Do what is needed on your part. Focus on the joy and love you want to feel (which is the reason you want this birth). Let God handle the details. Think about this. When you met your wife, did you think that you had to have her? Did you inform her that she must be with you.

No. I let her make up her own mind. If I had pressured her and pushed her to be with me, she probably would have run in the other direction.

God does not respond to pushing either. No one likes to be taken from, but everyone likes the opportunity to freely give of what they have. Let God give freely to you.

Do we have to go through all the stuff you talked about?

If you continue your present path, it is a possible future.

So, if we let go now, we won't have to go through the hard times you mentioned.

Letting go means you are willing to go through the hard times if it represents the highest good for your Soul.

Okay, I get it. I'll let go. I want to experience peace and joy. Letting go is the only way to do that.

This does not mean you will feel peace and joy all of the time.

I know, I know. There is always something to let go of.

Always something new to learn.

This is why you are a good teacher—you are a good student. You learn. You examine yourself and you make changes based on the awareness you gain.

Thanks. It's the least you can say after telling me I have to give up my wife, my income, my business, and my future child.

Giving them up is the only way to truly enjoy them, to truly have them. It is also a way of facing your fears.

And what fears are those?

"What if my marriage failed? What if we never have a child? What if my business goes down? What if I go into debt?" These are your underlying fears. Face them. Look at them and come to a place where you are willing for them to happen if these events would be in the highest good for your Soul. You are not asking for these things to happen. You are simply willing.

When I think of letting go, of experiencing these things I fear, I feel lost. I mean, I feel no control over my life. I have no idea what the future will bring. That scares me.

Is it not possible you could lose every earthly thing you value and still find joy and prosperity? Does your joy and prosperity depend on these situations? Are there not infinite possibilities in the Universe?

Yes, there are infinite possibilities, but I can't conceive of what they are.

You as your personality can not conceive it. When you decide that this marriage, this career path, and this source and level of income will make you happy, you limit yourself. This kind of thinking creates fear. When this marriage seems threatened you fear losing it. When this career path seems threatened you fear losing it. When the money you expect does not arrive, you fear consequences. Your attachments create fear. Is this what you want, a life filled with fear?

No, I don't want fear.

Then free yourself from attachment to what <u>you</u> think you should have and to what <u>you</u> think should happen.

Bill's Journal

When it comes down to it, I am afraid of my life falling apart. It has happened before. What would everyone think? I would be a failure in my view. I am afraid to fail because it would be embarrassing.

My life has fallen apart before, yet I am still here (better than ever). Say my life, as I know it, does fall apart. If I trust God; if I love; I will be given what I need. God is providing for me and for my wife. No matter what happens in the physical world we'll be okay. We are loved, prospered and guided. Loving my wife doesn't mean hanging on to her no matter what. It means wanting the highest good for her and for me. And if the highest good is that we live separate lives, then so be it. If the highest good means not having a baby, then so be it.

If the highest good means not having a lot of money at this time, then so be it. After all, had I found money too soon years ago, I would not have learned to be grateful.

I can let go. I am letting go. Deep down I trust God, so what is there to be fearful about? What's that old prayer: "Dear God, I believe, but help me with my unbelief." Okay, so I feel some apprehension, but I'm doing this anyway. I feel like I am standing on the edge of a precipice and God is saying "Leap, Bill! Leap. I'll catch you." So here I go, leaping into the unknown. Oh well, I've been pretty comfortable for the past five years. But just tell me one thing I can focus on that will help me to leap into the unknown.

Be a light!

What do you mean, be a light?

Do not wait for the light to shine on you; be a light. Shine. You are a radiating center of love and creativity. Be that. Be a light in all of your relationships and in your work. Do not worry about your needs. They will be met. All you must do is be a light. Write; speak; sing; love; help others; listen deeply; express gratitude; utilize your talents to the fullest in service to God, to other souls, and to life. Be a fountain of joy. Be so much of a light that people will love to be around you. Do this and you will be free of fear. When you are expressing your God given abilities with abandon; when you are trusting fully in your Creator; what is there to fear? You are a shining light, Bill. You help others to realize that they are shining lights. We would like to see you shine more.

There is a line in life that many people today do not cross. You have straddled this line for some time. We ask that you cross it. We know you are ready. On one side of the line you are needy. Your thoughts and your energy are focused on your wants and your needs. To be in this place is a necessary phase, but not your whole destiny. On the other side of the line your focus is on how you may serve—others, your Soul, God. As needs and desires arise you establish intentions, turn over your concerns to God, and you act. You need not invest time and energy into worry. Worry not about what you should get; think about what you can give.

To be happy; to live a spiritual life; to experience true joy; to know and feel Divine Love; to be at peace; focus not on getting. Focus on giving.

Thank you. You are right. I have spent so much time in need. I can let go of my needs and focus on giving. I can trust that my needs and desires are being handled.

Bill's Journal *(One month later)*

I spent today creating invoices for services rendered. My focus has been on giving these past few weeks. I am receiving more, and I am grateful.

I have been reading over all that I have written these past years. My focus has so often been on external things that I have wanted. One thing I have learned is that life is lived from the inside out, therefore, shouldn't I be focusing on internals?

I read a verse in the Course in Miracles: "I am surrounded by the Love of God." I have expanded this verse to "I am surrounded and fulfilled by the Love of God." I am contemplating this verse every day. I ask, "How does this apply to what is happening right now in my life?" I consciously look for evidence that this statement is true. I continually ask what being surrounded and fulfilled by the Love of God means. Sometimes I think of all of the ways I am not loving. What stops me? Other times I feel well loved and encouraged by people around me. I am grateful.

It brings me joy when I focus on thoughts of love.

To focus your thoughts on a statement of Truth is an excellent way to grow spiritually. What you focus on expands. As you contemplate and learn what love truly is, you become love. Were you to contemplate trusting in God, or seeing God as your fulfillment in all things, you would become those truths. Hold steady in your contemplation, even when discomfort is created. Great good will come of this. Weave this statement of Truth into the the very fabric of your life. As you are surrounded by love, think how you may surround others with your love. Think how you may surround and fill every situation, every relationship with love. Continue to love in this way and you will be healed. Others will be healed. You have only to love a situation unconditionally for a moment and it will be healed.

That statement rings true in me. If I could love a situation unconditionally for a moment, it would be transformed. That sounds like a miracle. I have contemplated love as all around me and within me. It's not completely real to me yet. Something in me resists, and cannot accept love. I want healing from this. Can you help me?

We have said that words are not enough. You must find a way to heal. Your wounds, the dark places inside you, are deep. You contemplate love which brings up all that is not love within you. Your task is to face your pain. Create an intention to face it and heal it. You are being helped.

Later

I created my intention. An opportunity came up for me to visit a healer who does Reiki and esoteric healing. The session was helpful, but I do not feel healed. I do feel more aware. There is a part of me that refuses to be nurtured. In this dark place a voice says: "No one will nurture me. No one will love me, not even God. I have to do it myself." I know I can't do it alone. What should I do to open myself to being loved?

Stay open to what comes. Do not run away from this. You will be guided as long as you intend to heal. The moment you ask for healing, healing begins. The moment you leap into the loving care of God, God provides for you.

Chapter Twenty
Living with a Bold Heart - Compassion

Compassion will build the doorway to love and fulfillment. You have learned about gratitude and about filling your mind with loving thoughts. You have learned about forgiveness. You know that you create your every experience with your thoughts. You are aware that you are responsible for your life and affairs. You know that God is the source of all life and sustenance. You know it is best not to judge others, but to practice discernment when you make choices in life. You have learned much. You seek the compassion of your Creator, not understanding that it is already given to you. Therefore, you must discover this compassion.

How do I accomplish that?

You have experienced deep compassion these past few days.

I did? I mean, yes I did. It was yesterday. Early in the morning I hurt my lower back. I worked on it through exercise and stretching, which helped. I was in a low mood all day. I told myself that my mood was created by my thoughts. At the same time, the pain in my back helped to magnify and aggravate my low mood. It was difficult to carry on with the constant pain I was feeling and with the low mood.

A thought came to me that this is what it must be like for my sister. I have a sister who has had a chronic pain problem for four years. I have certainly cared about her and I have offered help. My understanding of her situation, though, was mostly academic. But yesterday, I felt what it was like to be her. I expressed my thoughts to her, and it was meaningful for her to hear what I said. I complimented her on her ability to stay positive in the face of all that pain. My back pain lasted a day or two. Her pain has gone on for much longer.

You did well, also. You might have focused on your own pain with no thought for others.

I saw my pain as an opportunity, and I wanted to find out what the opportunity was.

There is more treasure to be found in this opportunity. You have discovered what it is like to be your sister who lives in pain. What is it like to be other people in your life?

My wife doesn't live with constant physical pain, but she has carried a constant emotional pain. For years she has wanted to have a baby without success. A few years ago there was a miscarriage. This experience has contributed greatly to her spiritual and emotional growth, and to our growth in relationship. At the same time, there is this constant emptiness she has been learning to heal.

Feel what that would be like.

Well, it feels empty, like something that comes from the deepest of longings is missing. There is a hollowness inside that can be described as grieving. Someone I deeply care about is supposed to be here, but he's not. It's lonely, and I don't know why or how to change the situation. Everything has been tried, yet nothing has worked. It makes me think of that song by

Donovan, "Widow with a Shawl". Every day, for seven years, the widow walks to the seaside to look for her husband who is lost at sea. She feels a strong connection to him. Every night she walks home empty. Identifying with my wife, I walk hopefully into each month looking for this child I love. Each month I am disappointed all over again. Months come and go with no child, yet the longing lingers. It's hard to put into words, but that's about it.

Now you have a small idea about your wife's feelings. You come from a loving place where you want to help the people in your life. Help begins with compassion. Compassion is not feeling sorry for someone. It is acknowledging the feelings of others without judgment, without trying to fix them, without trying to one up them with your pain. You acknowledge with love and understanding. At the same time you see them as they truly are—a spiritual expression of God. You see the light within another and acknowledge it. This is how you become a light. Look deeply into each person you meet and see her darkness and her pain. Look deeper still and see her light.

I can do this. How does this help me to accept love for myself? How does this help me to know that God loves and nurtures me?

Acknowledge your own pain without judgment. Love your mistakes. Love yourself making mistakes. The One Who Knows you loves you unconditionally. We love you unconditionally. Acknowledge your human fallibilities. At the same time see your self as you truly are— a spiritual expression of God. See the light within you and acknowledge it. This is how you become a light. Look deeply into yourself and see your darkness and your pain. Look deeper still and see your light. You are totally loved. The Love of God surrounds and fills you.

I believe that the Love of God surrounds and fills me, but I don't really <u>know</u> it.

This is what you are healing. Your Soul desires to heal. Compassion has created a doorway. You feel a restlessness to walk through it. Your restlessness is the key. Use it to move forward.

I am restless, but I don't know what to do.

Act upon the opportunities presented to you.

I have stayed open for several months now, seeking healing opportunities. I saw an opportunity to go to Peru and I was excited. I'm going to Peru next week with a group of people. I have a feeling something good is going to happen in terms of healing that part of me which feels unloved. Is that the trick? I have to go half way around the world to find healing?

A pilgrimage can be helpful, if where you are going has meaning for you.

It does. I have wanted to go to Macchu Picchu for almost twenty years. This is a dream come true. This pilgrimage is also a conference led by Matthew Fox. I have wanted to hear him speak for some time, too. The funny thing is that I don't really know why I have wanted to go to Macchu Picchu, or why I have wanted to hear Matthew. I just do.

You are following your heart. We will be with you and look forward to your journal writings about this pilgrimage. This journey will teach you something about compassion and healing for yourself.

Bill's Journal

So much has happened on this trip. I felt uncomfortable at times during the first two days. I often feel uncomfortable in groups, except when I am the leader. I stepped outside of myself and observed me. My actions seemed to alternate between reaching out and seeking isolation. The strongest urge was to isolate myself. I decided that wasn't a good plan.

Both Matthew and the other speaker, Carol Vacciarello from El Paso, Texas, talked about indigenous peoples and their spirituality. Carol had us build a medicine wheel. We each chose a spirit animal and found a stone that represented it. Each animal symbolized a specified quality. I chose the wolf as my spirit animal. I learned that the wolf represented love. I found a beautiful red stone that was somewhat heart shaped. I called it my heart stone and held it to my chest. It seemed to fit there, like a puzzle piece in a puzzle. We conducted a ceremony where we placed our stones on the circle and spoke about how we felt. I spoke of my tendency to distance myself from others, to move through life with few close friends, of my contentment to be a loner. I talked about seeking connection with others as an alternative to isolation. Somehow the ceremony and my speech were meaningful. I felt a deep compassion for my self, for that part of me which needed nurturing. It was not until two days later that I took the next step.

In our morning session Matthew spoke about balancing the masculine and the feminine in our spirituality, finding the sacred in life, and the importance of ritual. We discussed the difference between being a pilgrim and being a tourist. A pilgrim leaves a place a changed person. A tourist is distant, removed from what he is viewing, and leaves unchanged. I planned to leave this place a changed person. We talked about people being wounded and having no way, no ritual for healing. Next, Matt asked us to create a mandala. It was to be divided into three parts: one to represent the past; one to represent a present insight we have received; and one to represent the future. I took my crayons and paper and started drawing.

The Mandala

I represented the past with a broken, raggedy heart (left). It is bleeding. My strategy for dealing with this hurt, as I've said, has often been isolation. The present insight (bottom) is that rather than isolate, I need to connect— with myself, with other people, with the earth, and with Spirit (represented by the sun in the center). The future is represented by a Bold Heart (right). The future heart has legs on it to connect it to the earth and to move it forward into the unknown. The eye in the Bold Heart represents discernment. The bold heart loves, yet is discerning in its choices. It is a seeing heart, a wise heart. This kind of love is not blind, nor mushy, nor indiscriminate. The sun (Spirit) is shining on all parts of me (past, present, future).

Next, we discussed our mandalas with a partner. It is difficult to explain how much this drawing means to me. It depicts my healing journey. I now have a bold heart. Maybe I've always had it, but now I feel it. This process is a healing ritual for me.

There may still be work for me to do, but this gets me over the hump. It is here that I make the transition from thinking that the Love of God surrounds and fills me to feeling it. It is difficult, maybe impossible, for a wounded heart to know this God Love. I felt it temporarily many times, for an hour, for a day. Now it is part of me. I feel a powerful, quiet confidence simmering in my chest.

Looking at the mandala I created, I recognize my wounded heart from my childhood. I see how I have maintained it through my adult years. I sought solutions in resentment and isolation. I created relationships and situations that reinforced my wounded condition. This is not the first time I've had a revelation like this. Why would I continue to carry the wound? I must have thought there was a value in it, a payoff of some kind. I don't need to analyze it. Seeing it all on paper, I know I don't want to continue acting like a wounded child. There is something better for me.

I realized that people acting in evil ways comes from a sense of being wounded. The hurt child decides that he will be hurt no more. Instead he will do the hurting. We shut ourselves off to our vulnerability and seek to control the world so it cannot hurt us. Money, violence, political power, authority over others become tools with which to control our world. They help us to feel powerful. In my life I have resented others who I felt took advantage of me. At times I have been the one who took advantage of someone weaker, someone less intelligent, or someone who trusted me.

No longer need I travel through life with a wounded heart. A wounded heart needs to be given to. A wounded heart cannot love fully because it is broken. A wounded heart is always looking for that which will fix it—seeking nurturance or healing in other people, in riches or accomplishment, in situations, in controlling others, in food or sweets, in drugs or alcohol, in drama or self pity, in injury or sickness. A bold heart seeks to offer itself, to express love and to express that love creatively. A bold heart is a big heart. It can not and it will not play at being small. It does not offend intentionally, yet it will not back down. A bold heart is not tentative, nor hesitant. It moves forward, trusting it will have what it needs.

I left my heart stone in the Sacred Valley of the Incas, but I have brought my bold heart home with me. I feel this in my body, in my cells. It is much more than an intellectual affirmation. It is very real to me.

In the afternoon of that same day, we did a Shamanic Journey with Carol. My mind usually wanders during these kinds of things, and I don't get much out of them. However, once before I had done a Shamanic Journey with some success. Success to me is to have more than a daydream. I wanted this experience to be real and to have an impact.

This journey was a visualization process where one enters another dimension, guided by one's spirit animal. The purpose was to seek an answer to an important question. We lay on the floor while Carol beat a drum. I closed my eyes and visualized a place we had visited the day before called the Interdimensional Portal, in a town called Ollantaytambo.

Incas used to sit in front of the portal and meditate. They would leave their bodies and enter the portal, traveling to another dimension. I began my journey. I called for my spirit animal, the wolf. Four wolves showed up. I felt well protected. I entered the portal immediately and found myself in a cave. It seemed so real that I felt the need to remind myself that I was lying on the floor in a room at a hotel, safe. It took some convincing to get myself to go with the flow, to let go of my need for safety. After a few minutes I was again involved in my journey. My wolf friends and I proceeded through a series of dimly lit, narrow passageways. Each path undulated and curved alternately to the left and to the right. We traveled quickly and easily. After several minutes of walking I saw a silvery white light shining through an opening. The opening was at least fifteen feet up. The wolves and I climbed up the rocky wall and through the opening. We found ourselves standing on a plateau.

We were greeted by a star filled sky. In the distance, a sun was just beginning to rise. I recognized this place as the underworld. I'm not sure how I knew. Clearly this place was not part of my everyday reality. It was beautiful. I approached the edge of a cliff and sat down. My wolves sat beside and behind me. I could feel their breathing on my neck, and I could feel soft fur against each of my arms. It was comforting. I looked skyward and asked, "What is there for me to do next in my life?" Immediately four pictures were shown to me in rapid succession. First, I saw myself doing a book signing with this book. Second, I saw myself producing a musical. Third, I saw myself going to Israel, doing research on my next book. Fourth, I saw myself holding two beautiful little children—they were ours (my wife's and mine). Next, I heard a voice say: "These are your dreams, and they are to manifest if you want them. It is up to you." I came back to physical reality in the hotel room. I felt strong and confident.

The Shamanic Journey was vivid, not like my normal visualizations. It was like a part of me was really there. Maybe I was. Usually, when I visualize, I create the pictures consciously. No part of this journey was created by my conscious mind. Instead, I felt drawn into a story unfolding. It made a strong impression on me.

The following day we visited the ancient Inca city of Macchu Picchu. I breathed in its grandeur. My eyes were filled with its wondrous and sacred images. Macchu Picchu rests on a mountain surrounded by mountains. A verdant river valley lies below. Maybe it is because I am mountain-deprived living in Michigan, but I just wanted to drink it in, to get drunk on it. I was in awe of the scenery, of the genius of the Inca people, of the fact that I was fortunate enough to be there. I will never forget it.

I hope I can keep this going. I mean, this is more than a conference high, isn't it?

You know better. Do not allow doubts to creep into your mind. Your healing is very real. You will still feel unsure at times, but you will process these emotions much faster now. It is important that you move forward and do the work that is before you. Finish the book. Complete the musical. Love your wife. When the time is right, plan for Israel. If you can dream it, you can do it. Never doubt that a dream which is in alignment with who you are and what your life is about can come true.

Thank you. I feel more whole now. After years of spiritual and psychological work I have grown in confidence and in awareness. I knew that I needed to cross the line—to cross the line from needing to giving. Now I feel like I have done it. My heart literally feels stronger.

Your heart is stronger. You have crossed the line. You now have a giving heart, one that is not concerned about its needs being met. You know that God provides, and so you do not worry. You have little need to find wholeness outside of yourself. You are healed. You are ready to go to the next level.

What is the next level?

New challenges will arise. We have said you are healed, not enlightened. There is more to learn. You have completed your growing up process. You are an adult in all ways now. Many people carry the weight of childhood wounds. Therefore, in many ways, they are still hurt children. You are not a hurt child any more. Be compassionate toward those who are wounded. Help them to heal. Share your story, and help them to write their own stories of healing. Go out into the world and heal through your teaching, writing, and relationships. Whatever healing you offer will benefit you. Whatever teaching you present will be learned by you.

A bold heart makes you a man of power. There is nothing you cannot do with love. Therefore, visualize that which you desire and surround it with love. It will become manifest. The power of attraction will bring to you that which you desire. Visualize, love, and release all concern and attachment.

I have come a long way. I used to think that spiritual growth meant that I would manifest wealth and loving relationships. It is true that I do not lack in the areas of money or love. I have an abundance of both. More importantly, I feel at peace, full of love, and confident. I am grateful every day for what I have, but my true joy comes from the way I feel. I feel powerful. I feel like I can create anything I desire. I desire only that which will bring joy to myself and others.

Bill's Journal

I am ready to end this writing. I have accomplished what I set out to do. I am grateful to the Holy Presence of God, including my Soul, my guides, and my teachers which have helped me. I am blessed with a beautiful life, filled with an abundance of love and joy. The journey has been both painful and joyous. Such is life. I am coming home to my Self. I am beginning to know who I am. Still there is much to learn, much to express before I leave this body. At this moment I am happy. Most days, for no external reason, not for riches nor recognition, I am filled with joy. My heart overflows with love because I am.

I am happy because I am. The fear I carried for many years, the sense of feeling diminished no longer plagues me.

Before I leave this journal, would you like the last word?

This is not an ending, because things are just beginning for you, Bill. Life is about to get a little more exciting. This is good. Do not worry. Know that we are with you always. Call upon us often. You are never without that which you need. You are never alone. Be at peace. Namaste'.

Epilogue

Bill's Journal

One millennium has ended and another has begun. This past year has been a year of miracles. I had plenty of business, yet I still had time to travel, read, and do the things I enjoy. My income increased well beyond previous years. I have found great joy in my work and at home.

Last summer my wife and I traveled to France. We made a pilgrimage to the Cathedral at Chartres. Matthew Fox had talked about Chartres, and I had read about it previously. Something within me was drawing me to this magnificent place. Once there, it felt like I was home. I walked the 800 year old labyrinth carved into the stone floor. I spent hours gazing into stained glass windows. I experienced a feeling of awe and reverence. I felt a tremendous respect and appreciation for the generations of people who built and maintained Chartres. I was awed by the sculpture, the 185 stained glass windows, and the feeling of the place. Each stained glass window told a story with a lesson. Each sculpted vignette made the Bible come alive. My appreciation for the Christian faith increased. I have read so much about the horrendous things done by Christianity in the past. The Cathedral at Chartres helped me to balance my view and to see the Creator expressed through the hands and hearts of so many artisans and Christians.

I look back on the year with great satisfaction. I am pleased with the growth in myself, my marriage, and my work. Yet no one thing I have mentioned has impacted my life as much as our baby girl.

Last spring we tentatively looked at international

adoption agencies. We came to realize that our vision of creating a family did not have to come through our bodies. The vision was to become parents together, and adoption was another means by which to accomplish it. In May of 2000 we applied to adopt a baby girl from Russia. After what seemed like tons of paperwork we traveled to Russia at Thanksgiving. We stayed in Moscow and enjoyed many of the sites, the Kremlin, Russian Orthodox Churches, and art museums. We traveled to the city of Smolensk to meet our then future daughter and apply for her adoption. She was beautiful. Unfortunately we had to leave her and go back home.

We returned to Russia a few weeks later, and we brought our nine month old baby girl home just before Christmas. She brings so much joy to our home. Her joy and laughter add music to our lives. My love for her grows each day. Loving her as I do, I become even more aware of the love I feel for my two grown children. Memories of loving moments with them when they were babies often come flooding in. Seeing them hold and nurture their adoptive sister brings me joy. Seeing my wife mother our child gives me a deep feeling of happiness for her and for us.

My greatest achievement in the past several years has been learning to love myself. My experience in Peru created a shift in my thinking and feeling. However, it was not that experience alone that helped me. I prepared for that experience; I asked for that experience. For many months I challenged my unloving thoughts every time they surfaced. I refused to allow fears to drive my behavior. If the little voice was telling me I was unworthy, I offered a more sane response. Most people carry self hatred inside themselves. This self hatred is not logical nor is it sane. On that basis, I found grounds to question the fears driven by self hatred. I asked the Creator for healing, and I nurtured the intention to heal. Had I not prepared in this way, I think the workshop in Peru would have been just another workshop.

Healing doesn't mean that I never feel depressed, or unsure, or doubtful. It doesn't mean that I won't have to deal with things like death, illness, relationship issues, money challenges, and a tumultuous world. It means that I process these feelings more completely and more quickly. It means that when times are tough, I'm in a mental and emotional position to give to others. I still need to be vigilant, noticing my thoughts and where they are leading me. I still entertain "insane" or negative thoughts which I must address. I now have a foundation upon which I can build a healthy, loving approach to any situation. My foundation includes self love, a strong knowing that God is ever present, and the awareness that I am a spiritual being. I always have a choice between approaching life's issues from a perspective of fear or love. These days, I rarely allow fear to drive my behavior.

Learning to love myself; growing closer to God; feeling a strong sense that I am always provided for; growing my business; having more money; and bringing our baby home are all miracles in my life. These miracles did not happen instantly, but they did happen. There was no quick fix. There was no magic program I followed. There was work. It was my work, and I continue to be employed at it. Life is my spiritual coursework.

In order to grow spiritually we cultivate loving thoughts toward self, others, and the Creator. We discipline our minds, and we gain the courage to visualize and act on our dreams. I know that we are so much more than we think we are. How do I know this? I know it because I am so much more than I was when I began this book. I know that, in years to come, my awareness will grow, and I will see myself as greater than I am now.

Yes, this past year has been a year of dreams coming true. I enter this new year with enthusiasm, with reverence for all life, with intentions to express God in every way possible. I am committed to being open to and willing to learn from each experience in my life. Every problem has it's answer within my mind. I am grateful for life — all of it. This may sound like a happily ever after ending. It isn't. This is a beginning. Life continues to unfold. I continue to live and to love.

A baby pigeon stands on the edge of a nest all day.
Then he hears a whistle, Come to me.
How could he not fly toward that?
Wings tear through the body's robe
when the letter arrives that says,
"You've flapped and fluttered against limits
long enough.
You've been a bird without wings in a house without doors
or windows.
Compassion builds a door.
Restlessness cuts a key.
Ask!
Step off
proudly into sunlight,
not looking back.
Take sips of this pure wine being poured.
Don't mind that you've been given a dirty cup."

Rumi

THE ILLUSTRATED RUMI, Coleman Barks and Michael Green,
Broadway Books, 1997

.

Acknowledgments

There are many people who encouraged and helped me in the writing of this book. I am thankful to Reverend Beth Monteith for her suggestions, encouragement and support. Thank you to Erwin Braker for his critique and encouragement. I thank Jane Zussman for her editing expertise. I am especially thankful to my son, Joshua Diedrich, for teaching me so much about writing through his detailed editing and critique. Additionally, I am thankful to Joshua for his cover art and all of the artwork in this book.

I am thankful to my wife, Peggy, for supporting me on this project and putting up with my seven year obsession with this book. Friends encouraged me in the early days of this project and I am grateful to them. Thank you to Constance Godmair, Patricia Hopkins, Rod Rodriguez, and Tom Gannon. I am indebted to Grethel Ruth Brown for her wise counsel and encouragement.

Thank you to friends and family, especially those I have mentioned in this book. You have each enriched my life in so many ways. The love you have each given me is a gift.

I am thankful to Matthew Fox and the Reverend Carol Vacciarello for teaching me the importance of ritual to healing. I am thankful to Alan Mesher, for *Journey of Love*, and for inspiring me to think about the Prodigal Son story in different ways. Thank you to the many authors and teachers whose works have contributed to my learning, including John Randolph Price, Ernest Holmes, Dr. Wayne Dyer, Sanaya Roman (Orin), and the authors and editors of *A Course in Miracles*. Thank you to Aung Sang Suu Kiy for her living example and the wisdom of her words. Lastly, I am thankful to the angels and spirits who surround me for their wisdom, love, and understanding.